JOURNAL OF MORAL THEOLOGY

VOLUME 10, SPECIAL ISSUE 1
SPRING 2021

SCRIPTURE AND MORAL THEOLOGY

EDITED BY
WILLIAM C. MATTISON, III
AND MATTHEW LEVERING

JOURNAL · OF MORAL THEOLOGY

Journal of Moral Theology is published semiannually, with regular issues in January and June. Our mission is to publish scholarly articles in the field of Catholic moral theology, as well as theological treat-ments of related topics in philosophy, economics, political philosophy, and psychology.

Articles published in the *Journal of Moral Theology* undergo at least two double blind peer reviews. To submit an article for the journal, please visit the "For Authors" page on our website at jmt.scholasticahq.com/for-authors.

Journal of Moral Theology is available full text in the *ATLA Religion Database with ATLASerials®* (RDB®), a product of the American Theological Library Association.
Email: atla@atla.com, www: http://www.atla.com.
ISSN 2166-2851 (print)
ISSN 2166-2118 (online)

Journal of Moral Theology is published by Mount St. Mary's University, 16300 Old Emmitsburg Road, Emmitsburg, MD 21727.

Copyright© 2021 individual authors and Mount St. Mary's University. All rights reserved.

Pickwick Publications, An Imprint of Wipf and Stock Publishers, 199 W. 8th Ave., Suite 3, Eugene, OR 97401.
www.wipfandstock.com. ISBN 13: 978-1-6667-3092-0

JOURNAL · OF
M · O · R · A · L
THEOLOGY

EDITOR EMERITUS AND UNIVERSITY LIAISON
David M. McCarthy, *Mount St. Mary's University*

EDITOR
Jason King, *Saint Vincent College*

SENIOR EDITOR
William J. Collinge, *Mount St. Mary's University*

ASSOCIATE EDITOR
M. Therese Lysaught, *Loyola University Chicago*

MANAGING EDITOR
Kathy Criasia, *Mount St. Mary's University*

BOOK REVIEW EDITORS
Kent Lasnoski, *Wyoming Catholic College*
Mari Rapela Heidt, *Notre Dame of Maryland University*

EDITORIAL BOARD
Christine Astorga, *University of Portland*
Jana M. Bennett, *University of Dayton*
Mara Brecht, *Loyola University Chicago*
Jim Caccamo, *St. Joseph's University*
Carolyn A. Chan, *King's University College at Western University, Ontario, Canada*
Meghan Clark, *St. John's University*
David Cloutier, *The Catholic University of America*
Christopher Denny, *St. John's University*
Mary M. Doyle Roche, *College of the Holy Cross*
Joseph Flipper, *Bellarmine College*
Nichole M. Flores, *University of Virginia*
Matthew J. Gaudet, *Santa Clara University*
Kelly Johnson, *University of Dayton*
Andrew Kim, *Marquette University*
Warren Kinghorn, *Duke University*
Ramon Luzarraga, *Benedictine University, Mesa*
Alexandre Martins, CM, *Marquette University*
William C. Mattison III, *University of Notre Dame*
Christopher McMahon, *Saint Vincent College*
Cory D. Mitchell, *Mercy Health Muskegon*
Suzanne Mulligan, *Liaison with Catholic Theological Ethics in the World Church Pontifical University, Maynooth, Co. Kildare, Ireland*
Matthew Shadle, *Marymount University*
Joel Shuman, *Kings College*
Christopher P. Vogt, *St. John's University*
Paul Wadell, *St. Norbert College*

JOURNAL OF MORAL THEOLOGY
VOLUME 10, SPECIAL ISSUE 1
SPRING 2021

CONTENTS

Introduction: Trends in Post-Vatican II Scholarship on
    Scripture and Moral Theology
    William C. Mattison III... 1

On Pilgrimage with Abraham: How a Patriarch Leads Us in Formation in Faith
    Jana M. Bennett 20

Joseph the Just and Matthew's Matrix of Mercy: The Redefinition of Righteousness
    Jonathan T. Pennington.. 40

"Repent for the Kingdom of Heaven is at Hand!" (Mt 3:1 and 4:17): Conversion in the Gospel and the Christian Life
    Anton ten Klooster.. 51

"Those He Predestined He Also Called" (Romans 8:30): Aquinas on the Liberating Grace of Conversion
    Daria Spezzano 67

Almsgiving as an Integral Practice of Repentance for Christian Discipleship: The Gospel of Luke and Daniel 4:24
    James W. Stroud 84

A Defense of the Command/Counsel Distinction Based on Matthew 19 and 1 Corinthians 7
    John Meinert 104

Newness of Life and Grace Enabled Recovery from Addiction: Walking the Road to Recovery with Romans 7
    Andrew Kim 124

Trends in Post-Vatican II Scholarship on Scripture and Moral Theology

William C. Mattison III

Few lines from Magisterial documents are more frequently quoted in post-conciliar Catholic moral theology than this one from *Optatam Totius* 16:

> Special care must be given to the perfecting of moral theology. Its scientific exposition, nourished more on the teaching of the Bible, should shed light on the loftiness of the calling of the faithful in Christ and the obligation that is theirs of bearing fruit in charity for the life of the world.

In the roughly five decades since the close of Vatican II, moral theology has been undergoing a vigorous renewal. Few, if anyone, denies that pre-conciliar Catholic moral theology required such renewal. As to what constitutes authentic renewal, what has led to deviation, and what the role of *Veritatis Splendor* is in that renewal, there is significant disagreement. One of the more specific directives regarding the renewal of moral theology in *Optatam Totius*—namely, that its scientific presentation be "nourished more on the teaching of Scripture"—would be denied by few and yet has received inconsistent attention in Catholic moral theology since the Council.

This volume includes a set of essays that attempt to respond to the call of Vatican II to do Catholic moral theology in a manner nourished more by the teaching of Scripture. The authors of the essays contained herein do not explicitly reflect on the need for such an endeavor, to what extent it has been carried out in various ways over the last half century, or how their own essays constitute such an endeavor. They simply go about doing it. Yet, how they do so invites reflection on the ways that this set of essays is illustrative of both the contemporary *status quaestionis* of scholarship on Scripture and moral theology and of certain thematic emphases in Catholic moral theology more broadly. Thus, while the main task of this essay is to introduce the essays contained in this volume, it first offers some reflections on one trajectory of development in scholarship on Scripture and moral theology in the half century since Vatican II.

Perhaps it would help to note what this essay is *not*. It is not a *Theological Studies* genre "Notes in Moral Theology" that names all important scholarship on this topic in a certain period. Nor it is it an assessment of scholarship on Scripture in moral theology in the past half century. Such an argument would have to address, for instance, what trends in that scholarship constitute genuine continuity with the Biblical renewal in the years preceding Vatican II. It would also have to address several important post-conciliar trends not treated here, including the ascendancy of liberationist accounts of Scripture and (particularly political) moral theology. Rather, the task of this essay is to introduce the essays herein, and to contextualize them by narrating one trajectory in post-Vatican II scholarship on Scripture and moral theology. That trajectory is the move from a preoccupation with method in the deluge of scholarship on Scripture and ethics in the 1970s–90s, to a contemporary emphasis on virtue and formation without such preoccupation on method. To narrate that trajectory this essay proceeds in three sections. Section One offers an account of this focus on method in the initial wave of post-Vatican II scholarship on Scripture and ethics. Section Two examines certain "hinge figures" who bring this initial wave of scholarship to its fruition and/or portend future emphases. Section Three identifies a common emphasis in contemporary scholarship on Scripture and moral theology, as exemplified in both recent works on the Sermon on the Mount and the essays in this volume.

SECTION ONE: DELUGE OF SCHOLARSHIP AFTER VATICAN II

In the roughly three decades following the Second Vatican Council, there was an explosion of scholarship on the topic of Scripture and moral theology.[1] Yet in the ensuing two decades, the degree of attention to this topic has fallen precipitously. The purpose of this section is to offer a brief overview of that initial wave of scholarship on Scripture and moral theology.[2] No attempt is made here at anything approaching a comprehensive bibliography of scholarship on Scripture

---

[1] Others commonly speak of this topic with phrases such as Scripture (or the Bible) and (Christian) ethics, or Biblical morality. Though "Scripture and moral theology" is used here, it is not used as a way to distinguish this scholarship from scholarship self-described with such other terms.

[2] There have been other post-conciliar attempts at describing this body of scholarship in stages. See for instance, Edouard Hamel, "Scripture and Moral Theology: 1940–1980," *Theology Digest* 36, no. 3 (1989): 203–207. See also James Bretzke, SJ, "Scripture: The 'Soul' of Moral Theology? The Second Stage" *Irish Theological Quarterly* 60, no. 4 (1994): 259–271. Most recently, see Lucas Chan, SJ, "Biblical Ethics: 3D," in *The Bible and Catholic Theological Ethics*, eds. Yiu Sing Lucas Chan, SJ, and James F. Keenan, SJ, and Ronaldo Zacharias (Maryknoll, NY: Orbis, 2017), 17–33. For examples of scholarship that surveys the topic based on prominent figures,

and moral theology.³ Rather, important features and contributors at various stages are narrated here in order to place this volume's essays in post-conciliar context.

In the 1970s there began a veritable deluge of scholarship on Scripture and moral theology. A helpful collection of essays presenting the *status quaestionis* at this time is Charles Curran and Richard McCormick, SJ's *Readings in Moral Theology, vol. 4: The Use of Scripture in Moral Theology*.⁴ This volume exemplifies certain characteristic features of this wave of research on Scripture and moral theology. A first noteworthy feature concerns the participants in this scholarship. The essays in this volume are representative of the ecumenical character of research on this topic, with the essays split nearly in half between Catholics and Protestants. Furthermore, the volume is indicative of collaboration between moralists and Biblical scholars.⁵ Finally, this volume contains seeds of the concern to include historically under-represented perspectives on the Biblical narrative.⁶

A second characteristic of this scholarship is the extent to which it served as a platform for pressing moral theological issues of the time. Consonant with a renewal in Catholic moral theology at this time was a broader inquiry into establishing the bases for morality. For instance, what are the justifications for and role of rules in morality more broadly? There was a common distinction between Scripture as "revealed morality" and "revealed reality"—in other words, between the Scripture as source of moral norms as distinct from Scripture as revealing the truth about reality which results in normative claims. This distinction evidences inquiry into the basis and function of moral norms.⁷ There was a clear focus on the hermeneutical task of engaging

---

see Lucas Chan, *Biblical Ethics in the 21ˢᵗ Century: Developments, Emerging Consensus and Future Directions* (Mahwah, NJ: Paulist Press, 2013). See also Jeffrey Siker, *Scripture and Ethics: Twentieth Century Portraits* (Oxford: Oxford University Press, 1997).
³ Fortunately, this task has been taken up with tremendous thoroughness by James Bretzke, SJ. See his *Bibliography on Scripture and Ethics* (Lewiston, NY: Edwin Mellen Press, 1997), which is now updated (2017) and available electronically at www2.bc.edu/james-bretzke/ScriptureAndEthicsBibliography.pdf.
⁴ Charles Curran, SJ, and Richard McCormick, SJ eds. *Readings in Moral Theology*, vol. 4: *The Use of Scripture in Moral Theology* (Ramsey, NJ: Paulist Press, 1984).
⁵ See the following essays by Biblical scholars in *The Use of Scripture in Moral Theology*: Richard Hiers, "Jesus, Ethics, and the Present Situation," 1–20; Jack Sanders, "The Question of the Relevance of Jesus for Ethics Today," 45–65; and Elizabeth Schussler Fiorenza, "Toward a Feminist Biblical Hermeneutic: Biblical Interpretation and Liberation Theology," 354–382.
⁶ See the following essays in *The Use of Scripture in Moral Theology*: James Cone, "Biblical Revelation and Social Existence," 21–44; Alfred Hennelly, "The Biblical Hermeneutics of Juan Luis Segundo," 303–320; and Elizabeth Schussler Fiorenza, cited in n. 5.
⁷ See James Gustafson, "The Changing Use of the Bible in Christian Ethics," in *The Use of Scripture in Moral Theology*, 133–150, at 140–141. Note that his depiction of

Scripture for moral guidance, and inquiry into the authoritative role of the community in doing so, as well as the need for "outside" sources.[8] This inquiry had a distinct inflection among Catholic scholars given debates over authority in the wake of *Humanae Vitae*. Also prevalent at this time, especially among Catholics, was an inquiry into the distinctiveness of the Biblical ethic and Christian morality more broadly.[9] We see therefore a second feature of this first wave of scholarship on Scripture and moral theology, namely, that it reflected broader moral theological inquiry of the day.

These first two features of post-conciliar scholarship persist today. It is the next one that is noteworthy in this introductory essay, given its difference from more recent scholarship on Scripture and moral theology as evidenced by the essays in this volume. Third and finally, this initial stage of scholarship on Scripture and moral theology was dominated by the identification of a method for "using" Scripture and an attempt to encyclopedically "cover" all Scripture (or one of the Testaments).[10] Comprehensive surveys of various approaches to Bible and morality, or the distinct tasks in doing so, were common at the time. It was common to speak of how to "use" Scripture in moral theology.[11] It was also common to speak of Scripture as one of the "sources" of morality, especially as part of the so-called Wesleyan

---

revealed morality was focused on moral norms. For his four types of using Scripture in such a way, see his "The Place of Scripture in Christian Ethics: A Methodological Study," in *The Use of Scripture in Moral Theology*, 151–177, at 159–168.

[8] For an example of the hermeneutical import of the Christian community, see Stanley Hauerwas, "The Moral Authority of Scripture: The Politics and Ethics of Remembering," in *Use of Scripture in Moral Theology*, 242–275.

[9] Charles Curran's essay focuses squarely on this topic. See "The Role and Function of the Scriptures in Moral Theology," in *Use of Scripture in Moral Theology*, 178–212. See also the roughly contemporaneous volume edited by Charles Curran and Richard McCormick, *Readings in Moral Theology* vol. 2: *The Distinctiveness of Christian Ethics* (Ramsey, NJ: Paulist Press, 1980).

[10] By encyclopedic here, I reference not the length or quantity but the genre as described by Alasdair MacIntyre in *Three Rival Versions of Moral Inquiry* (Notre Dame, IN: University of Notre Dame Press, 1990). Such approaches try not only to cover everything in the field of scholarship, but to organize or categorize that field through a schema of comprehensive categories. For such examples see: James Gustafson, "The Place of Scripture in Christian Ethics: Methodological Study," in *Use of Scripture in Moral Theology*, 151–177, especially at 159–168; Sandra Schneiders, "From Exegesis to Hermeneutics: The Problem of the Contemporary Meaning of Scripture," *Horizons* 8, no. 1 (1981): 23–39; and Kenneth Himes, "Scripture and Ethics: A Review Essay," *Biblical Theology Bulletin* 15, no. 2 (1985): 65–73.

[11] This phrasing is found in the subtitle of the Curran, SJ, and McCormick, SJ, volume on this topic. See also another important book on the topic from this era, Thomas Ogletree's *The Use of the Bible in Christian Ethics: A Constructive Essay* (Philadelphia, PA: Fortress, 1983).

quadrangle including also tradition, reason, and experience.[12] Gustafson speaks in this context of Scripture as providing "data."[13] The breadth and complexity of schematizations of a method or of various methods, figures, or tasks during this period of scholarship were quite impressive. Yet an irony of such an emphasis is that there was often very little engagement with particular texts of Scripture. Of course, exposure to and formation by Scripture presumably drove such scholarship. In fact, at times scholarship focused precisely on this dynamic.[14] But even in these cases, scholars most commonly addressed and analyzed how to use Scripture for morality rather than focus on particular Scriptural texts themselves.

SECTION TWO: HINGE FIGURES ON SCRIPTURE AND MORAL THEOLOGY

Certain works in the 1990s warrant closer examination, as they serve as hinges between the first wave of scholarship in the decades after Vatican II and work in the twenty-first century. They represent a sort of culmination of the aforementioned emphasis in the first period and/or signals of the next wave of scholarship. One example of the former is Frank Matera's *New Testament Ethics*.[15] This book perfectly represents the encyclopedic character of the first wave of scholarship as it covers nearly the entire New Testament. Here we have a master Biblical scholar who distills from each Gospel and Pauline letter an overarching theme to help break open that book's ethical guidance. Matera's command of Biblical scholarship grounds his analysis of each book. He does not reflect extensively on the exegetical and hermeneutical tasks, though his mastery of these tasks as a Scripture scholar seeps through each chapter. In some ways, he signals future scholarship that focuses more squarely on particular texts rather than method. Yet his status as a Biblical scholar working on Scripture and

---

[12] Gustafson seems to be the source of this approach to Christian ethics in this era. See his *Protestant and Roman Catholic Ethics: Prospects for Rapprochement* (Chicago: University of Chicago Press, 1982), 139–144. See also Lisa Cahill, *Between the Sexes: Foundations for a Christian Ethics of Sexuality* (Philadelphia, PA: Fortress, 1985), 5. In her far more recent *Just Love: A Framework for Christian Sexual Ethics* (New York: Continuum, 2008), Margaret Farley deploys this method and claims her students for decades would recognize it from her teaching; see 182, n. 22. For an example of Catholic moral theology that continues to deploy this quadrangle today, see Todd Salzman and Michael Lawler, *Virtue and Theological Ethics: Toward a Renewed Ethical Method* (New York: Orbis, 2018). For description of Scripture as a source in quite a distinct context, alongside tradition and Magisterium, see Servais Pinckaers, OP, *L'Evangile et la Morale* (Paris: Cerf, 1990), 83–100.

[13] See James Gustafson, "The Place of Scripture in Christian Ethics," 166.

[14] In addition to Hauerwas's essay, see Richard McCormick's "Scripture, Liturgy, Character, and Morality," in *The Use of Scripture in Moral Theology*, 289–302.

[15] Frank Matera, *New Testament Ethics* (Louisville, KY: Westminister John Knox Press, 1996).

moral theology, and especially the comprehensive nature of his research on the topic, make his classic book a culmination of that first wave of scholarship.

The very same year as Matera's *New Testament Ethics*, Protestant Biblical scholar Richard Hays released his *Moral Vision of the New Testament*.[16] This book so successfully brought to fruition the goals of the late twentieth century wave of scholarship on Scripture and moral theology that it may be responsible for the decline in scholarship on the topic. This book is that definitive. It is divided into four tasks. The first one, the descriptive task, identifies in a manner akin to Matera the key themes in each of the Gospels as well as the Pauline and Johannine epistles. It even wades into the heated debate of that time over the historical Jesus. As with Matera, here we see a master Biblical scholar at work, grounding his ethical claims in a command of Scriptural scholarship. The book then turns to the second, "synthetic," task and identifies three overarching themes that are at the center of the ethical vision of the entire New Testament: new creation, cross, and community. His third task, the "hermeneutical," explicitly attends to method, or how Scripture is "used." After a chapter overviewing five important approaches to Scripture by twentieth century scholars (Niebuhr, Barth, Yoder, Hauerwas, and Schussler Fiorenza), he presents his own method including a set of clear guidelines. Here we have attention to method that is both comprehensive and trajectory-setting. The final task, the "pragmatic," attends to how Scripture shapes and informs certain contentious issues in moral theology (e.g., divorce and remarriage, homosexuality, warfare, ethnic conflict and anti-Semitism, and abortion).

Hays's magisterial work represents the clear culmination of a characteristic feature of scholarship in the years preceding his work. It evidences all the key features of the methodological focus of such scholarship, including: an encyclopedic approach to the New Testament; explicit attention to the hermeneutical task approached both through a sample of prominent scholars and a constructive method; a constructive synthesis of what the New Testament says about ethics; and attention to ethical quandaries so characteristic of late twentieth century moral theology. It would be too much to claim that Hays's book decisively ended all debate on Scripture and ethics. Indeed, there were importantly different approaches to the topic even at this time. Though some of them are addressed by Hays (e.g., Yoder, Hauerwas), they would not be accurately described as part of Hays's project, which is far more encyclopedic in method.[17] Yet it is certainly the case that for

---

[16] Richard Hays, *Moral Vision of the New Testament* (San Francisco: HarperOne, 1996).

[17] In addition to the work of Yoder and Hauerwas, see also Stephen Fowl and Gregory Jones, *Reading in Communion* (Grand Rapids, MI: Eerdmans, 1991) and Stephen

anyone reading scholarship on Scripture and moral theology in this period, Hays's book would have to be on the reading list. As with Matera, there are hints of future directions. For instance, although neither of the terms "virtue" nor "character" appear in the index, the constructive synthetic proposal of cross, new creation, and community portends future scholarship emphasizing the role of Scripture in ongoing formation in the life of discipleship.[18] Characteristically focused on methodology and hermeneutics, Hays addresses Biblical texts primarily encyclopedically, although his final section on contested moral issues starts with the relevant particular texts.

A third work that deserves further attention as a hinge to the next wave of scholarship is William Spohn's 1999 *Go and Do Likewise: Jesus and Ethics*. Though he entered the scholarly discourse on Scripture and moral theology after that initial spate in the 1970s, this Catholic student of Gustafson is as important a contributor to that scholarship as anyone. He burst on to the scene with his 1984 *What are They Saying About Scripture and Ethics?*, which offers a six-fold summary of various approaches to Scripture and moral theology—yet ironically very little engagement with particular Scriptural texts, as was common for scholarship at the time.[19] He wrote influential scholarly articles on the topic in ensuing years, and his scholarship culminated in *Go and Do Likewise* before his tragic passing in 2005.[20] In some ways, this book is characteristic of the first wave of scholarship on Scripture and moral theology. It is an argument for method. And although Scriptural texts such as the Psalms, the parable of the Good Samaritan, the Proclamation of the Kingdom, and the Lord's Prayer feature prominently, they support the methodological claims rather than structure the argument. That said, the book is importantly innovative in its explicit attempt to do ethics based on the person of Jesus Christ, accessed in large part through the Scriptures, and followed in a life of discipleship that Spohn terms "spirituality." His method is explicitly virtue-centered, and he is concerned throughout the book to address how encountering Jesus shapes one's perceptions, dispositions, and identity.

Fowl's *Engaging Scripture: A Model for Theological Interpretation* (Malden, MA: Blackwell, 1998). In these approaches Nicholas Lash's "Performing the Scriptures," *The Furrow* 33, no. 8 (1982): 467–474, is cited prominently.

[18] Hays's section on Hauerwas mentions the latter's treatments of these topics; see 253–265.

[19] William C. Spohn, SJ, *What Are They Saying About Scripture and Ethics?* (Mahwah, NJ: Paulist Press, 1984, 1996). For a recent examination of Spohn's work in the context of twentieth century Catholic moral theology, see James F. Keenan, SJ, *A History of Catholic Moral Theology in the Twentieth Century: From Confessing Sins to Liberating Consciences* (New York: Continuum, 2010), 75–77.

[20] William C. Spohn, SJ, *Go and Do Likewise* (New York: Continuum, 1999).

In these latter ways the book is an important contribution to scholarship on Scripture and ethics that represents both a culmination of prior work on the topic and a premonition of future directions in that field.

One final scholar warrants mention as a hinge figure for Scripture and moral theology. A case can be made that Servais Pinckaers, OP's 1995 *Sources of Christian Ethics* is the most important and influential book in Catholic moral theology after Vatican II.[21] Though the book contains chapters on the Sermon on the Mount and Pauline ethics, the book's focus is not the topic of Scripture and moral theology per se, but rather constitutes a larger project aiming to restore happiness and virtue to their previously prominent place in Catholic moral theology. So, while his project is thoroughly informed by Scripture, it is not a book primarily on Scripture and moral theology. This is even true of his 1990 *L'Evangile et la morale*.[22] This latter book (like *Sources*) contains no significant treatment of methodology. It is an account of the Spirit-animated life, containing essays on topics such as the new law, infused virtues, gifts of the Holy Spirit, Church, and evangelical counsels, as well as classic moral topics and issues such as the moral act, conscience, marriage, and violence. Though there are brief treatments of (again) both the Sermon on the Mount and Paul's ethics, one would be hard pressed to describe either of these books, absent their titles, as works on Scripture and moral theology. Rather, they represent Pinckaers' overall project of a Thomistic moral theology firmly rooted in sources that include Sacred Scripture; particularly in his focus on the Sermon on the Mount, but also in his account of the moral life and a Spirit-animated formation in virtue, Pinckaers augurs and informs future scholarship on Scripture and moral theology.

SECTION THREE: CONTEMPORARY RESEARCH ON SCRIPTURE AND MORAL THEOLOGY

Perhaps the most noteworthy feature of a survey of scholarship on Scripture and moral theology over the past five decades is the marked difference in quantity of research on the topic. The initial explosion of research in the 1970s lasted through the 1980s and into the 1990s. Yet the volume of such work drops precipitously after 2000.[23] Anecdotally, during my own doctoral studies at Notre Dame in the late 1990s,

---

[21] Servais Pinckaers, OP, *Sources of Christian Ethics*, trans. Mary Thomas Noble, OP (Washington, DC: The Catholic University of America Press, 1995). For an example of just such a case, see David Cloutier and William C. Mattison III, "The Resurgence of Virtue in Recent Moral Theology," *Journal of Moral Theology* 3, no. 1 (2014): 228–259, at 238–241. Note that Pinckaers' book is the English translation of the French *Les sources de la morale chrétienne* (Paris: Cerf, 1986).

[22] Servais Pinckaers, O.P., *L'Evangile et la morale* (Paris: Cerf, 1990).

[23] Quantitative support for this observation comes from a review of Bretzke's bibliography. Though updated in 2017, the enormous amount of scholarship before 2000 is massively disproportionate to that after 2000.

doctoral candidacy exams in moral theology always featured a question on Scripture and moral theology, and the body of scholarship on the topic was robust and well-known. Twenty years later, students far less frequently choose to do Scripture and moral theology as one of their topics, and when they do it is more difficult to assemble a robust bibliography with materials from the past two decades.

That said, the work does continue, and observations about the ways it is similar and yet distinct from that earlier burst of scholarship are warranted. As for similarities, this continues to be a markedly ecumenical area of research, with important contributions by both Catholics and Protestants, at times in collaboration. The work is also still being done in a cross-sub-disciplinary manner, with contributions from both moralists and Biblical scholars. Finally, a focus on liberationist topics and inclusion of under-represented voices has not only continued but greatly expanded.[24] This is unsurprising since research on Scripture and moral theology continues to reflect current trends in moral theology more broadly. To name one such trend that characterizes the essays in this volume, there has been a massive surge in attention to virtue in treatments of Scripture and moral theology, reflective of a resurgence in attention to virtue in Catholic moral theology beginning just before the turn of the century.[25]

As for differences, the most immediately obvious one was noted above, i.e., the significant decrease in amount of scholarship on the topic. But the conceptually interesting differences identified here and exemplified in this volume's essays are a far greater focus on specific Biblical texts rather than an attempt to comprehensively "cover" all of Scripture, and significantly less explicit attention to questions of hermeneutics and methodology, generally in favor of a focus on formation and virtue. Put bluntly, recent scholarship focuses less on *how* to do Scripture and moral theology. It simply does it. This is not of course a claim that recent scholarship achieves some sort of immediate access to the true meaning of the text without need of hermeneutical

---

[24] Indeed, an analysis of this trend warrants an essay of its own. A review of Bretzke, SJ's bibliography reveals that though there are proportionally fewer works on Scripture and moral theology post-2000, among those works a larger proportion explicitly addresses the topic with a concern for under-represented voices, and it seems also true that proportionally more of the work is being done *by* scholars from under-represented groups. Though it is not focused directly on Scripture and moral theology, mention should be made here of James F. Keenan, SJ's Catholic Theological Ethics in a World Church initiative (CTEWC), which has fostered greater awareness of scholarship from beyond Europe and North America, and engendered greater collaboration among ethicists internationally. An essay on increased emphasis on liberationist themes and contextual theology in recent scholarship on Scripture and moral theology could surely focus on the fifth volume to come from CTEWC, Chan, Keenan, and Zacharias, eds., *The Bible and Catholic Theological Ethics* (Maryknoll, NY: Orbis Book, 2017).
[25] For more on this resurgence, see Cloutier and Mattison, "The Resurgence of Virtue in Recent Moral Theology."

acumen and nuance. Yet when scholarship such as the essays in this volume turn to Scripture to inform contemporary moral issues, that is generally done absent any extended inquiry into method. Rather than such an emphasis primarily on method and concerned to cover all of Scripture, recent scholarship is increasingly characterized by an emphasis on *formation* and focus on specific texts.

These features, a focus on both formation and particular texts rather than method and/or more comprehensive focus on the whole of Scripture (or the New Testament), represent one important difference between twenty-first century scholarship and late twentieth century scholarship, one that is evidenced in the essays of this volume.[26] The following two parts of this section further examine these features of contemporary scholarship on Scripture and ethics. The second part turns to the enclosed essays in this volume. The first part utilizes a sample of this scholarship focused on the Sermon on the Mount. Once again, the goal here is neither to offer a comprehensive review of all excellent recent scholarship on Scripture and ethics, nor to claim that the features identified here are the only important features of that scholarship.[27] Rather, the goal is to situate the essays in this volume in the context of one trend in that scholarship.

Recent Scholarship on Scripture and Moral Theology: The Sermon on the Mount

Why focus on scholarship on the Sermon on the Mount? After all, if one claim of this essay is that more recent work on Scripture and

---

[26] There are exceptions to the increasingly common focus on specific texts in recent scholarship. Ben Witherington III has embarked on a quite encyclopedic project on Scripture (the New Testament) and ethics. See his *The Indelible Image: The Theological and Ethical Thought World of the New Testament*, vol. 1: *The Individual Witness*, and vol. 2: *The Collective Witness* (Downers Grove, IL: IVP Academic, 2009, 2010). For a comparable project on the Old Testament, see Christopher J. H. Wright, *Old Testament Ethics for the People of God* (Downers Grove, IL: IVP Academic, 2004). Wright's book is reminiscent of an earlier wave of scholarship in its survey of various methods of doing Old Testament Ethics. His approach is encyclopedic in tackling the entire Old Testament, though he approaches it via themes rather than all of its books or sections of books. For another recent book that encyclopedically attends to the entirety of the Bible through various moral topics, see John Collins, *What Are Biblical Values? What the Bible Says on Key Ethical Issues* (New Haven, CT: Yale University Press, 2019).

[27] For instance, another category of books on Scripture and moral theology left unaddressed in this essay are those that trace one theme through the entirety of Scripture (or one Testament). In addition to the works (e.g., Gary Anderson) treated below in the context of Stroud's essay, consider several such works by (this volume's co-editor) Matthew Levering, including *Biblical Natural Law: A Theocentric and Teleological Approach* (New York: Oxford University Press, 2008); *The Betrayal of Charity: The Sins that Sabotage Divine Love* (Waco, TX: Baylor University Press, 2011); and *Aquinas's Eschatological Ethics and the Virtue of Temperance* (Notre Dame, IN: University of Notre Dame Press, 2019).

moral theology focuses on specific texts, it seems question-begging to focus the inquiry this way. There are two reasons for this basis for a sample of recent scholarship. First, at the conference from which the enclosed essays are drawn, there was a session on two of the following books on the Sermon. Second and more importantly, the selection of this topic reflects a growing focus on that text in the past two decades, a focus that was missing in that earlier surge of scholarship, and that constitutes a return to prominence of this text in the broader context of the Christian tradition. Augustine said the Sermon offers "the complete way of living the Christian life," containing "all the precepts that inform such a life" (*De sermo domini in monte*, 1.1.1).[28] Thomas Aquinas regarded it as the written version of the new law (ST I-II q. 108, a. 3 and I-II q. 106, a. 1). So perhaps it should be no surprise that there has been a return to particular focus on the Sermon in recent scholarship on Scripture and moral theology. Four books that do so are examined here.[29]

In 2003, Glen Stassen and David Gushee, both Protestant ethicists, published *Kingdom Ethics*. The book is heavily shaped by the Sermon, if not "on" the Sermon, and thus it is a sort of "hinge" book for this section akin to those books in Section Two.[30] Its approach to Christian ethics is based on the Kingdom of God and forming a Kingdom people, but it does so primarily through the beatitudes (which it calls "virtues for the Kingdom") and through attention to character. It then turns to certain methodological issues in Christian ethics, including authority and Scripture as well as the status of moral norms, both common topics in that first wave of scholarship reviewed in Section One. Its review of a dozen or so commonly addressed issues in Christian ethics is more framed *by* the Sermon than *on* the Sermon. But two features of this book portend recent scholarship on Scripture and ethics. First, it offers a careful reading of the beatitudes that is attentive to Biblical

---

[28] Accessed at www.augustinus.it/latino/montagna/index2.htm; translation mine: "*perfectam vitae christianae modum*" and "*praecepta esse omnia quae ad informandam vitam pertinent.*"

[29] Though just four such books are treated here, they by no means represent the whole of scholarship on Scripture and moral theology focusing on the Sermon. See also Charles Talbert, *Reading the Sermon on the Mount: Character and Decision-Making in Matthew 5–7* (Ada, MI: Baker Books, 2006); Dale C. Allison, *The Sermon on the Mount: Inspiring the Moral Imagination* (New York: Herder & Herder, 1999); Frank Matera, *The Sermon on the Mount: The Perfect Measure of the Christian Life* (Collegeville, MN: Liturgical Press, 2013). Finally, see the excellent sets of essays in various issues of volume 22 (2009) of *Studies in Christian Ethics*.

[30] David Gushee published a second edition of this book in 2017, after Glen Stassen's passing. He re-organized the book into two main parts, the first on methodology and the second on particular issues. This is more representative of the earlier wave of scholarship on Scripture and ethics. But, interestingly enough, he also renamed the various "issue" chapters to more explicitly conform to passages in the Sermon on the Mount.

scholarship.[31] Second, it quite consciously adopts a virtue approach to morality.[32] This approach, it is safe to say, dominates the next three books examined here.

The next book is Lucas Chan, SJ's *The Ten Commandments and the Beatitudes: Biblical Studies and Ethics for Real Life*.[33] It is actually not a book on the Sermon of the Mount per se. Yet, its focus on the beatitudes and the commandments, both of which dominate Matthew 5 in the Sermon on the Mount, make it a fitting inclusion in this section. Before examining this book, a word is in order on Chan's work more broadly.[34] Before his tragic premature passing in 2015, Lucas was establishing himself as an authority in Scripture and ethics. His revised dissertation, *Biblical Ethics in the 21st Century: Developments, Emerging Consensus, and Future Directions* offers an encyclopedic overview of this field through an analysis of four Scripture scholars doing ethics and four moralists working on Scripture.[35] Its encyclopedic scope and focus on method were more characteristic of earlier work on Scripture and moral theology, but he made two important contributions that continue to characterize more recent work. First, he emphasized how important it is that Biblical scholarship and moral theology be done in conjunction with one another, even making this a basis for his account of the stages in recent scholarship on Scripture

---

[31] Whether the beatitudes are understood as virtues (as in this book) or as related to the virtues (see Chan as well as Mattison below), a focus on the beatitudes is common in the turn to virtue in recent work on Scripture and moral theology. For another "hinge" text where the beatitudes feature prominently even as the rest of the text focuses primarily on methodological criteria for doing Scripture and moral theology, see the Pontifical Biblical Commission's *The Bible and Morality: The Biblical Roots of Christian Conduct* (Vatican City: Libreria Editrice Vaticana, 2008). Interestingly enough, it aligns each of its six specific methodological criteria with a virtue (104).

[32] The growing prominence of a virtue approach to morality in scholarship on Scripture and moral theology is evident in the two books on virtue and Scripture published by moral theologian James F. Keenan, SJ, and Biblical scholar Daniel Harrington's *Jesus and Virtue Ethics* (New York: Sheed and Ward, 2002) and *Paul and Virtue Ethics* (Lanham, MD: Rowman and Littlefield, 2010). As noted in the introduction to *Paul and Virtue Ethics*, the claim is that a virtue approach to morality can help readers better understand Paul (or the Gospels), and in turn that the Scriptures provide a "lens" to understand virtue ethics (xii).

[33] Lucas Chan, SJ, *The Ten Commandments and the Beatitudes: Biblical Studies and Ethics for Real Life* (Lanham, MD: Rowman and Littlefield, 2012).

[34] For a review of Chan's work in a recent volume dedicated to him, see James F. Keenan, SJ, "Hospitality: Interpreting Lucas Chan's Work Through a Timely, Biblical Virtue from the Book of Ruth," in *Bridging Scripture and Moral Theology: Essays in Dialogue with Yiu Sing Lucas Chan, SJ*, eds. Michael Cover, John Theide, and Joshua Ezra Burns (Lanham, MD: Rowman & Littlefield, 2019), 3–22.

[35] Lucas Chan, SJ, *Biblical Ethics in the 21st Century: Developments, Emerging Consensus, and Future Directions* (Mahweh, NJ: Paulist Press, 2013).

and moral theology.[36] Second, he makes a case for the particular importance of virtue in doing Scripture and moral theology, a position that features prominently in recent scholarship on the topic.

As for Chan's book under spotlight here, his focus on particular Scriptural texts models the collaboration with Biblical scholars that he lauds in other work. He engages several prominent recent Biblical scholars in his interpretations, especially of the beatitudes. His concern for formation is evident in the subtitle, which accurately depicts the book's accessibility and formative nature. Perhaps its most creative aspect is its proposal of a virtue for each commandment or beatitude. Alignments of various Scriptural "sets" in the Christian moral tradition have a long and distinguished history extending at least to Augustine's alignment of beatitudes, gifts of the Holy Spirit, and petitions of the Lord's Prayer. Chan's effort thus represents a deeply traditional move, and also a way to present the convergence of a virtue-centered approach to morality with the beatitudes and especially the commandments, the latter of which are too often regarded as non-teleological norms that are only artificially connected to virtues.

Another recent book, my own monograph *The Sermon on the Mount and Moral Theology: A Virtue Perspective*, similarly exhibits characteristic features of recent work on Scripture and moral theology. It obviously focuses on a particular text and evidences the robust engagement with Biblical scholarship that has continued to characterize scholarship in Scripture and moral theology. Like most recent scholarship in this area, its focus is less on method than on what the text at hand offers as to formation in the Christian life. That is not to say it has no method. Similar to other such recent works, it adopts what it calls a "virtue-centered approach to morality." The consistent claim of the book is that bringing such an approach to the Sermon illuminates moral claims that might otherwise be missed. Conversely, this authoritative gospel text does not simply endorse classical virtue ethics claims, but rather offers an account of them transformed in the life of graced discipleship.

This book uses various sections of the Sermon on the Mount to launch Scripturally-informed inquiries into foundational questions in a virtue-centered approach to moral theology. For instance, the beatitudes prompt an examination of the relationship between good action and happiness. The antitheses prompt inquiry not only into the way Jesus fulfills the old law, but how rules can in various ways depict activities constitutive of the goals toward which they point. The Matthew 6 passages on prayer, fasting, and almsgiving offer a sort of disciplined process of habituation endemic to any classical virtue ethics, even as their ordering all things toward love of our heavenly Father

---

[36] See Chan, "Biblical Ethics: 3D," 18–22.

offers an account of charity commanding all our activities that is foreign to classical virtue. The same may be said by the various sayings in Matthew 6 and 7 on the last end, prudence and justice, all of which are classical virtue ethics topics but are radically transformed in the context of faith in a God of provident gratuity. The consistent approach of the book is to deploy the resources of classical virtue ethics to understand the formation offered in the Sermon, a formation radically transformed in the context of faith in and love of our heavenly Father.[37]

As with Chan's book, this book offers some constructive alignments of virtues with various parts of the Sermon, in a manner that harks back to Augustine even as it focuses on the three theological and four cardinal virtues. The Introduction offers an alignment of parts of the entire Sermon text with the seven theological and cardinal virtues, and the concluding chapter aligns the petitions of the Lord's Prayer with these seven virtues. These alignments are more playful and mutually illuminating than restrictive or reductive, suggesting a "synergy between Scripture and the tradition of the virtues [that] 'breaks open a new space for apprehending and contemplating the beauty of the wisdom that is present in these words.'"[38] Regardless of the fruitfulness of that endeavor, it is yet another indication of how heavily virtue is used in recent work to break open the Scriptures for guidance on moral formation.

A fourth and final important recent contribution to Scripture and moral theology that displays characteristics common to such scholarship today is Jonathan Pennington's *The Sermon on the Mount and Human Flourishing: A Theological Commentary*.[39] Pennington is a Protestant Scripture scholar, and thus this work demonstrates the ongoing ecumenical and cross-sub-disciplinary nature of this field. In fact, it is even evident in the format of the book itself. As befitting a Scripture scholar, half of the book's chapters offer a standard genre verse-by-verse commentary of the Sermon.[40] Yet the other half of the chapters, which include two on context and structure more common to Scripture scholarship, address foundational moral topics such as

---

[37] For another example of assimilating classical virtue ethics and a Scriptural text on formation, see N. T. Wright's focus on character and formation in *After You Believe: Why Christian Character Matters* (New York: HarperCollins, 2010).
[37] William C. Mattison, III, *The Sermon on the Mount and Moral Theology: A Virtue Perspective* (Cambridge: Cambridge University Press, 2017).
[38] Mattison, *The Sermon on the Mount and Moral Theology*, 15, citing Patrick Clark.
[39] Jonathan Pennington, *The Sermon on the Mount and Human Flourishing: A Theological Commentary* (Grand Rapids, MI: Baker Academic, 2017).
[40] For a comparable book from Protestant Scripture scholarship that examines ethics through a particular text in the style of commentary, see Brian Brock and Bernd Wannenwetsch, *The Malady of the Christian Body: A Theological Exposition of Paul's First Letter to the Corinthians*, vol. 1 (Eugene, OR: Cascade Press, 2016).

makarios, teleios, and a variety of other key moral terms in the Sermon. The climactic chapter even offers a "sketch" of the Sermon's account of human flourishing, and the (literal) last words of the book are given to Pinckaers. Such is the thoroughness of integration of Biblical and moral scholarship in this book.

Though all of these chapters reward close reading, the chapter on *makarios* as used in the beatitudes—which Pennington chooses to translate "Flourishing are …"—is a masterpiece of harmonic Biblical and moral scholarship. Through examination of the continuity and difference between the Hebrew and Greek terms for active flourishing of people (*asre, makarios*) on the one hand and the terms for more receptive blessing by God (*brk, eulogetos*) on the other hand, Pennington demonstrates how the common practice of using the English term "blessed" for both obscures the sense of flourishing. Though the use of a common term is a helpful reminder that it is only through God's blessing (grace) that people flourish, *"the English term 'blessed' is so heavily loaded with the narrower sense of 'divine favor' that the sense of human flourishing is almost always lost."*[41] This early argument of Pennington's book is not only a linchpin of the rest of the book, but a perfect example of Biblical and moral scholarship in concert, the deployment of virtue methodology for the latter, and a focus on a particular text with concern for formation in the life of discipleship.

It is precisely these features that characterize scholarship on Scripture and moral theology today. In continuity with earlier, post-Vatican II scholarship, we find an emphasis on the contributions of both Biblical and moral scholarship. We similarly find ongoing ecumenical contributions. There is far less explicit focus on methodology and hermeneutics today. This is obviously not to say there is no method. In fact, the use of a virtue-centered approach to morality and Scripture has become rather dominant and seems to focus particularly on the importance of Scripture for formation in the life of discipleship. But surveying various methods and offering encyclopedic coverage of Scripture are far less prominent than in earlier scholarship. Focus on particular texts and a virtue-based concern for formation are evident also in the essays included in this volume, to which we now turn.

Current Scholarship on Scripture and Moral Theology:
Enclosed Essays

The first section of essays in this volume perfectly exemplifies the features of recent scholarship on Scripture and moral theology above. Jana Bennett, a Catholic moral theologian, and Jonathan Pennington, a Protestant Scripture scholar, examine faith and mercy in Abraham

---

[41] Pennington, *The Sermon on the Mount and Human Flourishing,* 50, italics in original.

and Joseph, respectively, focusing not only on particular texts but also on exemplary figures.

Bennett's essay begins with recent research on the increasing number of "Nones," people who self-identify with no particular faith tradition. She finds that such people grasp a rather attenuated notion of the faith, which they disavow. At least as disturbingly, she finds a comparable account of faith even in those who self-identify as Christian. This portends that, to the extent this inadequate account of faith is a contributing factor, there is far more disaffiliation to come. Bennett describes a common contemporary view of faith as deductively rational (or alternatively subjective and internal), individualistic, and lacking in its account of God. In response, Bennett looks to the father of faith, Abraham, and distills four features from Genesis 11-22 that counter this attenuated account. She finds in Abraham an account of faith as an ongoing journey, an encounter with a God both hidden and revealed, a communal endeavor, and a response to God who shares God's own life. Her essay is a perfect example of turning to Scripture to remedy a contemporary need for formation in faith.

Catholic moralists who appreciate Pope Francis's emphasis on mercy will find an ally in Protestant Scripture scholar Jonathan Pennington. Pennington's essay presents a case that the primary project of the Gospels is one of *paideia*, which he translates as "formation," and that a crucial tool in that endeavor is the presentation of exemplars, particularly certain "round" characters throughout the Gospels. Pennington also makes a case for righteousness ("justice") and mercy as the heart of Jesus' proclamation of the Kingdom in the Gospel of Matthew. Though Jesus is of course the central protagonist of that mission, Pennington explains how disciples of Jesus in all ages are given exemplars of discipleship in the Gospels. He makes a case that

> Joseph proves to be the exemplar who sets the tone for Jesus' primary moral teaching—that to enter into the kingdom of heaven one must have a righteousness greater than the scribes and Pharisees (5:20), a righteousness marked by mercy, compassion, forgiveness, and love.

Though we never hear words from Joseph, and he recedes after the first two chapters of Matthew, Pennington documents the ways Joseph exemplifies the justice and mercy that emerge as the heart of Jesus' teaching, particularly as articulated in the Sermon on the Mount.

After this opening pair of essays on exemplar figures from the Scriptures, three essays focus on various aspects of conversion in the life of discipleship, each with a focus on certain Scripture passages. Anton ten Klooster observes that the opening words in Matthew's Gospel for both John the Baptist (3:1) and Jesus (4:17) are calls for conversion, to repent. He uses Lonergan to situate the centrality of conversion for the life of discipleship and turns to recent Biblical scholarship on these passages as well as Thomas Aquinas's *Commentary on Matthew* to detail both the necessary relationship between conversion and repentance, and the necessity of God's grace throughout the conversion process. These themes, along with his finding that conversion is as much an ongoing process as an initiating event, present an account of conversion that mines the Scriptural witness for ongoing formation in the life of discipleship.

This theme of conversion as ongoing dominates Daria Spezzano's essay on conversion. She examines the Scriptural basis—from Lamentations, John, and especially Romans—for Aquinas's account of conversion. Spezzano demonstrates in her essay that God's grace is needed for all parts of the "progressive journey" that is conversion, not just at its very start, but also through the whole of one's life. As with other essays in this collection, she manages to do rather technical (in this case Thomistic) moral theology in a manner suffused with Scripture, showing how key moves in Thomas' account of grace, even if using terms not found in Scripture, are thoroughly shaped by his understanding of these Scripture passages.

James Stroud continues the emphasis on conversion in this volume through an examination of the inherent connection between repentance and almsgiving. He first examines Old Testament scholarship on the book of Daniel, as well as Gary Anderson's works on *Sin* and *Charity*, to make a case for the ways that almsgiving is requisite for the ongoing process of conversion and in turn further disposes one to receive God's grace.[42] He similarly examines the tight connection in Luke's Gospel between change of heart and almsgiving, further supporting his claim that almsgiving is "not simply a work of charity or justice but serves as an important formative practice of repentance for the Christian disciple that leads the disciple to place one's faith in God, to seek repentance for one's sins, and subsequently disposes one to the reception of grace."

As should be clear in these three essays, conversion is not a "one and done" phenomenon, but an ongoing, active process powered by God's grace. This is reminiscent of the exemplars addressed in the first pair of essays, especially Abraham, whose faith is presented as a journey. This view of conversion militates against any sharp division between conversion and ongoing growth in the life of discipleship. In

---

[42] See Gary A. Anderson, *Sin: A History* (New Haven, CT: Yale University Press, 2009) and *Charity: The Place of the Poor in the Biblical Tradition* (New Haven, CT: Yale University Press, 2013). Anderson's work on morally important themes across Biblical passages has stimulated further valuable studies, including Nathan Eubank, *Wages of Cross-Bearing and Debt of Sin: The Economy of Heaven in Matthew's Gospel* (Berlin: De Gruyter, 2013); David J. Downs, *Alms: Charity, Reward, and Atonement in Early Christianity* (Waco, TX: Baylor University Press, 2016); and Anthony Giambrone, *Sacramental Charity, Creditor Christology, and the Economy of Salvation in Luke's Gospel* (Tübingen: Mohr Siebeck, 2017).

that sense, the final group of two essays, each of which focuses on an aspect of that ongoing growth, fits seamlessly with the preceding essays.

John Meinert examines the command-counsel distinction based on Matthew 19 and 1 Corinthians 7. As with other contributors to this volume, he exemplifies rigorous attention to both moral and biblical scholarship. Rather than proof-texting these passages to support moral theological positions determined prior to engagement with the text, or simply seeking moral rules in the text, Meinert engages the texts as authoritatively illuminating the difficult moral issue he treats, namely, the extent to which a distinction between command and counsel is necessarily laden with certain assumptions now recognized as problematic in contemporary moral theology. Meinert masterfully salvages the command-counsel distinction, shorn of problematic corollaries such as a "two-tiered ethic," precisely by reviewing pre-modern and contemporary Biblical interpretation of the relevant passages. Meinert offers an account of the counsels that delineates in what sense they are for all and in what sense they are not. He deploys Pinckaers's notions of morality of happiness and freedom for excellence to show how the counsels serve a role in growth and perfection (Matthew 5:48 and 19:21) in the life of discipleship.

In certain ways, this volume of essays ends (with Andrew Kim) where it began (with Jana Bennett): namely, by examining inadequacy in a common contemporary notion and turning to Scriptural resources to correct it. Whereas Bennett examined faith, Kim examines addiction, and his essay begins with an assessment of the accuracy and inaccuracy of common contemporary accounts of addiction as a disease. Exemplifying the scholastic dictum that grace perfects nature, Kim turns to Paul's account of his slavery to sin and freedom through Christ in Romans 7:13–25 for guidance in articulating a four-stage account of a grace-enabled recovery from addiction, understood as analogous with disease but not reducible to it. Drawing also on Romans 1 and passages from James, Kim explores the compatibility of grace and ongoing sin, all with an eye toward assisting addicts on the path of recovery.

Although presented here in three loose groups, the seven essays of this volume are unified not only by the methodological considerations examined in the bulk of this introductory essay. They are also unified in their focus on how Scripture informs the life of discipleship in a manner that is sustained by God's grace as perfecting nature, and which continues in an ongoing manner—even after conversion—as there ever remains room for growth in faith, hope, and love in this life. To that extent these essays, even while delving into technical issues in moral theology, constitute a common effort to draw on God's Word to nourish formation in the graced life of discipleship to Jesus Christ, the Word of God.⁴³ Ⓜ

William C. Mattison III is Associate Professor of Theology at the University of Notre Dame, Indiana, with a joint appointment in the Alliance for Catholic Education. He spent ten years at The Catholic University of America, where he served as interim Dean of the School of Theology and Religious Studies. He is the author of *Introducing Moral Theology: True Happiness and the Virtues* (2008) and *The Sermon on the Mount and Moral Theology* (2017).

---

[43] Thanks to Matthew Levering and David Cloutier for extensive comments on earlier drafts of this essay, without which it would be far more impoverished. Obviously, any lacks remaining are my own.

On Pilgrimage with Abraham: How a Patriarch Leads Us in Formation in Faith

Jana M. Bennett

THE CONTEMPORARY PLIGHT OF FAITH

IN CHRISTIAN TRADITION, THE THEOLOGICAL VIRTUE of faith describes an epistemology, a way of interpreting scripture, a worldview of history and culture, an ethics, and more. St. Augustine's *Confessions*, for example, depicts Augustine's journey toward God as requiring intellectual as well as faith-based assent to a scriptural worldview, and a bodily way of life that supports, and is supported by, that worldview. The famous line "Lord, make me chaste and continent, but not yet" (*Conf.* 8.7.17), is faith actively seeking God in body and mind. For Christians, faith is a robust theological virtue that requires our whole selves, in concert with God's grace.

Twenty-first century accounts of faith fail to engage that Christian tradition well, however. What people tend to mean by faith has become attenuated largely to intellectual assent to certain beliefs. Faith's contemporary meanings tend not to bear the full weight of Catholic teaching on faith. Moreover, these attenuated versions of faith do not meet people's deepest hungers for God, and therefore have the effect, often, of turning people away from Christianity altogether.

For example, a common contemporary statement made about the term "faith" is that it is merely another name for "organized religion." Organized religion, in turn, is often understood as a set of ideas that one must believe to belong. In studies about people who have eschewed Christianity, people's answers to questions about faith assume both that faith is an organized religion named Christianity, and that belonging to this mere organization means having belief in a set of specific teachings about faith. Further, such statements have often turned people away from the "Christian organization." A recent Pew Research Forum study observes that those who are unaffiliated are so because: "I question a lot of religious teachings" (51 percent), "I don't like the positions churches take on social/political issues" (4 percent), and "I don't like religious organizations" (34 percent).[1] Insofar as faith

---

[1] Becka Alper, "Why America's 'Nones' Don't Identify with a Religion," Pew Research Forum, last updated August 8, 2018, http://www.pewresearch.org/fact-tank/2018/08/08/why-americas-nones-dont-identify-with-a-religion/.

is equated with religious institutions, Americans increasingly want no part. The unaffiliated often name Catholicism and other religious traditions as irrelevant.[2]

The shift from a robust, holistic, theological virtue toward the attenuated view just described stems from Enlightenment traditions of thought that emphasized rational thought, especially as espoused in scientific evidence and logical statements. Religious belief came to be understood by some as irrational and personal to the holder of that belief, rather than rational and (therefore) universal. What is interesting is that around the same time, and in response to Enlightenment traditions, Christians tended to package their beliefs into neat sets of questions and answers, and catechisms. Nineteenth-century conservative and liberal Christians alike aimed to develop rational theories that demonstrated proof that Christianity is true, such as archeological digs to find the real Noah's ark and attempts to find the "historical Jesus." Such activities continue today, perhaps most famously in the Hobby Lobby Bible Museum, which has devoted itself to showing that archeology and the historical record demonstrate the unchanging Word of God in the Bible. The Jesus Seminar continues the search for the historical Jesus. Despite, or maybe because of, such intense desire to prove tenets of faith with historical and scientific proofs, contemporary unaffiliated people are unconvinced, and have left.

Such deductive faith is not the only version of faith present in contemporary discourse. The same Pew Research Forum study also indicates that the vast majority of the unaffiliated profess belief in a god—though not quite the God of Christian teaching. Almost 80 percent of the unaffiliated appear to have a belief in some kind of god.[3] Faith of this kind has an individualistic character: people desire to be free to believe in God in ways that are not apparently ensnared in traditional religious views. Journalist Caroline Kitchener studied the rise of the unaffiliated:

> Americans are leaving organized religion in droves: they disagree with their churches on political issues; they feel restricted by dogma; they're deserting formal organizations of all kinds. Instead of atheism, however, they're moving toward an identity captured by the term "spirituality." Approximately sixty-four million Americans—one in five—identify as "spiritual but not religious," or SBNR. They, like Beare, reject organized religion but maintain a belief in something

---

[2] Nicolette Manglos-Weber and Christian Smith, *Understanding Former Young Catholics: Findings from a National Study of Emerging Young Adults* (University of Notre Dame, 2013).

[3] Alper, "Why America's Nones Don't Identify with a Religion."

larger than themselves. That "something" can range from Jesus to art, music, and poetry. There is often yoga involved.[4]

The apparent individual development of spiritual practices is not the whole picture. There also seems to be rather a collective sense of religious belief. Over a decade ago, sociologists Christian Smith and Melinda Lundquist Denton observed American teenagers and discovered that many held several common conceptions of faith, irrespective of the particular faith tradition they belonged to, or even whether they saw themselves as seekers or nothing. They termed this collection of ideas "moralistic therapeutic deism." They summed up these beliefs as:

1. A God exists who created and orders the world and watches over human life on earth.

2. God wants people to be good, nice, and fair to each other, as taught in the Bible and by most world religions.

3. The central goal of life is to be happy and to feel good about oneself.

4. God does not need to be particularly involved in one's life except when God is needed to resolve a problem.

5. Good people go to heaven when they die.[5]

Smith and Denton also suggest regardless of faith status or background, moralistic therapeutic deism is not limited to a specific generation; adults, too, share several of these conceptions of God.[6]

In a later study, sociologists Nicolette Manglos-Weber and Christian Smith dug into more details and suggested that both Christians and unaffiliated have more in common on their views of faith than we might otherwise presume. Smith and Manglos-Weber studied young adults who left the church, as well as Catholics who had not left. The ways unaffiliated people describe what faith looks like to them has much in common with the ways professing Catholics describe faith. For example, both groups are likely to name God as merely an object in the universe, like other objects. They are also about equally likely to see scientific and religious questions at odds with each other: "Science and logic are how we 'really' know things about our world, and religious faith either violates or falls short of the standards of scientific

---

[4] Caroline Kitchener, "What it Means to be Spiritual but not Religious: One in Five Americans Reject Organized Religion but Maintain Some Kind of Faith," *The Atlantic*, 11 January 2018, http://www.theatlantic.com/membership/archive/2018/01/what-it-means-to-be-spiritual-but-not-religious/550337/.
[5] Christian Smith and Melinda Lundquist Denton, *Soul Searching: The Religious and Spiritual Lives of American Teenagers* (New York/London: Oxford University Press, 2005), 162–163.
[6] Smith and Lundquist Denton, *Soul Searching*, 169–170.

knowledge."[7] Because religion thus operates on irrational subjective ideas, many also see religion as a main source of conflict between people.[8] Both Catholics and unaffiliated express the views that God acts for me (as an individual), and on my behalf, largely in ways that I perceive to be positive and self-beneficial.[9] God is seen as benevolent and all-loving, but in ways that are individually-directed. Such individualism stands in direct contrast to Catholic thinking about the common good, or the Catholic view that all people are made in the image and likeness of God and therefore have inherent dignity and worth. Indeed, my worry is that, in a secular culture that prefers to eschew both the common good and the inherent worth of all people, belief in a personal, individualistic god further enables secular culture to work, including on professing Catholics.

The commonalities between professing Catholic young adults and young adults who name themselves as unaffiliated should be highly concerning. For many church observers, a key issue for Catholicism is about numbers: number of baptisms, number of mass attendees, number of people who get married and raise their children in church, and more. Unaffiliated people now surpass Catholics in terms of numbers.[10] Scholars have suggested that if the problem is the increase in the numbers of unaffiliated, the solution needs to be finding ways to bring more people into the church.

Yet what if the church to which we are bringing unaffiliated people back is merely displaying some of the same basic, and very troubling, visions of faith, regardless of stated affiliation? If that is the case, I contend that faith is getting watered down into concepts that are not, in fact, compatible with traditional Christian beliefs about God. Yet it is precisely those kinds of beliefs that both groups hold—that seeming incompatibility between science and religion, that view of God as a mere object—that only serve to reinforce unaffiliated people's dissatisfaction with propositional beliefs, and that place the beliefs of professing Catholics on increasingly shaky ground, especially as they encounter secular cultures that raise questions for which a deductive faith has no answers.

---

[7] Manglos-Weber and Smith, *Understanding Former Young Catholics*, 14.
[8] Manglos-Weber and Smith, *Understanding Former Young Catholics,* 10–11. See also Christian Smith, Kyle Longest, Jonathan Hill, and Kari Christoffersen, *Young Catholic America: Emerging Adults In, Out of, and Gone from the Church* (New York: Oxford University Press, 2014).
[9] Mangos-Weber and Smith, *Understanding Former Young Catholics*, 9.
[10] Jack Jenkins, "Nones Now as Big as Evangelicals, Catholics," *Religion News Service*, March 22, 2019, http://www.ncronline.org/news/people/nones-now-big-evangelicals-catholics-us.

Abraham, the Father of the Faith

In this article, I aim for a return to that more robust account of faith of Christian tradition. My account of faith draws from one of the fathers of faith in scripture, Abraham. By pondering Abraham's journey of faith in Genesis, I argue for four points about faith that need to be articulated in our contemporary world. First, faith must be seen as a journey, a pilgrimage, that one undertakes as a response to God, rather than a set of simplistic propositions. Secondly, faith, perhaps especially in the initial journey stages, encounters God who is largely hidden, especially in modern context, yet as faith grows, we find ourselves gradually seeing God face-to-face. Third, faith requires a community that shows us that God is a God of life, but that also nurtures our faithful pilgrimage toward God. Thus finally, faith shall lead us inexorably toward God's own life. Taken together, the journey, God's hiddenness but emerging presentness, the ways faith must become communal, and the fact that faith draws us toward God's own life, become great. Indeed, we shall see that faith really is like the mustard seed that grows into a tree so large birds can make nests in it.

Stories about Abraham provide potential windows to other views of faith because Abraham is so clearly not a modern person. Contemporary readers of Abraham must do some work to think through Abraham—migrant, desert wanderer, important man of his time, husband to Sarah, lover of Hagar, father of Ishmael and Isaac, near-sacrificer of his own son.

Of course, we contemporary readers can and do bring our Enlightenment and contemporary interpretations to Abraham's stories. Many modern thinkers have myopically focused on Abraham's near-sacrifice of Isaac, precisely because that is the moment when Abraham's story turns irrational, the moment when Abraham's God appears as so violent and vicious that no clear-thinking, compassionate, rational person ought to believe. Thus, the early-modern philosopher Immanuel Kant "could not reconcile a command to kill one's son with a universal moral duty within us."[11] In Kant's account, Abraham's obedience to God's voice contradicts obedience to the universal moral law of not killing a human being. Kant calls into question the goodness of even having faith; rather, Kant argues that an individual must separate religious beliefs from universal moral principles, thereby disconnecting morality from faith. The later philosopher Soren Kierkegaard emphasizes the same sacrificial story as Kant and sees in it some of the horror that Kant sees. For Kierkegaard, the story becomes a potential moment for more profound faith: "Let us then either consign Abraham to oblivion, or let us learn to be dismayed by the tremendous paradox which

---

[11] Carey Ellen Walsh, "Christian Theological Interpretations of God's Grace in the Binding of Isaac," *Perichoresis* 10, no. 1 (2012): 43.

constitutes the significance of Abraham's life, that we may understand that our age, like every age, can be joyful if it has faith."[12]

A different way to approach the questions about rationality in scripture has been via historical-critical method. Historical-critical methods of Scripture interpretation developed in the nineteenth century; there are multiple methods that have in common emphasizing scripture as a historical book. Some methods have taken up old questions about discrepancies that exist between similar Scriptures (the different accounts of Jesus's crucifixion and resurrection, for example), but now doing so in new ways. Other methods have relied on the development of archaeology as affirming or denying both scientific and historical facts that may be present in Scripture. This turn in scriptural study encompasses both liberal and conservative voices. One scholar describes how "certain famous archaeologists began to dig up sites in Palestine to find proof that the Bible was true in a modern historical sense. What had been known as a textual story to that date was now reconstructed as real history."[13] Yet other scholars will find in archeological record little or no evidence, or open questions, regarding Scripture.

Historical-critical methods have a large impact on how we read Abraham and have held very real cultural and political consequences to the present day. For example, a historical-critical reading from a more evangelical Protestant, and often conservative, sensibility, argues that Abraham's call from God and the gift of a promised land show a political impact on Zionism, the drive for a modern state of Israel, and the current evangelical Protestant push to identify contemporary Israel with evangelical claims about the end of times. Abraham becomes political, under the guise of faith.[14]

Historical-critical methods can be helpful, and of course historical context provides important details about scripture. Yet for the contemporary plight of faith, especially the relative thinness of faith as I described above, the focus on using facts and archeology to prove or disprove scriptural veracity does not illumine how Christians might approach faith theologically.

My method is to do direct readings of some texts from Abraham. Direct reading of the Scriptures, for me, will mean making use of both plain sense of scripture as well as, at times, the multiple kinds of typological readings that patristic scholarship understood. Truly typological readings of scripture, on my view, encompass all the four senses of reading scripture that patristic and medieval fathers extolled:

---

[12] Søren Kierkegaard, *Fear and Trembling and The Book on Adler* (New York: Alfred Knopf, 1994), 43.
[13] Ulrike Bechmann, "Genesis 12 and the Abraham Paradigm Concerning the Promised Land," *The Ecumenical Review* (2016): 63.
[14] See Bechmann, "Genesis 12."

the plain sense, the allegorical sense, the moral sense, and the eschatological senses.[15] I will also draw on some of the patristic interpretations of Genesis, to show how some of earliest Christian typological readings shaped Christian life. Each of these readings from Genesis draw us into salvation history and call us to see our own lives—past, present, and future—imprinted with God's word. Typological readings have been criticized in recent decades for supporting supersessionist claims about Judaism, or similarly, for perpetuating troubling and serious anti-Semitic attitudes that the Church has denounced.[16] Yet I think that typological readings, done carefully, can also call Christians to greater love and appreciation of Jewish traditions of reading scriptures, as well as acknowledging Jews as the chosen people of God. Typological readings seek an awareness of time, place, and culture, in order to know what the author might have meant in the initial telling of the story. Typological readings can also draw us into a range of interpretations, including rabbinic interpretations. From that kind of reading, we can then search spiritually for how that story connects to us today, and then even further, to think through how it might read for the future of the Kingdom of God and our place in God's Kingdom.

READING ABRAHAM'S FAITH

In the following four subsections, I focus sequentially on four passages in Abraham's story that demonstrate the four points about faith named above: faith as journey, God as hidden, the way the faithful community reveals a God of life, and what it means to be drawn into God's own life. These stories are: Abraham's beginning journey from Hebron to Canaan, his successive covenants with God especially as shown in the story of Lot, his practice of the virtues of hospitality to the three visitors, and his near sacrifice of Isaac.

A Journey of Small Steps (Genesis 11–12)

The beginning of Abraham's story demonstrates that faith is better seen as a journey or pilgrimage than a set of reductive criteria. Like Abraham, we who thirst for God are invited to follow God. The journey motif, however, will help us see that faith might best be understood in terms of small, even halting steps that we take toward the voice of God as we currently apprehend it. Our faithful response to

---

[15] In my view, Thomas's discussions of the senses of reading scripture intersect with each other, and all use "types." The types may signify how the New Testament relates to the Old Testament (allegory), or they may signify Christ, which gives us what we ought to do (moral sense), or they may signify eternal things, thereby offering a type of our blessed end in God. See Aquinas, ST I q. 1, a. 10.

[16] Christopher Leighton offers an overview in "Christian Theology after the Shoah," *Christianity in Jewish Terms*, eds. Tivka Frymer-Kensky, David Novak, Peter Ochs, David Fox Sandmel, and Michael A. Signer (Boulder, CO: Westview Press, 2000): 36–48.

God may deepen and change over time; our vision of God that is our guide and goal on the journey may likewise deepen and change.

Thus, Abraham's story runs contrary to the way we contemporaries approach faith. Like Kant, or like the more contemporary theologian Paul Tillich, moderns are tempted to see faith as an ultimate decision, in which one must make a choice to assent to or dissent from God (in whatever form one chooses to believe in God). Tillich writes: "Faith as ultimate concern is an act of the total personality. It . . . is the most centered act of the human mind. ... It participates in the dynamics of personal life."[17] By contrast, Abraham's faith does not show as a centered act of the human mind as much as one simple step on a journey that began, in fact, long before Abraham even existed.

Abraham's (Abram's) beginnings are in Genesis, Chapter 11, where we find that he and his father Terah have been on the move from Ur in Chaldea (v. 31). In Chapter 11, it seems that Terah had intended to travel all the way to Canaan, but for some reason he stops and remains in Haran. The knowledge that this journey has been undertaken before sets us up for Chapter 12, then, where God first says to Abraham:

> Go from your country and your kindred and your father's house to the land that I will show you. I will make of you a great nation, and I will bless you, and make your name great, so that you will be a blessing. I will bless those who bless you, and the one who curses you I will curse; and in you all the families of the earth shall be blessed. (12:1)

Notice that Abraham's journey is *both* one of leaving behind his family, friends, and country but is *also* one of continuing the journey that his father had begun so many years before.

Abraham's response and action here is that he simply takes up a journey that has already begun. He takes the steps of a life that he has already been living, follows the voice of a God he has been following and yet does not entirely know. Abraham's is not a brand-new journey that he, personally, has undertaken. This is a fact that surely wreaks havoc with us moderns who believe our spiritual seeking after God to be entirely ours, entirely an individualistic choice that we made in favor of (or against) belief in a certain, kind of god. Abraham's step of faith already suggests to modern readers a more distinctive vision of faith than is seen in the moralistic therapeutic deist view that God "does not need to be particularly involved in one's life" and that a "central goal of life is to be happy and to feel good about oneself."[18]

---

[17] Paul Tillich, *The Dynamics of Faith* (New York: Harper and Row, 1957), 4.
[18] Christian Smith, "On 'Moralistic Therapeutic Deism' as Teenagers' Actual, Tacit, De Facto Religious Faith," *Catholic Education Resource Center*, www.catholiceducation.org/en/controversy/common-misconceptions/on-moralistic-therapeutic-deism-as-u-s-teenagers-actual-tacit-de-facto-religious-faith.html.

Rather, God engages directly in Abraham's life. In contrast to his father Terah's journey, God directly calls Abraham. We do not know if God had similarly called Terah, but we do know definitively that God has called Abraham to follow the path of his father, but with a new purpose. The journey God calls Abraham to undertake is simply to be a continuation of the person that Abraham already has been: he is a semi-nomad, a pilgrim, and he grew up in that way.

It is significant that in this passage, Abraham does not see God, he only hears God's voice, yet he recognizes the voice as God's. Some accounts of Abraham suggest that he did not really know God until God first calls him in Chapter 12; but some accounts, like the Jewish Midrash, suggest that Abraham searched for God from the time he was young, and that "ultimately he apprehended the way of truth and understood the path of righteousness through his accurate comprehension. He realized that there was one God who controlled the sphere, that He had created everything, and that there is no other God among all the other entities."[19] I suggest that the reason Abraham is willing to leave his family, his friends, and the land of his father behind and journey to Canaan on God's command is because he has already been listening to God's voice for many years, at least in a nascent sense; yet now he will undertake the journey that—as we shall see—steadily encourages him to know God more and more. He shall steadily journey more and more toward becoming God's friend.

One key element is to note the nature of the call, the way that God speaks to Abraham and the way he responds. We live in a culture where it is difficult to hear God's voice. We live in a post-Kantian culture that is prone to believing that the voice of God may simply be our own intuition, or willful mind, or internal thoughts—only Christians are so stupid (culture suggests) as to put a name like "God" to those thoughts. Such a view of God makes sense in a post-Enlightenment world that has imbibed ideas like "man makes religion."[20]

For modern sensibilities, I suggest that we need recollection of the fact that hearing God's voice is not always a clarion call, and in fact, that we can be entirely wrong in our perception of God's voice. Just as we are prone to seeing faith as a clear and final decision, so listening for God's voice can seem like it must be clear and loud. Such an assertion about God's speaking to us is precisely one of the aspects of faith that causes Nones to assume they must not have faith. Yet Abraham witnesses to the possibility of hearing God's voice in a time when hearing God's voice is not valued. Abraham's position as father of the faith also enables us to read his story alongside all the scriptures that

---

[19] Joseph B. Soloveitchik, *Abraham's Journey: Reflections on the Life of the Founding Patriarch* (New York: KTAV Publishing House, 2008), 40.
[20] Karl Marx, *Introduction to the Critique of Hegel's Philosophy of Right* (Cambridge: Cambridge University Press, 1970), 127.

witness to those times when God's voice is precisely not heard (for example, the prophets in Kings and Chronicles who merely speak the words the kings want to hear). Such recognition of both God's call to Abraham and the fact that we humans do not always (or even often?) hear God's voice well, is to remember that following God's voice is a matter of discernment.

One final point I observe about Abraham's call in chapter 12 is that God calls Abraham out from the ordinariness of his life at Ur. The journey takes place as part of Abraham's ordinary life, which again emphasizes that faith is so often the small steps we make in the midst of the life we are given. God does not usually ask us to make gigantic leaps but rather asks us to go this way rather than that way. Faith might best be seen as a journey of exploration, waiting to see what one small step may lead to by the end of a person's life. This shall become more significant as we continue through Abraham's story. While we know the end of this story—we know that God's call to Abraham will continuously expand even to the point of near-sacrifice of his only son, in chapter 12—here, he is simply a son following in his father's footsteps.

Responding to the Hidden God (Genesis 13:1–18)

The second scripture passage to examine is Genesis 13:1–18. In this passage, Abraham responds in faith to a God who is, at least at the moment, hidden from him. Abraham's response to God includes responses of virtuous action toward others, even when that action appears to leave Abraham in a worse position than before his action.

The thirteenth chapter tells the story of when Abraham—still referred to as Abram in the text—and his nephew, Lot, separate. Up to this point, Lot has come right alongside Abraham, with all his family and flocks. In these verses we see that Abraham has amassed some wealth ("Now Abram was very rich in livestock, silver, and gold" [13:2]), and so has Lot ("Lot, who went with Abram, also had flocks and herds and tents, so that the land could not support them if they stayed together" [13:5–6a]). Perhaps it is inevitable that arguments would arise: "There were quarrels between the herders of Abraham's livestock and the herders of Lot's livestock" (13:7). In a semi-nomadic community, such arguments over land would be quite ordinary.

Abraham chooses to settle the dispute by deciding that he and Lot should part ways. So Abraham proclaims to Lot: "Is not the whole land available? Please separate from me. If you prefer the left, I will go to the right; if you prefer the right, I will go to the left" (13:9). Lot, being quite human, chooses what looks like the best of the land. "Lot looked about and saw how abundantly watered the whole Jordan Plain was as far as Zoar, like the Lord's own garden, or like Egypt." Lot sets out on the most fertile of land; Abraham's portion looks more like... desert.

In the next verses, in fact, God plays on the fact that Abraham's land is desert land. "After Lot had parted from him, the Lord said to Abraham: Look about you, and from where you are, gaze to the north and south, east and west; all the land that you see I will give to you and your descendants forever. I will make your descendants like the *dust of the earth*; if anyone could count the dust of the earth, your descendants too might be counted" (13:14–15). Abraham's descendants will be like the desert sands that he sees. Abraham here lives faith as the practice of things not seen, for desert sands suggest nothing of fertility, yet Abraham appears to maintain his faith. Abraham is the one to whom is promised the fertility of being the father of many— even set against the backdrop of his young and fertile nephew, who lives in the young, fertile, and green land.

How does Abraham's faith manifest itself? It does so precisely in Abraham's practice of virtue. In this passage we see most clearly Abraham's practice of generosity because we also see his faith. Faith in God's promises enables Abraham to practice generosity to others, even to the point that someone else gets the choicest cut of land. Later, Abraham demonstrates a similar kind of generosity when Abraham's men have a dispute with the Canaan ruler Abimelech over water (Chapter 21). Abimelech's men have taken a well that Abraham himself had dug. What does Abraham do? He does not insist, "No fair, I am the one who built the well." He does not kill Abimelech's men. Rather he offers seven lambs to Abimelech so that the man will publicly state that it is Abraham's well. They make a covenant together; Abraham gets control of *his* own water well in that desert land through *his* own generosity toward Abimelech. Abraham can be generous to the point of showing a different relationship to Lot, to Abimelech, and to others around him.

Such actions of generosity (or other virtues) are difficult to do, and often impossible to comprehend, in a contemporary context. Abraham's action makes him seem to lose out, rather than achieve any great gain. As noted above, the contemporary moralistic therapeutic deism acknowledges God's existence only when clear signs of therapeutic happiness appear, and we feel generally good about ourselves. Only when people can name the direct blessings God bestows in money or other direct answers to human wants, can they also name God as present. Abraham's story suggests quite the contrary: we must learn to see God not in the tangible blessings, but precisely in the opposite, in the desert sands that rage and seem bleak.

It should, therefore, be no surprise that faith is in crisis. God will seem utterly hidden to people, especially for a modern culture that tends to insist rationality and faith in God do not belong together. The theodical questions compel people to align apparent rational accounts of a desolate world with the fact of God's existence. God often loses in that equation, at least from the human perspective. It is on this point, though, that we must look to a deeper understanding of who God is, as revealed in scripture and in the life, death, and resurrection of Jesus Christ. God will not call attention to Himself, will not present bravado and self-aggrandizing as the modes of being. As the contemporary theologian Katherine Sonderegger writes, God is "content to be the Truth, the Wisdom, the Reality of all things, yet be unrecognized in the manifold truths and discoveries of an age. He is content to be unseen.... He does not cry out or lift His voice in the marketplace; we pass Him by as of no account; from Him we turn away our faces. And He bears this."[21] So if we wish to walk in faith, we shall have to remember that God is simply not going to do and be the things we expect.

Yet if we are willing to take the small steps toward generosity (as just one among many virtues), even in times and places when others are not being virtuous toward us, our faith may gradually become more and more attuned to the God who is hidden. Patristic scholars discussed that aspect of faith in Abraham. In *City of God*, Augustine notes,

> For the keener the observer's sight, the more stars he sees; and so we are justified in supposing that some stars are invisible even to the keenest eyes, quite apart from those stars which, we are assured, rise and set in another part of the world far removed from us....This, it should be noticed, is the context of the statement which the Apostle recalls for the purpose of emphasizing God's grace: "Abraham believed in God, and this was accounted to him for righteousness." (*City of God*, XVI 23)

We cannot see all the stars that might show us all the descendants, but that fact, for Augustine, shows us the depth of Abraham's faith and faithful response to God.

Contemporary Christians, as I suggested above, have a truncated view of God and faith. Christians who want to help themselves, and others, on the path of faith might use Abraham's faith to name that the hiddenness, and even the resulting doubt, are means for perseverance in faith. Perhaps the lack of sight is similar in some respects to St. John of the Cross's "dark night of the soul." A generation that demands faith to be confirmed—whether by way of moralistic therapeutic deism or by means of immediate, tangible, scientific reassurances of God's presence in the creation/evolution debate—is not a generation that has learned to be formed in the faith of Abraham. It is not a generation that really believes in either mystery or the very fallible nature

---

[21] Katherine Sonderegger, *Systematic Theology: The Doctrine of God*, vol. 1 (Minneapolis, MN: Fortress Press, 2015), 143.

of its own knowledge. Yet perhaps if we too practice the kinds of virtues that Abraham exhibits on his pilgrimage toward God, we might find ourselves stumbling toward our final, blessed end in God, as well.

Building Communities of Life (Genesis 17–18:15)

The third scripture segment we consider is Genesis 17–Genesis 18:15. As we continue in Abraham's journey, we shall see that God becomes less hidden, but we also begin to see other aspects of faith that we might not have understood before. For example, faith is not an individual enterprise, but a communal one.

Genesis 17 depicts the covenant of circumcision that God effects with Abram, who here becomes Abraham, and then Genesis 18 gives us the famous passage of the visit from the three strangers. Here, God does become tangibly present to Abraham in a protracted way, and Abraham likewise makes a tangible offering to God. In Genesis 17–18, Abraham's faith shows us the ways he comes to know God as a God of life. That knowledge of the God of life will then lead further, toward guiding and shaping our neighbors and indeed our whole community. In contrast to the individualistic contemporary versions of faith that abound, here we see that faith is not meant to be individual; it is meant to be a communal witness to the God of life.

One of the first points to note in chapter 17 is that, as opposed to the earlier scriptures, God directly *appears* to Abraham and says, "Walk in my presence and be blameless." Previously, we had only seen hints of God, but God had remained hidden. In God's initial attempts to covenant with Abraham, God's presence remains more abstract. For example, in chapter 15, God makes a covenant under the guise of a smoking pot and a flaming torch, in which he gives Abraham the land his descendants will inhabit, yet still does not precisely name any one individual who will be Abraham's descendant. In fact, God's promise is more to Abraham's descendants than to Abraham himself: "To your descendants I give this land, from the Wadi of Egypt to the Great River, the Euphrates, the land of the Kenites, the Kenizzites, the Kadmonites, the Hittites, the Perizzites, the Rephaim, the Amorites, the Canaanites, the Girgashites, and the Jebusites" (Gen. 15:18–20).

Here, as Abraham's faith grows, faith is confirmed by a beatific vision. In addition, in chapter 17, God adds to the previous covenants. Readers learn that Abraham will be the father of a multitude of nations and will be "exceedingly fertile; I will make nations of you; kings will stem from you," God says (17:6). *This* covenant is marked by circumcision, surely a physical and specific reference to fertility, but also a direct physical response to God that coincides with God's own direct appearance. This covenant also features a name change for Abraham, who had been Abram and now becomes Abraham, the fertile father of many. The name change signifies the continuously changing relationship with God; the relationship between God and Abraham is now much more immediate and intimate. In chapter 17, the covenant of circumcision, it is Abraham the *individual* who receives the special relationship. Alongside the covenant of circumcision, this is the first time we hear that Abraham will have a specific person who will become an heir of the covenant, Isaac. The importance of circumcision is not only that it is a physical mark of the special relationship that Abraham and God have. The importance of circumcision is its connection to Abraham's procreativity and to God's great gift of life.

Yet there is more. God is giving the gift of faith here, not just to Abraham, but to his descendants. The connection between God and Abraham will need to be passed along to Abraham's specific future descendants. In verse 10, we read: "This is the covenant between me and you and your descendants after you that you must keep: every male among you shall be circumcised." Abraham's new covenant carries with it a responsibility, which is formation of others in faith. Rabbi Soloveitchik helps re-envisage Abraham and his call: "With circumcision, another mission was assigned to Abraham: the formation and education of a covenantal community, a community that would be close to God and would follow a new way of life...."[22] Faith is not only about one's individual relationship with God, but it is about nurturing others' faith as well.

Patristic writers recognized such a gift. The *Letter of Barnabas* goes on at some length about the way development of a community of faith occurred:

> Learn abundantly, therefore, children of love, about everything: Abraham, who first instituted circumcision, looked forward in the spirit to Jesus when he circumcised, having received the teaching of the three letters. For it says, 'And Abraham circumcised ten and eight and three hundred men of his household.' What then is the knowledge that was given to him? Observe that it mentions the 'ten and eight' first, and then after an interval the 'three hundred.' As for the 'ten and eight,' the I is ten and the H is eight; thus you have Jesus. And because the cross, which is shaped like the T, was destined to convey grace, it mentions also the 'three hundred.' So he reveals Jesus in the two letters, and the cross in the other one." (9:7)

Abraham is father of Christian faith because typologically, he hands on faith in Christ. His formation of Isaac, and through Isaac whole generations of Israelites, also includes us and our own formation.

The community of faith in the God of life becomes even more clear in the next chapter, Chapter 18, the passage where Abraham and Sarah

---

[22] Soloveitchik, *Abraham's Journey*, 158.

receive three strangers, whom commenters frequently name as God. So again, God becomes no abstraction, but pays a protracted visit to Abraham and Sarah. Isaac is again introduced as the child of promise, but this time to Sarah and Abraham both, rather than just to Abraham. Despite being at an age that seems to contradict new life, Sarah will be the mother, and Abraham the father, and they shall together show the world that God is a God of life.

The passage emphasizes that just as God is a God of life, our faithful human response must also be in service of life. We see this in the ways Abraham and Sarah practice the virtue of hospitality, especially in verses 6–8. The haste with which Sarah prepares the food showcases how important hospitality is in this harsh land, where strangers have walked miles and really do stand in need of sustenance, both food and water, at every possible venue. To fail to bestow hospitality is to fail to bestow life on wayfarers.

When the New Testament authors discuss Abraham, they emphasize this connection to life. Abraham is referenced in both the gospels and the letters as someone who "will be raised from the dead."[23] The author of the *Letter to the Hebrews* directly names the stories from Genesis 17 and 18 to "demonstrate that Abraham himself is the 'first shadow' of the resurrection from the dead."[24] The renewal of Abraham and Sarah's procreative faculties are seen typologically as connected to resurrection of the body, and the New Testament writers name this often. In Romans 4:19, we see Paul using the word "*nenekromenon*" to refer to Abraham's procreative capacity before Isaac: that is, procreation is *dead* for him; essentially, he is a dead man. Similarly, in the *Letter to the Hebrews*: "By faith Sarah herself received power to conceive, even when she was past the age, since she considered him faithful who had promised. Therefore, from one man, and him as good as dead, were born descendants as many as the stars of heaven and as many as the innumerable grains of sand by the seashore" (Hebrews 11:11–12, ESV). Life overcomes death for Abraham and Sarah; faith in God is emphasized as faith in the God of life.

The building of Abraham's narrative, then, draws us ever closer to the God of life. Abraham's journey of faith has developed from virtuous response to a hidden God now to a point where now he sees and witnesses to God Himself through circumcision and hospitality. Abraham's practice of virtue has always been with others, and thus communally focused, but now God's covenant is being shown as the beginnings of a community of faith. Abraham's embrace of covenant and community draws him into God's life, which in fact is a celebration of

---

[23] David H. Wenkel, "Abraham's Typological Resurrection from the Dead in Hebrews 11," *Criswell Theological Review* 15, no. 2 (Spring 2018): 55.
[24] Wenkel, "Abraham's Typological Resurrection from the Dead in Hebrews 11," 51.

life. Dry desert sands, aging and apparently infertile bodies, still have the capacity to show us God's own life. For contemporary Christians, this again helps us take up the theme of hiddenness discussed before, as well as emphasizes that properly speaking faith in God means faith in a particular, living God who loves life.

Drawn into God's Own Story (Genesis 22:1–19)

That knowledge of the God of life leads, finally, to the Abraham/Isaac sacrifice story contained in Genesis 22:1–19. The problem of the story begins directly in verse 1: "Some time later. God tested Abraham." Multiple questions arise from this test. First, why would God, who knows all, need to test Abraham? Then verse 12 only adds to the questions: the angel of the Lord proclaims, as the mouth of God, "Do not lay a hand on the boy. ... Now I know that you fear God." God knows now, since Abraham has brought his son to the very brink of sacrifice—but God did not know then. Then, too, there is the question of sacrifice itself, and how a God who appears not to know, would require human sacrifice in order to know. In terms of faith, a difficulty is that God appears to be unstable, which then suggests an instability to faith in God.

The thin general faith of the contemporary period meshes well neither with the idea of testing (which contradicts the moralistic and therapeutic aspects of moralistic therapeutic deism) nor with the idea of sacrifice of the son, as indicated above. As I alluded above in my discussion of Enlightenment views of faith, this particular story has appeared as irrational, in part for its account of faith. Our age of seeing religion as the opposite of science, would likely push us to reject that God who demands a parental sacrifice of a child. Christians whose faith displays some of the weaknesses indicated earlier, can seem to be assenting, in faith, to an inexplicable God that they cannot justify in relation to science. Further, the response of moralistic therapeutic deism suggests a faith that allows us to hold God down, to see him as a "nice" god who really would never test faith in such a way, which does not allow for the fullness of faith that Abraham exhibits in this passage. When we focus on the sacrifice, without all that has come before, it can seem that faith only or mostly tends toward moments of heightened decision, rather than the journey of small steps that I indicated earlier. Yet if we have been attentively on the pilgrimage with Abraham thus far, this story of sacrifice shows, instead, that the whole journey of faith leads, finally, to a whole life in God.

Readers over the centuries have contended with the problem of the test, but typically answer by suggesting that God already knew that Abraham would prove himself. The fifth-century bishop Theodoret of Cyrus writes:

> God did not test Abraham in order to learn something that He already knew, but to teach everyone else that He had good reason to love Abraham. That was why he tested his love of God for three days and nights. Abraham, torn between nature and faith and pulled both ways, decided favor of faith. Now, this was a shadow of the divine plan implemented for our benefit; for the sake of the world, the Father offered his beloved Son. Isaac was a type of the divinity, the ram of the humanity. The actual time was also of equal length; three days and nights both cases.[25]

Theodoret's typological reading suggests not only that God already knows Abraham, but also that God already knows about the sacrifices that lie in the future, via God's own Son. Theodoret also provides one possible way forward on the question of testing, that notably connects to what has been discussed above. Abraham has already exhibited faith; here his step-by-step pilgrimage in faith leads inexorably to a vision of God's own life, in which we learn that God in Christ gives Himself eternally to humanity.

Even if this is the answer to the question of "Why the test?" there remains the question of the manner of the test. Yet, in light of all we have considered thus far in scripture, we might consider whether the test is: will Abraham continue to believe that God is a God of life, that God will choose for Isaac? The author of the *Letter to the Hebrews* clearly sees this; the author appreciates Abraham's faith in simply setting out on the journey from Terah. Hebrews in fact spends several verses commenting on the faith of Abraham and Sarah before arriving at the sacrifice of Isaac: "By faith Abraham, when put to the test, offered up Isaac, and he who had received the promises was ready to offer his only son, of whom it was said, 'Through Isaac descendants shall bear your name.' He reasoned that God was able to raise even from the dead, and he received Isaac back as a symbol" (Heb. 11:18–19). For Hebrews, Isaac is the symbol that prefigures Jesus's resurrection from the dead. Thomas Aquinas writes as well:

> Abraham in his old age believed God promising that in Isaac he would be blessed in his seed. He also believed that God could raise the dead. Therefore, since he believed that God's commands must be obeyed, nothing else remained but to believe that He would revive Isaac, by whom his seed would be called. (*Commentary on the Letter to the Hebrews*, 11.605)

---

[25] Theodoret of Cyrus, *The Questions on the Octateuch: On Genesis and Exodus*, vol. 1, Greek text revised by John F. Petruccione, trans. Robert C. Hill (Washington DC: The Catholic University of America Press, 2007), Q. 74. Also interesting here is Theodoret's typology of the hypostatic union of Christ using ram and Isaac together.

Here, we witness again that God is a God of life, especially via the Resurrection. Isaac's sacrifice therefore witnesses to God's own self-sacrifice, but also to God's conquering of death.

Second, on the question about sacrifice of one's son, we might note that Genesis 22:1–19 is not only about Isaac's sacrifice but also about Abraham's own self-sacrifice. "Take your son Isaac, your only one, the one whom you love" (22:2). Even the thought is costly, but the text lingers on the fact that Isaac is Abraham's only, irreplaceable heir. Rabbi Soloveitchik expresses with eloquence the kind of self-sacrifice he envisions of Abraham as parent:

> "Offer your sacrifice!" That is the main command given to the person of religion.... The Holy One, Blessed be He, says to Abraham, "Take your son, your only one, Isaac, etc." In other words, I demand of you the supreme sacrifice.... Don't fool yourself that after you heed my voice I will give you another son in place of Isaac.... You will think about him every day. I want your son whom you loved and whom you will love for ever.... Your life will turn into a long chain of suffering of your soul. All of this notwithstanding, I demand this sacrifice.[26]

To be faithful is to become self-sacrificial in small and large ways. We turn away from our own love of self and love of the world as we want it to be, toward love of God and others, and a world that remains mysterious. Abraham could not know what God would do with the ram. Yet he had come to know God, and because he knows God, he is able to see the world as mysterious, but God as present in the mystery, nonetheless. He continues to take steps in faith.

In verse 3, Abraham silently assents to God's request to take his only son and sacrifice him. Here his faith has no words; Abraham simply assents. Later, Abraham and Isaac discuss the coming worship of God that they will do together. Notice that there is a collective sense of worship. Green's study of rabbinic resources suggests that there is also a collective sense of sacrifice here, such that "the sacrifice of Isaac and Abraham's personal self-sacrifice are morally analogous."[27] Even more, a midrash on Genesis 22:1–19 describes Isaac as someone who, with his father, *chooses* self-sacrifice, so that both are following God.[28] Such a view of sacrifice extends my earlier discussion of Abraham's faith as becoming something that is communally focused rather than individually ascribed. Faith becomes something that we practice together.

---

[26] Joseph B. Soloveitchik, in *BeSod haYachid ve-haYachad*, ed. Pinchas Peli (Jerusalem: Orot Press, 1975), 427–28.
[27] Ronald Green, "Abraham, Isaac, and the Jewish Tradition: An Ethical Reappraisal," *Journal of Religious Ethics* 10, no. 1 (1982): 8.
[28] Green, "Abraham, Isaac, and the Jewish Tradition," 8–9.

In verse 7, Isaac asks where the sacrifice is, and Abraham proclaims: "God will provide the sheep for the burnt offering" (22:8), which in fact is what we see happen in verses 11–13. The first-born son is not, in fact, the sacrifice that God desires in his covenant relationship with Abraham; God provides the sacrifice, and will do so again, with Jesus Christ.

Isaac's near sacrifice does offer a climactic point in the story, so it makes sense that Kant, Kierkegaard, and others should have fastened on this point. In a typological reading, however, Isaac's near-sacrifice, and the typological revelation of Jesus's sacrificial love on the cross, become the touchstone. Yet if that sacrifice is all that is seen, readers may miss that the whole of Abraham's narrative demonstrates a life of faith, begun with small steps. Those small steps of faith may yet lead to great faith, which is seen in small and large acts of generosity, hospitality, and other virtues. Readers miss, indeed, that Abraham's response to God is one of recognizing and trusting in the God of life who had already been revealed to him, and with whom he had already been living.

It is significant that Christians read this part of Abraham's story at the Easter Vigil, meant to help us reflect still more deeply on Christ's sacrificial love, on the depths of God's love for us, the "scandal of the cross" (as Paul has it in 1 Cor. 1:23). We notice how so much of Abraham's story is God's own story: Isaac carries the wood for the sacrifice; Abraham and Isaac travel three days. At the Easter Vigil, we are faced with the courageous momentous decision to choose this God in great faith; we are asked to be like Abraham. So many of the lives of the saints depend, too, on this kind of heightened utter courage: who can risk all on behalf of God? Yet also in this context, we seem to be asked quite a momentous question: Who can truly be a martyr, give away all possessions, go and live with the poor, drink the pus of plague victims, and more? What makes so many of the saints' stories so great to tell is that they, like Abraham, exhibit a shock value kind of faith.

For all those who wrestle with faith in God in modernity, it is the small steps and even the halting steps that will eventually become a recognizable pattern of faith in God. Recognizing the significance of those small steps, perhaps as part of gradual reflection on (for example) how science and faith belong together, is important for contemporary faith formation.

Conclusion

It remains, then, to offer some conclusions regarding my reading of Abraham and the question I began with, about how Christians might emphasize a much thicker, more complex, and stronger faith. I suggest that Abraham's step-by-step pilgrimage that led him ever more toward God offers a practical approach. Rationalistic, deductive faith insists on people already being able to assent to what may seem impossible or at odds with science, culture, and more. Abraham's pilgrimage suggests we can counsel people to begin with small steps from where they are. What small steps in faith might we offer to those young adults who profess Christ yet hold a view of God that is not a Christian view? What small steps toward discussing the Church's understanding of science and faith as integrally related might we offer? In the case of unaffiliated people, the conversation may begin much differently, at a place where a person expresses serious doubts. We might acknowledge the doubts and find ways to enable even the tiniest of steps in faith.

Moreover, Abraham gives us an opening and opportunity to discuss the modern dislike of "organized religion" with those who may have some account of faith but who are unable to see the benefit of a community of faith. However, while community is something with which Abraham surrounds himself throughout his journey, it is important to note that the particular community of faith does not show up till he is further along in the journey. In other words, a straight up invitation to church may not be a small enough step for some of the people we encounter.

That small step, in turn, requires our own faith as scholars and teachers. We must be willing to acknowledge that we can never foresee a person's whole journey in faith, nor are we the author of any part of their faith. God alone is the teacher, author, and shepherd. We shall definitely be called upon to respond to our faith with generosity and hospitality toward others. We shall have the opportunity to proclaim the Gospel in all the ways that we can, including through sharing Abraham's pilgrimage of what it means to be drawn into God's own life.

What if, via Abraham, the decision people are asked to make about faith is not about the decisions made at crisis points, but rather about the continuous decision to see the God of life everywhere that despair seems to exist instead? The Christian life that moral theologians need to describe is about being willing to step into the light of faith, even with small, halting steps, and persist for the long haul. Abraham truly is a father of our faith because he leads us, step by halting step, toward our Risen Lord and Savior. Ⓜ

Jana M. Bennett is professor and chairperson of the Department of Religious Studies at the University of Dayton. She is the co-author (with David Cloutier) of *Naming Our Sins: How Recognizing the Seven Deadly Vices Can Renew the Sacrament of Reconciliation* (Catholic University of America Press, 2019), and author of *Singleness and the Church: A New Theology of the Single Life* (Oxford, 2017).

Joseph the Just and Matthew's Matrix of Mercy: The Redefinition of Righteousness

Jonathan T. Pennington

The majority of the world's population today lives surrounded by electric light, making the ancient human habits of stargazing and constellation-recognition harder to find and harder to do. Light pollution and limited experience make it difficult for most people to identify much more than the Big Dipper and a couple of planets. A few years ago, when I was in New Zealand, up near the tip of the North Island, far away from any city, wading in the Southern Hemisphere's warm January ocean, I was able to experience stargazing in a new way. With some guidance, I beheld something few people in North America or Europe have had the privilege of seeing in all its glory—the Southern Cross (the constellation, "Crux"). For those of us who live north of the equator, the Southern Cross is only partially visible in the spring at the latitudes of southern Florida and the tip of Texas. In the southern hemisphere, however, the Southern Cross is their Big Dipper, their South Pole version of the central constellation that guided the native Maori and then, much later, the first Europeans who were sailing south.

This essay is not my misplaced notes for a travelogue presentation at my local observatory, however, but the fruit of my delightful reflections on the role of Scripture in moral theology. I start with this discussion of heavenly bodies as a framing metaphor for the moves in my argument. The constellation metaphor is about coming to see connections that one is not accustomed to see, but that can be discerned with guidance. There are four shining points in Matthew that, when connected, form a constellation—one that we will analogize with the Southern Cross. These four shining stars are recognizable in Matthew by themselves, but as your guide for this exploration, I will take the role of the heavenly docent and point out that when we look at each of these stars in relation to each other we can see that they connect to form something that is more than their individual brightness. The contribution of this essay is not so much to provide something new in any of my four points but rather, out of the thousands of stars in the First Gospel, I will point us to see a connected constellation that will add to our understanding of both Scripture and moral theology.

FOUR HEAVENLY BODIES THAT FORM A MATTHEAN CONSTELLATION OF MORAL THEOLOGY

The bulk of my argument consists in directing our gaze to four observations about Matthew that do not at first appear to be connected, at least not all four together. The first and fourth points concern how the gospels function, starting with what I call the great *paideia* project of the gospels and ending with a brief discussion of how characters in the story serve as moral exemplars. The second and third points concern themes in Matthew—righteousness and mercy—that may seem distinct at first but prove to be mutually-informing concepts in the First Gospel. Together these four shining points in Matthew form a constellation that envisions a particular moral theology.

(1) The Great Paideia Project of the Gospels

The first point of light in our constellation in Matthew comes from the purpose of the Gospels overall, as part of the *paideia* project of the Gospels. When hearing the phrase "*paideia* project" some readers will recall the impressive post-WWII Mortimer Adler/University of Chicago effort to rediscover the Great Books and shape society accordingly, what Adler called *The Paideia Proposal*.[1] Borrowing happily from the Greek tradition, Adler and others crafted a plan to reshape and rebuild post-war American society by focusing on training the sensibilities of young adults through exploring the great ideas—truth, goodness, beauty, liberty, equality, justice.[2] This is *paideia*, the shaping of society by the education of people in particular ways with great ideas. Even though I am talking about the Gospels, not Adler's Great Books, it is no mere coincidence that both of these corpora can be connected to the notion of *paideia*.

What I am referring to is the great *paideia* project by the ultimate Pedagogue, Jesus himself. Central to the moral theology of Scripture is the idea that Jesus is the pedagogue, the pioneer and teacher in righteousness. When we ask the important question, "What is the purpose of the gospels?" I recommend that the simplest and most comprehensive answer is that the gospels are given to the Church to shape and form people to inhabit the world in a certain way based on Jesus's life and teachings. This is *paideia*. Elsewhere I have summed up the gospels with this description:

---

[1] Mortimer J. Adler, *The Paideia Proposal: An Educational Manifesto* (New York: Macmillan, 1982).
[2] A fascinating account that sets the kind of vision Adler had into a larger intellectual trend of Christian humanism is found in Alan Jacobs's *The Year of Our Lord 1943: Christian Humanism in an Age of Crisis* (Oxford: Oxford University Press, 2018).

> Our Gospels are the historical, theological, aretegenic (virtue-forming) biographical narratives that retell the story and proclaim the significance of Jesus Christ, who through the power of the Holy Spirit is the Restorer of God's reign.[3]

All three of those opening adjectives are operative and important. "Historical" refers to the gospels making claims about a real person in real time, the in-fleshed Son of God whose entry into human history transformed it. "Theological" refers to the gospels making claims of a profoundly theological nature, revealing who God is; the gospels are not merely history, leaving the theology to Paul and the rest of the New Testament. "Aretegenic" names the purpose of the gospels, namely, to shape people to a way of seeing and being in the world, the life of God-ward, Christ-shaped, kingdom-oriented virtue that alone promises life and life abundantly.

It is this last and ultimate goal that is our focus here. Why does one write a biography (like the gospels) in the ancient world?[4] To record the teaching and actions of a noteworthy person *for the purpose of calling people to be transformed through becoming disciples*. The reason the vast majority of the literary real estate of the New Testament is given to biographical narratives is because the focus of Christianity is first and foremost on a Person, not a set of doctrines and morals abstracted (as important as those also are secondarily)—and a Person whose words and actions instruct and model the proper way of seeing and being for disciples.

We might describe this as a project of individual and corporate re-enculturation into an alternative community, a re-socializing of people to a different set of values, sensibilities, loves, habits, virtues; in short, an invitation to see and be in the world in a certain way. This is discipleship. This is moral theology. This is the great *paideia* project that is at the heart and *telos* of Christianity. I suggest that the Gospels are at the center of this project; they are the first fruits of Scripture, as Origen describes the *Tetraeuangelion*.[5]

This large sun-sized star is the first to highlight as we consider Matthew because, of all the Gospels, Matthew is particularly concerned to present Jesus as a Pedagogue who is forming a people to live

---

[3] Jonathan T. Pennington, *Reading the Gospels Wisely: A Narrative and Theological Introduction* (Grand Rapids, MI: Baker Academic, 2012), 35.

[4] New Testament scholarship in the last couple of decades has largely come to agree on the importance of recognizing the similarity of the Gospels to ancient *bioi*, largely influenced by Richard Burridge, *What are the Gospels? A Comparison with Greco-Roman Biography* (25th Anniversary ed., Waco, TX: Baylor University Press, 2018). See also the recent and comprehensive work of Craig Keener, *Christobiography: Memory, History, and the Reliability of the Gospels* (Grand Rapids, MI: Eerdmans, 2019).

[5] Origen, *Commentary on John* 1.4.

differently in the world. This is emphasized by Matthew's employment of five major blocks of teaching located at crucial places in his narrative—teaching blocks that each provide a locus and focus for training in being a disciple.[6] Understanding this *paideia* project of the Gospels sets the tone for how we read the stories, expecting that they are given to shape our sensibilities, habits, and loves in particular (and often unexpected) ways.

(2) True Righteousness

The second star in the Matthean constellation concerns the question of true righteousness. Human religions and philosophies of all stripes have long asked the question of the good: What is the good and how should one pursue it? Jesus and earliest Christianity have their own answer to this universal human question, typically using the biblical language of "righteousness."

"Righteousness" in the Bible has a semantic range that is large and complex. It can refer to justice in social relations, upstanding behavior, and a position of justified honor.[7] In the Old Testament, *ṣaddîq/ṣədāqâ* often has the idea of restorative justice, understood in the context of covenant with God. This covenantal justice is ultimately God's work of setting the world to right, his saving activity, though we are called to participate in this and are the beneficiaries of it. Related, righteousness—both God's and humanity's—is a matter of honor.[8] Following suit, in the subsequent Tannaitic literature righteousness "is uniformly a term for man's conduct in accord with God's will."[9]

When we turn to the First Gospel we find that righteousness is one of the major themes in Matthew, and that the evangelist is carefully

---

[6] Matthew's five major teaching blocks are identified as (1) Chapters 5–7, (2) Chapter 10, (3) Chapter 13, (4) Chapter 18, and (5) Chapters 23–25.

[7] The following discussion is based on my *The Sermon on the Mount and Human Flourishing: A Theological Commentary* (Grand Rapids, MI: Baker Academic, 2018), 87–91.

[8] See Jackson Wu, *Saving God's Face: A Chinese Contextualization of Salvation through Honor and Shame*, EMSDS (Pasadena, CA: William Carey International University Press, 2013); Jerome H. Neyrey, *Honor and Shame in the Gospel of Matthew* (Louisville, KY: Westminster John Knox, 1998); David A. deSilva, *Honor, Patronage, Kinship Purity: Unlocking New Testament Culture* (Downers Grove, IL: IVP Academic, 2000); and Leland White, "Grid and Group in Matthew's Community: The Righteousness/Honor Code in the Sermon on the Mount," *Semeia* 35 (1986): 61–89. White points out that Jesus's disciples and Matthew's hearers are not considered "honorable" in their own society precisely because "the community claims Jesus the crucified as its leader. *Members of the community share the public esteem or blame in which the crucified is held*" (80). The Beatitudes (and the rest of the Sermon) provide a quasi-public forum where the disciples can be seen to be truly the righteous and honorable ones, despite what the society around them says.

[9] Kari Syreeni, *The Making of the Sermon: A Procedural Analysis of Matthew's Redactoral Activity* (Suomalainen Tiedeakatemia, 1987), 207, quoted in Pennington, *The Sermon on the Mount and Human Flourishing*, 90.

directing our attention to understand it in a particular way.[10] Within the range of ways in which righteousness can function, Matthew uses it in its natural ethical sense of behavior that is right, in short, "doing the will of God" (Mt 7:21, 24; 12:50; cf. 6:10; 7:12; 18:14; 26:39, 42), the righteousness that is required to enter the kingdom of heaven (5:19–20; 7:21). Mt 21:28–32 is a good example of the concatenation of these overlapping expressions — "doing the will of the father," "entering the kingdom of God," and "the way of righteousness."

In sum, we can define "righteousness" in Matthew as *whole-person behavior that accords with God's nature, will, and coming kingdom.* The "righteous" person, according to Matthew, is the one who follows Jesus in this way of being in the world. The righteous person is the whole (*teleios*) person (5:48) who does not only do the will of God externally but, most importantly, from the heart. This is at the heart of the Sermon on the Mount's teachings and continues throughout Matthew, highlighted again in contrast with the scribes and Pharisees in Mt 23:1–36. When the pious young synagogue leader comes to Jesus and asks about the good, about the righteousness required to be in relationship to God, Jesus affirms the good of the external behavior of the man (keeping the commandments) while also pushing him to the matter of his heart, his loves (Mt 19:16–22). This external plus internal righteousness is once again described as *teleios* (19:21), as the kind of whole-person righteousness God wants for his creatures.

On the one hand, Matthew's emphasis on and description of righteousness is continuous with that of the Hebrew Scriptures. On the other hand, this emphasis on righteousness as *teleios,* as necessarily both external and internal, becomes a point of contention between Jesus and his primary interlocutors, the scribes and Pharisees. Jesus implicitly and explicitly condemns the scribes' and Pharisees' lack of true righteousness because of a cardial problem. They are obeying God's commands and continuing the traditions, but they lack the most important thing—a heart of love for God and love for others, which are the first and second greatest commandments (Mt 22:34–40). Thus, central to Matthew's theology and polemic is a kind of redefinition or clarifying of what righteousness is, particularly on the point of how one treats others in love and mercy. And this leads us to our next point.

---

[10] The Greek root *dikai-* appears 26 times in Matthew. Very commonly this is about "the righteous ones," an important category of people in Matthew. These righteous ones, or disciples, are often put into contrast with other people and things, such as the unrighteous (*adikous*, 5:45), sinners (*hamartōlous*, 9:13), the evil ones (*ponērous*, 13:49), hypocrisy and lawlessness (*hypokriseōs, anomias*, 23:28), and (most interestingly) "those of good repute" (*euōnymōn*, 25:41). See further discussion in my *Sermon on the Mount and Human Flourishing*, 88–89.

(3) The Matrix of Mercy

With our third heavenly body, the bright theme of mercy, our Matthean constellation begins to take shape. Matthean scholars have offered many options for the major theme in the First Gospel, and there are indeed many good candidates. Strong contenders include fulfillment, righteousness, and discipleship. A theme that is often overlooked initially but proves to be very important is the theme of mercy. Or better than just the singular word, "mercy" is what may be called Matthew's "matrix of mercy"—a series of distinct but deeply overlapping postures of heart and habits of life that Jesus regularly models and commends: *mercy, compassion, forgiveness,* and *love*. We can think of these concepts in a Venn diagram relationship of mercy-compassion-forgiveness, with the overlapping area in the middle as love.

This Matthean matrix of mercy unfolds through several key words and descriptions of Jesus's actions. First is the *eleos* word group. "Mercy" (*eleos*) is the manifestation of a state of heart that makes peace with others, shows compassion toward others, and forgives. It is a generous action that delivers others from some need or bondage. In the Beatitudes, Jesus commends this way of being with the macarisms about showing mercy (5:7) and making peace (5:9). In Matthew 6, one of the spiritual practices to be done with a whole heart is giving alms or showing mercy to those in physical need (6:1–6), the opposite of which is the harsh judging that is condemned in 7:1–5. Mercy typifies Jesus's way of righteousness, especially as it fulfills the second greatest commandment, love for others (22:34–40). Jesus places great weight on showing compassion to others in need as highlighted twice with Matthew's strategic use of Hosea 6:6 (Matt. 9:13; 12:7)—"I desire mercy/compassion, not sacrifice." Additionally, disciples are exhorted to help those in need (6:3; 25:35–36), an exhortation connected to mercy (*eleos*) in terms of the word for "giving alms to the poor" (*eleēmosynēn*). We might think of Matthew's theme of mercy by comparing it to a volume slider on a mixing board—Matthew has turned up the volume on mercy in his theological mix.

Closely related, Matthew regularly emphasizes Jesus's compassion toward others in both emotion and action. Five times in Matthew, Jesus is described with the verb *splanchnizomai*, having compassion (directly in 9:36; 14:14; 15:32; 20:34; indirectly in 18:27). Jesus's continual healing ministry is a sign of his compassion. By way of contrast, Jesus's conflict with his self-appointed enemies, the scribes and Pharisees, often centers on their lack of compassion for others (12:1–14; 23:4, 23). As Dale Allison points out, Jesus puts much emphasis on showing mercy to others—both in commanding it (9:13; 12:7; 23:23; 18:21–35; 25:31–46) and modeling it (9:27–31; 15:21–28; 7:14–18;

20:29–34). In this he stands in the biblical and Jewish tradition which places compassion "near the center of the moral life."[11]

Also, part of this matrix of mercy is the Matthean emphasis on forgiveness toward others. Jesus repeatedly speaks of the necessity and beauty of forgiving other people who have sinned against us (6:14–15; 18:15–20, 35), often tying it inextricably to receiving forgiveness from God himself. Forgiveness toward those who have wronged us is central to being a disciple of Jesus because it is living in the way that God himself does, forgiving others and making the sun and rain come upon all people, even the wicked (5:45).

As it relates to the argument of this essay, the point is to highlight this commonly overlooked star in Matthew—a deeply-embedded and widely-woven matrix of mercy. Put together with Matthew's goal in reshaping disciples' sensibilities and the theme of righteousness, the theme of mercy provides a third point that begins to bring our constellation into a recognizable shape. There is one more star for the picture to become clear.

(4) Characters as Exemplars

We noted above that the purpose of ancient biographies was intentionally to shape the sensibilities and habits of would-be disciples. The reason biographies are particularly important as a tool for formation is because, more powerfully than providing precepts and moral instructions in didactic form, human examples deeply shape character. As Seneca said it, "The way is long if one follows precepts, but short and helpful if one follows patterns."[12]

Matthew is full of characters that are meant to serve as short and effective examples. While there are current debates both within and outside of biblical studies about the proper methodology and conceptualization of the function of characters in stories, there is still benefit in an older categorization that goes back to E.M. Forster.[13] This approach classifies narrative characters into two types—*flat* and *round*. Flat characters are types who undergo no development and whose internal processes are not usually discussed. Instead, they serve as foils or simple exemplars, as a supporting cast to the main characters and events. Round characters, by contrast, do undergo development. They learn, change, grow, and, depending on the era of the writers, we may get to peek into the internal psychology of such characters. One current scholar in characterization studies is Cornelis Bennema, who appreciates the value of this scheme of flat and round characters, and

---

[11] Dale C. Allison, Jr., *The Sermon on the Mount: Inspiring the Moral Imagination* (Chestnut Ridge, NY: Crossroad Publishing, 1999), 50.
[12] Seneca, *Ad Lucilium* 6.5, trans. Richard Gummere (Harvard University Press, 1917), 25.
[13] E. M. Forster, *Aspects of the Novel* (San Diego, CA: Harcourt & Brace, 1927).

recommends we think in terms of a spectrum—with flat and round characters on either end and other characters often serving some in between role (oblong?).[14]

In Matthew there are many flat characters on both sides of Jesus who serve as examples both good and bad. These include people of great faith such as the Canaanite woman, the centurion who seeks Jesus for healing, and the two blind men. The primary negative flat characters are the scribes and Pharisees, who consistently play the role as foils to Jesus's teaching and example. The principal round characters in Matthew are the twelve disciples, but especially Peter, who plays an increasingly important role as the narrative progresses and who develops through failures and successes.

Paying attention to the characters in Matthew is important not just as part of a literary analysis, but especially for how the characters function as moral examples, both good and bad. Even though modern literary analysis is less likely to make any moral claims based on how characters function, there is no doubt that in their ancient context, this is how characters function in biographies: as exemplars of virtue and vice. These characters are models for the purpose of shaping the character of readers, not only by the power of example, but also in articulating and clarifying what are the vices and virtues that are to be avoided and adopted.

THE CONSTELLATION – WHOSE PICTURE?

With these four star-points identified—the *paideia* project of the Gospels, the themes of righteousness and mercy, and Matthean characters as exemplars—we can begin to discern that there is a pattern, a discernible constellation. The question is what image the constellation presents, or better, whose picture is it?

A good Christian answer to this question will always be Jesus. According to the New Testament, Jesus is the ultimate exemplar, the one who fulfills all righteousness (5:17), the one fully-pleasing-to-God beloved Son (3:17), who is full of compassion, mercy, and forgiveness, serving as the Model and Pioneer of the faith.

But while Jesus is the ultimate moral exemplar, there are other exemplars that Holy Scripture provides. He is the first-born of many brothers and sisters (Rom 8:29). As the Gospel of Matthew unfolds it is noteworthy to observe that the first characters we meet after the prefatory genealogy (Mt 1:1–17) are Joseph and Mary. Mary is mentioned first and that is significant (1:18), but Matthew focuses the narrative not on Mary (as does Luke) but on Joseph. While Joseph never speaks, he is the first active character of Matthew (and therefore of the canonical New Testament).

---

[14] Cornelis Bennema, *A Theory of Character in New Testament Narrative* (Minneapolis, MN: Fortress, 2014).

If we were to engage in a "quest for the historical Joseph," we would have an arduous task, not because he is unimportant to Christian tradition but because of various lines of interpretation that gather to Joseph by accretion over the centuries. Joseph as a character appears only briefly in the opening of Matthew and Luke but then vanishes from the narratives.[15] Naturally, Christian tradition was not content with such a paucity of information and the *Wirkungsgeschichte* regarding Joseph is rich in the non-canonical literature as well as sacred art.[16] From the biblical texts we understand that Joseph was recognized as the legal father of Jesus (Lk 2:4–7, 22–24; Jn 1:45; 6:42), though not the biological (Mt 1:20–25). Like his namesake in Genesis (Gen 37, 40–41), he was the recipient of angelic revelation and direction via dreams (Mt 1:20; 2:13, 19–23).[17] He was a *tektōn*, a craftsman in wood or stone, which according to the Talmud could also be a metaphor for a man learned in the Law.[18] While he is not explicitly mentioned in Matthew 19, Joseph is likely also in view when Jesus provides the exception clause for a justified divorce for the case of immorality (19:9) and the high calling of being a eunuch for the kingdom of heaven (19:12).

The most important description of Joseph is found in what Matthew identifies as the ground for his actions regarding Mary. Joseph was "righteous": "Joseph her husband, because he was a righteous man and did not desire to shame her, planned to divorce her quietly."[19]

---

[15] He is referenced as the father of Jesus in a number of subsequent texts (Mt 13:55; Lk 4:22) and twice early in the Gospel of John when Jesus is being introduced (Jn 1:45, 6:42). It is often assumed that Joseph died when Jesus is young, and this explains why he does not appear as a character in any other Gospel episodes. While this is possible, it should be noted that the references to Jesus as the son of Joseph that occur when Jesus is an adult are in the present tense (Mt 13:55; Lk 4:22; Jn 6:42) and could be read as referring to current knowledge of Joseph, not just past knowledge of him. The evidence in the New Testament is inconclusive.

[16] Joseph appears as a character in The Infancy Gospel of James, The Infancy Gospel of Thomas, the History of Joseph the Carpenter, and the Gospel of Pseudo-Matthew, in addition to countless works of visual art. For a detailed survey, see Philip Walker Jacobs, "The Reception History and Interpretation of the New Testament Portrayals of Joseph the Carpenter in Nativity and Infancy Portrayals in Early Christian and Early Medieval Narratives and Art from the Second Century to the Ninth Century CE," (PhD Dissertation, Bangor University, 2013).

[17] Joseph Fitzmyer explores the portrayal of Joseph in both Matthew and Luke, including drawing parallels between Joseph the husband of Mary and the Joseph of Genesis as "guardians" who provide safety for Israel. Joseph Fitzmyer, *Saint Joseph in Matthew's Gospel* (Philadelphia: St. Joseph's University Press, 1997), 2–4, 12, 17–20.

[18] This is Géza Vermès's suggestion, based on the observation that in the Talmud, "carpenter" and "son of a carpenter" were used to signify a Torah-learned man. Géza Vermès, *Jesus the Jew: A Historian's Reading of the Gospels* (Collins, 1973), 21–22.

[19] Author's English translation. The Greek reads: Ἰωσὴφ δὲ ὁ ἀνὴρ αὐτῆς, δίκαιος ὢν καὶ μὴ θέλων αὐτὴν δειγματίσαι, ἐβουλήθη λάθρᾳ ἀπολῦσαι αὐτήν (Matt. 1:19).

Crucial to understanding the significance of this description is attention to the Greek participial phrase, δίκαιος ὢν. Some English translations interpret this participle as concessive, thus rendering the phrase, "although he was a righteous man." While this is a possible translation, much better is the causal rendering: "because he was a righteous man." The logic of Matthew's description, in accord with his theological emphases, is that Joseph's righteousness is manifested through his merciful and compassionate attitude toward Mary, who as far as he knows (the angel has not yet appeared to him) has been unfaithful to him. Joseph is righteous in the way that Jesus will go on throughout Matthew to define righteousness—as marked by the highest virtue of a compassionate, forgiving, and merciful love toward others. Rather than dragging Mary before the village and demanding her stoning or other punishment, the wrongly treated Joseph desires to *not* put her to shame but rather to end their betrothal with a quiet, unexplained termination. Some—such as the flat characters of the scribes and Pharisees in Matthew—may be inclined to interpret righteousness as focusing on justice and rights, condemning those who have done wrong according to God's Law. But Joseph stands as the first exemplar in Matthew's Gospel of a deeper truth—that mercy, compassion, forgiveness, and love are the greatest commandments and therefore, the greatest righteousness.

We do not find a great number of scholars wrestling with what the nature of Joseph's righteousness was, and this lacuna means that Joseph's role in Matthew's moral theology is often missed. One scholar who did ask the question is Dan Via. In his article about how the narrative of Matthew teaches ethics, Via suggests that Joseph's righteousness inclines him to obey the law and have Mary stoned, but that this is qualified by his compassion. Additionally, Joseph's character is shown in that he has the flexibility and openness to change his understanding of what God requires of him based on revelation.[20] Thus, Joseph's righteousness is exemplified as an existential openness to be instructed by God in doing what is right. Via's reflections here are typical of his thoughtful and challenging structuralist and existential reading of the biblical texts.[21] However, in this case there is something more profound and Matthew-wide that is going on. *Jesus is redefining righteousness as mercy, kindness, compassion, and love.* Joseph serves as the first example of this newly defined righteousness that is intended to re-orient the moral theology of the Christian community in Matthew's day and throughout the history of the Church.

---

[20] Dan O. Via, "Narrative World and Ethical Response: The Marvelous and Righteousness in Matthew 1–2," *Semeia* 12 (1978), 136–137.

[21] See also Dan O. Via, *Self-Deception and Wholeness in Paul and Matthew* (Minneapolis, MN: Fortress, 1990).

Fast forward a few decades in the narrative and the adult Jesus will commend the very virtues that Joseph manifests here, such as practicing mercy over justice (5:7—Blessed are the merciful; "I desire mercy not sacrifice" 9:13; 12:7, the latter two quoting Hos 6:6), and practicing his righteousness in secret rather than for the praise of others (6:4, 6, 18). Additionally, when Jesus says in 5:20 that people need to have a righteousness greater than the scribes and Pharisees, readers have already in the first story of the Gospel an exemplar of this way of inhabiting the world.

Conclusion

For Christians, Holy Scripture has always been the primary source for moral theology, not only in giving explicit commands and prohibitions but also in providing a rich panoply of characters who serve as exemplars of virtue and vices to be avoided. This includes round and primary characters such as Peter, Paul, and Jesus himself. It also includes flat and secondary characters who may not seem to play a significant role, but who serve as clear and powerful pictures of particular virtues or vices.

Joseph, the husband of Mary, does not take up much literary space in the Gospel of Matthew, but his role in the moral theology of the book is great. We may be tempted to think of him as only a flat character because his story is so compressed, but Joseph does undergo growth in understanding. Even though he disappears after the prologue to the story, Joseph's significance is highlighted by being the first active character in the story. Moreover, the particular virtue that he exemplifies, righteousness manifested as mercy, does not seem overly significant at first. But as Jesus's teachings and actions unfold throughout the narrative, it turns out to be central to Matthew's theology. Joseph proves to be the exemplar who sets the tone for Jesus's primary moral teaching—that to enter the kingdom of heaven one must have a righteousness greater than the scribes and Pharisees (5:20), a righteousness marked by mercy, compassion, forgiveness, and love. Joseph, the adoptive father of Jesus, who sat under the Star of Bethlehem and beheld its wondrous glory, is rightly seen as a constellation in Matthew's heavenly picture of moral theology. M

Jonathan T. Pennington, who holds a Ph.D. in New Testament Studies from the University of St. Andrews (Scotland), is associate professor of New Testament Interpretation at The Southern Baptist Theological Seminary. Pennington is the author of *The Sermon on the Mount and Human Flourishing*, *Reading the Gospels Wisely*, and *Heaven and Earth In the Gospel of Matthew*.

"Repent for the Kingdom of Heaven
is at Hand!" (Mt 3:1 and 4:17):
Conversion in the Gospel and
the Christian Life

Anton ten Klooster

CATHOLIC MORAL THEOLOGY SEEKS TO answer the question of how one can live a good life, and it draws its answer from a long theological, moral, and spiritual tradition. In this tradition, conversion is often understood as the way by which one begins the journey that is the Christian life. On the one hand, conversion is then something fundamental, the total change of one's life from non-belief to Christianity. It is a point in time, with a distinct difference between what came before and what came after. On the other hand, the Christian life itself has many moments where a person can change their ways. The slack believer decides to adopt an order that carves out time for prayer, a repentant sinner goes to confession, and after hearing a homily by the Pope a person decides to finally talk to the homeless person on their block. This too is conversion. In order to speak fruitfully and helpfully about the moral life we therefore need a way to speak about the topic of conversion that includes these smaller conversions. We need to understand conversion in all its complexity. People can change their ways because their hearts have been touched, as in the case of the one who speaks to the homeless person. On another occasion, conversion is the outcome of an intellectual process, such as when reading a reflection on the *Rule of Saint Benedict* is an impulse to give structure to one's personal prayer.

The aim of this contribution is to understand conversion as part of the Christian life, and to do so in light of Scripture and its interpretation in the Catholic theological tradition. We will begin and end with sections engaging the question of conversion as an everyday event and draw from Scripture in the middle sections for guidance as to what it means to 'convert.' Together, these sections help us to appreciate conversion as a radical transformation that touches upon all of the domains of one's life. In the first section, we will address the different aspects of the question of conversion. We will draw in particular from the work of Bernard Lonergan for this task. This brings us to section two, where we study the call to conversion, or *metanoia*, in the Gospel of Matthew. Both John the Baptist and Jesus call the people into the kingdom of God with the same words: "Repent, for the kingdom of heaven is at hand" (Mt 3:1, 4:17). For both, it marks the beginning of their public ministry, indicating how fundamental conversion is when we want to heed the call to the kingdom. We will study these passages considering recent New Testament scholarship, paying particular attention to the meaning of the word *metanoia* which is often translated as "repent." This study of the Gospel raises several questions on the process of conversion and its actors. We will take these up in section three where we bring the biblical commentaries of Thomas Aquinas into the discussion. In the fourth and final section, we will bring all these insights together and consider their bearing on moral theology.

EXPLORING THE QUESTION OF CONVERSION

A number of questions and intuitions guide our exploration of conversion in Scripture. When conversion is understood as something that pertains to all of the Christian life—and not just to its initial phase—we need to begin by distinguishing between conversion *into* that life and conversion *within* that life. This immediately raises the question of agency. Against Pelagian trends, Catholic theology has always maintained that God is the primary actor in the process of conversion and that any human response is contingent on the divine initiative. This emphasizes that each moment of conversion is a moment of grace, be it conversion into or within the faith. But the events that we call conversion are highly complex. It can indeed be experienced as a powerful instant of divine intervention, similar to the conversion of Saul on the road to Damascus. For many, however, conversion is a process that speaks to different aspects of one's life, and it can be excruciatingly slow. Augustine may have been intellectually prepared to live a life of virtue but still felt unwilling, as attested in the famous "give me chastity and continence, but not yet" (*Conf.* 8.7.17). Although different in intensity, in both these types of conversion the subject enters a new life and undergoes a radical transformation. In both instances, conversion is understood as a fundamental change, and it is this type of conversion that many people think of when they hear the word. It is also how a typical theological dictionary defines the term. The *Lexikon für Theologie und Kirche*, for example, takes conversion as a prototype of 'objective' religious experience that is often the result of a psychological crisis.[1] Others give precise definitions, following Aquinas in describing conversion as "turning towards God through

---

[1] Herbert Wahl, "Bekehrung: Psychologisch," in *Lexikon für Theologie und Kirche* vol. 2, ed. Walter Kasper (Freiburg im Breisgau, Germany: Herder-Verlag, 2009), 166–167.

a process of cognitive assent upwards from creatures to divine reality."[2] Although precise, such a definition does not acknowledge the human reality of conversion.

Examples and dictionary definitions may allow for different types of conversion into Christianity, yet there still remains the question of how conversion takes place within the Christian life, and how we can acknowledge these conversions as fully human experiences while at the same time acknowledging that it is God who brings us back to him so "that we may return" (Lamentations 5:21). Often, different levels of one's being are involved in the conversion experience. The example of Augustine showed that the intellect can seemingly arrive at a place where the will is not yet. And what to think of Christians who adopt the creed but fail to act accordingly? They seem to have converted only partially, professing truths with their tongue that their heart and hands are unable to live out. This speaks of the complexity of the process of conversion both for those becoming Christians and for those trying to live as Christians.

Bernard Lonergan has made an important contribution to a theological appraisal of conversion. He wrote:

> Fundamental to religious living is conversion. It is a topic little studied in traditional theology since there remains very little of it when one reaches the universal, the abstract, the static. For conversion occurs in the lives of individuals. It is not merely a change or even a development; rather, it is a radical transformation on which follows, on all levels of living, an interlocked series of changes and developments. What hitherto was unnoticed becomes vivid and present. What had been of no concern becomes a matter of high import. So great a change in one's apprehensions and one's values accompanies no less a change in oneself, in one's relations to other persons, and in one's relations to God.[3]

We can say that to Lonergan conversion denotes an upheaval of values and a deeply personal experience.

The experience described by Lonergan is akin to the one Augustine reflects on in his *Confessions*: "You were within, but I outside, seeking there for you; and upon the shapely things you have made I rushed headlong, I, misshapen. You were with me, but I was not with you. They held me back far from you, those things which would have no being were they not in you." Augustine describes how everything changes, and how he himself values creation differently. Yet, this

---

[2] Patrick Quinn, "St. Thomas Aquinas's Theory of Conversion," in *Christianizing Peoples and Converting Individuals,* ed. Guyda Armstrong and Ian N. Wood (Turnhout, Belgium: Brepols, 2000), 270.
[3] Bernard Lonergan, *A Second Collection: Papers* (Philadelphia, PA: Westminster Press, 1974), 65–66.

change began with grace, and it was God who called, shouted, flared, blazed: "You touched me, and I burned for your peace" (*Conf.* 10.27.38). Conversion is radical. Lonergan understood the complexity of the conversion process which he described as "a transformation of the subject and his world."[4] This transformation takes place on different levels.

Lonergan calls these levels the three types of conversion: intellectual, moral, and religious conversion. Intellectual conversion marks a "radical clarification, and consequently, the elimination of an exceedingly stubborn myth concerning reality, objectivity, and human knowledge."[5] Moral conversion denotes a change in "the criterion of one's decisions and choices from satisfactions to values." Where intellectual conversion is preoccupied with the value of truth, moral conversion is interested in values in general, and for Lonergan this means that it goes beyond intellectual conversion.[6] "Similarly, religious conversion goes beyond moral" since it "transforms the existential subject into a subject in love, a subject held, grasped, possessed, owned through a total and so an other-worldly love. Then there is a new basis for all valuing and doing good."[7] The three types of conversion are connected but "still each is a different type of event and has to be considered in itself before being related to the others."[8] These types help us to see the profundity of conversion, specifying just how 'radical' it is, because it goes to the roots of what one thinks, does and believes.

The work of Lonergan thus provides us with helpful distinctions in our discussion of conversion. Very often conversion is taken solely as religious conversion, a change in what we believe and how we relate or begin to relate to God. But this includes intellectual and moral conversion, a change in how we think and act. Religious conversion can entail a change of thought and action, whereas sometimes an intellectual process leads to a change of actions and religious belief. To Lonergan, "there is no fixed rule of antecedence and consequence, no necessity of simultaneity, no prescribed magnitude of change."[9] This broad understanding of conversion provides us with the vocabulary to further explore the topic, and it gives us the questions we can take into our reading of Scripture. What change does conversion effect in its subject? Who is or are the actor(s) in the process of conversion? And is the formal distinction between three types of conversion at all helpful to understand the biblical narrative? With these questions in mind, we try to heed the call to conversion as it comes to us in the Gospel.

---

[4] Bernard Lonergan, *Method in Theology* (Toronto: University of Toronto Press, 2013), 130.
[5] Lonergan, *Method in Theology*, 238.
[6] Lonergan, *Method in Theology*, 240–242.
[7] Lonergan, *Method in Theology*, 242.
[8] Lonergan, *Method in Theology*, 238.
[9] Lonergan, *A Second Collection*, 66.

METANOIA FOR THE KINGDOM OF HEAVEN

In the first section, we sought to grasp the issue at hand and raised questions about it. Now we move to listen to Scripture in order to address them. How can we do so fruitfully, learning from Scripture rather than imposing our own presuppositions on the holy words? Servais Pinckaers gave a number of suggestions to this end in *The Sources of Christian Ethics*. He calls on theologians "to give honest priority to a direct reading of Scripture over any type of commentary, exegetical, theological, or whatever it may be."[10] This reading requires an exact translation and a basic understanding of the background of the text. Commentaries "will refine, expand, and improve it, so as to facilitate a richer and more penetrating re-reading. The commentary is at the service of the immediate reading."[11] Pinckaers is adamant about the necessity to first read Scripture for ourselves so that we can be touched personally by the words rather than have the commentary serve as a substitute for personal reading. Theological commentary does enrich this personal reading: "The person who has received, through faith, the spark of an interior understanding of Scripture will all the better appreciate the authentic findings of modern exegesis and profit from them, using the necessary critical discernment and a right critical ordering of things."[12]

An interior understanding of Scripture calls for careful discernment, and it will be difficult to convey this type of understanding in a written contribution. What we can do is first present our chosen texts and try to let them speak to us before we subject them to further scrutiny. Our chosen texts to study the subject of conversion are taken from the Gospel of Matthew, which for the church fathers held pride of place as the first gospel.[13] Both John the Baptist and Jesus call for conversion at the beginning of this Gospel, and they do so in the exact same words. The Evangelist introduces John by immediately presenting his preaching:

> In those days, John the Baptist appeared, preaching in the desert of Judea saying "Repent for the kingdom of heaven is at hand!" It was of him that the prophet Isaiah had spoken when he said: "A voice is crying out in the desert, 'prepare the way of the Lord, make straight his paths'" (Mt 3:1–3).

When we pause to prayerfully reflect on these lines, there are a number of words that can speak to the heart. 'Preaching' may evoke urgency.

---

[10] Servais Pinckaers, *The Sources of Christian Ethics* (Washington, DC: Catholic University of America Press, 1995), 318.
[11] Pinckaers, *The Sources of Christian Ethics*, 319.
[12] Pinckaers, *The Sources of Christian Ethics*, 321.
[13] See, for example, Jerome's preface to his commentary on Matthew.

The word 'desert' can suggest solitude, desolation, spiritually arid times. The words of John call, invite, and urge. They call to repent; according to the circumstances of our lives the word 'repent' will speak to us differently. The invocation of the kingdom of heaven invites us to reflect on what that means, and to be a part of it. By adding 'at hand,' urgency is added to this call. These are but a few reflections on what the words of the Gospel may evoke; they will speak to each of us according to how we pray with them and to how the Holy Spirit speaks to our heart through them.

When we move on to the next chapter of the Gospel, the call to repentance reappears but now on the lips of Jesus. After his temptation in the desert and after John is arrested, Jesus begins to preach. As he did with John's ministry, Matthew presents this preaching as a fulfillment of the prophecy of Isaiah:

> He left Nazareth and went to live in Capernaum by the sea, in the region of Zebulun and Naphtali, that what had been said through Isaiah the prophet might be fulfilled: "Land of Zebulun and land of Naphtali, the way to the sea, beyond the Jordan, Galilee of the Gentiles, the people who sit in darkness have seen a great light, on those dwelling in a land overshadowed by death light has arisen." From that time on, Jesus began to preach and say, "Repent for the kingdom of heaven is at hand" (Mt 4:13–17).

The attentive and prayerful reader may be triggered by several things in this Gospel passage. Jesus moves to Capernaum, and the prophecy speaks of the land of the Gentiles: the preaching moves out in to the open and rings out to everyone who will listen. Darkness is pitted against light. If you feel that there are parts in your life that are dark and dead, the double mention of 'light' may strike a chord of hope. Even a word like 'fulfillment' may speak to a longing of your soul. Again, these are but a few reflections on how the Gospel might speak to us in an initial prayerful reading. Although it is difficult to incorporate this step into a theoretical discussion, we should at the very least acknowledge it, following the encouragement of Servais Pinckaers. Where this is fitting, we will touch upon elements of this reflection later.

Our discussion will focus on the meaning of the word 'repentance' in these chapters of Matthew. This means we will have to forgo more extensive discussions on what the kingdom of heaven entails, and on the theme of fulfillment of prophecy in the first Gospel. We do, however, need to explore the topic of conversion or repentance in the *Umwelt* of the New Testament and in the structure of the Gospel of Matthew. Therefore, we will first look closer at the word for repentance, the Greek μετάνοια (*metanoia*), and then make some observations about its function in the Gospel.

Metanoia appears as both a noun and part of a verb in the synoptic Gospels; of particular interest to us are Matthew 3:2, 3:6, 3:8, 4:17, Mark 1:4, 1:15, and Luke 3:3. It is often translated as 'repentance/repent' and can as such refer to the movement of the heart that we interpret as conversion. In ancient Greek it is often paired with καιρός (*kairos*), which means 'time' in the sense of 'the right time,' with connotations of urgency. These two words appear together in Mark 1, 14–15: "After John had been arrested, Jesus came to Galilee proclaiming the gospel of God: 'This is the time (*kairos*) of fulfillment. The kingdom of God is at hand. Repent (*metanoiete*), and believe in the gospel.'"[14] Already in Greek mythology these terms were related and used together. *Kairos* was personified as the Greek god of opportunity, who is followed by *Metanoia* who represents all the missed opportunities. In Greek *metanoia* literally means afterthought, and so the word has strong connotations of regret.[15] We may recall here the 'death' and 'darkness' in which the call to conversion rings in the Gospel. Regret is a motivation for change and these "elements and repentance become strongly amplified when *metanoia* takes on biblical significance," with one significant change: "whereas the Greek interpretation involves a return to a thought or experience, the New Testament *metanoia* calls for a turning (or returning) of the soul to God."[16] In this interpretation to convert is to seize the opportunity when it presents itself. The preaching of both John and Jesus then are a sign of the *kairos*, meaning that is the right time for conversion.

What is the place of the call to *metanoia* in the larger scheme of the Gospel of Matthew? The work of a few Biblical scholars will help us to shed light on this issue. Jonathan Pennington contends that the call to repentance by Jesus in Matthew 4:17 inaugurates the first of five discourse-narrative blocks, and this first one runs all the way through to Matthew 9:38. The unit is marked by the similar endings of chapters four and nine, which both summarize Jesus's ministry in Galilee.[17] Between these chapters stands the Sermon on the Mount which, according to Pennington, is closely related to the call to repentance in

---

[14] See Ulrich Luz, *Evangelisch-Katholischer Kommentar zum Neuen Testament I/1: Das Evangelium nach Matthäus (Mt 1–7)* (Zürich: Benziger Verlag, 1985), 173.

[15] Kelly A. Myers, "*Metanoia* and the Transformation of Opportunity," *Rhetoric Society Quarterly* 41, no. 1 (2011): 1–8. See Henry George Liddell and Robert Scott, eds., *A Greek-English Lexicon* (Oxford: Clarendon Press, 1983), lemma μετάνοια. They offer as possible translations of the term: change of mind or heart, repentance, regret. Lipsett argues in favor of interpretations that describe *metanoia* as "life enhancing and liberating," which I believe can be interpreted as following upon the aspect of penance: B. Diane Lipsett, *Desiring Conversion: Hermas, Thecla, Aseneth* (Oxford: Oxford University Press, 2011), 12.

[16] Myers, "*Metanoia* and the Transformation of Opportunity," 8–9.

[17] Jonathan Pennington, *The Sermon on the Mount and Human Flourishing: A Theological Commentary* (Grand Rapids, MI: Baker Academic, 2017), 101.

Matthew 4:17. He claims that "The sermon in many ways is an unpacking of what this call to repentance looks like … Repentance is about the whole person turning back to God and devotedness to him."[18] This repentance does not merely mean changing one's ways, but it requires the alignment of one's heart with God.[19] This is the radical transformation that we encountered in Lonergan, albeit without further specification.

Other scholars agree with this interpretation. Daniel Harrington describes repentance as something that "involves a willingness to turn one's life around in the sense of a complete reorientation," in this case done for reason of the nearness of God's kingdom.[20] Even more extensive is the discussion of Joachim Gnilka, who reflects on "the fruits of repentance" that John calls for (Mt 3:8). He translates *metanoia* with the German *Umkehr*, turning around, and defines it as "the radical acknowledgment of God, because He is rightfully angered, an entirely new orientation."[21] This is a helpful translation for two reasons: it includes the penitential aspect, and it makes clear that *metanoia* is an all-encompassing movement of one's life. By connecting the call to conversion to the wrath of God preached by John, Gnilka makes clear that the call is urgent and that its object is God. There is not simply a turn-around, but a turning toward God who is ready to judge the world. Pennington, reflecting on Jesus's preaching, calls this a meta-theme of the Gospel of Matthew: "God is revealing himself in Christ and… this revelation results in or creates two groups, those inside and those outside, based on faith-response to Jesus."[22]

The newness of Jesus's preaching is that the proclamation of the kingdom derives its strength from nothing but himself. He embodies the kingdom he proclaims, whereas John and later Jesus's disciples depend on Jesus for the power and veracity of their preaching. One indication of this is that the baptism of conversion that John offered is presented in the Gospel as ordered toward the baptism with fire and the Spirit of Jesus (Matthew 3:11).[23] *Metanoia* is then primarily a turning to the kingdom of Christ, it is "the vantage point from which the existence of the disciple, the Christian life begins."[24] What one turns away from, the Gospels of Mark and Luke make clear, is sin. Hence the reference to John's ministry as "preaching a baptism of repentance

---

[18] Pennington, *The Sermon on the Mount and Human Flourishing*, 144, see 101.
[19] Pennington, *The Sermon on the Mount and Human Flourishing*, 153, 224.
[20] Daniel J. Harrington, ed., *Sacra Pagina: The Gospel of Matthew* (Collegeville, MN: Liturgical Press), 51.
[21] Joachim Gnilka, *Herders Theologische Kommentar zum Neuen Testament: Das Matthäusevangelium 1,1–13,58* (Freiburg im Breisgau, Germany: Herder, Sonderausgabe, 2000), 69.
[22] Pennington, *The Sermon on the Mount and Human Flourishing*, 98.
[23] See Gnilka, *Das Matthäusevangelium*, 70, 100–101.
[24] Gnilka, *Das Matthäusevangelium*, 101.

for the forgiveness of sins" (Mark 1:4, Luke 3:3). What we can take away from this is that conversion is a response to an urgent call. The call is to God and away from sin. It is this latter connotation that becomes the overtone when *metanoia* is translated as 'penance.'

Returning to our questions at the end of the first section, we can see that Scripture helps us to formulate answers to a few of them. Although there is no formal distinction between intellectual, moral, and religious conversion, the term *metanoia* also denotes a transformation that is radical, touching upon all the domains of one's life. The primary actor in this process is God, who through his call moves the human person to conversion. By associating *metanoia* with regret, we venture into the domain of moral choices, and of moral conversion. These are but some preliminary observations that stand in need of further study and development.

Conversion is fundamental to the Christian life. It demands the full and complete reorientation of one's life to the kingdom of heaven and everything this includes. It is clearly seen as a transformative event, the beginning of something new. This new beginning is all-encompassing, so we can say that this includes the intellectual, moral, and religious levels of living. If *metanoia* is to be complete it needs to be radical, involving all capacities of the human existence. Perhaps it is best understood as a search for meaning or truth that sets everything else in motion. This brings with it the question of what happens after these beginnings and how we can speak of growth in the Christian life. These are the questions that are relevant when we wish to make the notion of conversion fruitful for moral theology, from a Scriptural perspective. Much of this section has been the study of the word *metanoia*, but its aim is to stand at the service of moral theology which pertains to our concrete actions and choices. When we distinguish between different types of conversion we can better guide moral deliberation. In light of the ecological crisis for example, perhaps what is called for first is an intellectual conversion vis-à-vis a sentimental approach that is primarily interested in maintaining the current lifestyle. When one begins to consider this matter differently, a different pattern of consumption is more likely to follow. This is the sort of radical change that speaks not just to the instant of becoming a believer but to the everyday conversions that form the life of the believer.

By studying Scripture and reflecting on human experience we can learn to discern what the good is we should pursue in our efforts to be followers of Jesus Christ. For now, we note that it involves turning all capacities toward discipleship and away from that which is darkness and death. In brief, *metanoia* is turning one's being from the domain of sin to the domain which we call the kingdom of God. But this requires more than an act of our own will, as we will see in the next section.

THOMAS AQUINAS'S COMMENTARY ON THE CALL TO CONVERSION IN MATTHEW

To further explore the call to *metanoia* in the Gospel of Matthew we turn to the biblical commentary of Thomas Aquinas. In the commentary we encounter Aquinas in his task of reading Scripture, which was foundational to his teaching office. He performed this task by drawing from the wisdom of the church fathers, paying close attention to the letter of the text.[25] The biblical commentaries of Aquinas give us his most immediate engagement with the texts that are of interest to us. We turn to his works in particular not because we *must* at all times go to him but rather because, as Otto Hermann Pesch said, he is a teacher who "*may* be quoted, with the underlying thought, 'What a joy to read that a theologian who lived, thought and worked hundreds of years before our time had something to say… that can still help us today.'"[26] Aquinas's interpretation of Scripture is a valuable source for several reasons. His academic career takes place at the crossroads of history: Aristotle is reintroduced into the west, Christians engage in discussions with Muslim scholars, and biblical interpretation has evolved from a monastic practice into an academic exercise.[27] As in our days, the church in the thirteenth century faced the need for renewal. The Franciscans and Dominicans contributed to this renewal by returning to the Gospel, in practice and in preaching.[28] Aquinas could draw from the wellspring of inspired authors before him. He had a vast knowledge of Greek and Latin church fathers, whose works he collected in his *Catena Aurea* and then incorporated in his own commentaries. We will see that this brings him to valuable insights that contribute to our understanding of conversion.

Reading a Biblical commentary of Aquinas is helpful, but it is also a daunting task for those unfamiliar with this type of text. Naturally, he follows the order of the book he is commenting upon, and the text of a commentary is therefore not a systematic exposition on a given topic but rather a reflection on the letter of Scripture and the questions it evokes. Therefore, we should pay attention to the structure of the commentary itself. We should also note that Aquinas read the Bible in

---

[25] See A.M. ten Klooster, *Thomas Aquinas on the Beatitudes: Reading Matthew, Disputing Grace and Virtue, Preaching Happiness* (Leuven, Belgium: Peeters, 2018), 1–29.

[26] Otto H. Pesch, "Thomas Aquinas and Contemporary Theology," in *Aquinas as Authority*, ed. Paul van Geest, Harm Goris, and Carlo Leget (Leuven, Belgium: Peeters, 2002), 143.

[27] Gilbert Dahan, *L'Exégese Chrétienne de la Bible en Occident Médiéval: XIIe–XIVe siècle* (Paris: Les Éditions du Cerf, 1999), 75ff.

[28] Carolyn Muessig, "Preaching the Beatitudes in the Late Middle Ages: Some Mendicant Examples," *Studies in Christian Ethics* 22, no. 2 (2009): 136–150; Margherita M. Rossi, "(L')Attenzione a Tommaso d'Aquino Esegeta," *Angelicum* 76 (1999), 78–79.

the Latin Vulgate translation. The preaching of John and Jesus is translated as "*Paenitentiam agite, appropinquavit enim regnum caelorum*" (Matthew 3:2, 4:17). The single word *metanoiete* is translated as "do penance," which evokes sin and regret in the same way that the common English translation "repent" does.

Chapters three and four of the Gospel of Matthew have a particular place in Aquinas's *divisio textus* of the Gospel. Basing himself loosely on John Chrysostom, he divides the Gospel into three large sections: the entrance of Christ in the world, his passing through it, and his exit from it, respectively *ingressus*, *processus*, and *exitus*. The first two chapters on the genealogy, annunciation, and the birth of Christ are part of the *ingressus*. In the second section, the *processus* is dealt with "according to the progress of his teaching, because for this he came" (John 18:37).[29] The teaching proper is set down from chapter five on, beginning with the Sermon on the Mount. Both chapter three and four are part of the preparation for the teaching of Christ in the *divisio* of Aquinas. This preparation consists of the preaching of John, the baptism and temptation of Christ, and the initial preaching of Christ and the calling of the first disciples. John is presented as the herald; just as the Father was announced by prophets, so Christ is announced by John (see Luke 1:76) (*Commentary on Matthew*, c. 3 l. 1 n. 243).

Aquinas's commentary on the preaching of John addresses some of the questions raised earlier. When he reflects on why John preached in the desert, Aquinas notes that this "fit with his preaching, since he preached penance. Now a place of penance ought to be that way, either bodily or mentally" (*Commentary on Matthew*, c. 3 l. 1 n. 246). He dwells on what repentance and penance entail. With his call to penance, John "announces a certain new life, as Augustine says in the book *On Penance:* 'No one who is established as the judge of his own will can begin a new life, unless he repents of the old life'" (*Commentary on Matthew*, c. 3 l. 1 n. 248). To repent, the Latin *paenitere*, is to weep over one's sins, "and one should know that the whole thing is referred to the intention in his mind, namely that he be dedicated, and not commit such deeds worthy of tears, i.e., intend not to commit such deeds; for penance requires this." To do penance, *paenitentiam agere*, is "to satisfy for sins" (*Commentary on Matthew*, c. 3 l. 1 n. 248).

The recognition of sin is the first incitement to penance; the second is fear of divine judgment (*Commentary on Matthew*, c. 3 l. 1 n. 265). Aquinas argues that John and Jesus do not merely call on those who listen to stop sinning but ask that they indeed satisfy for their sins. To the medieval student, whom Aquinas is addressing, this may seem

---

[29] Thomas Aquinas, *Commentary on the Gospel of Matthew*, trans. Jeremy Holmes and Beth Mortensen (Lander, WY: The Aquinas Institute for the Study of Sacred Doctrine, 2013), c. 3 l.1, n. 241.

strange because John foretells the baptism of Christ, and in this baptism, all sins are forgiven. He responds to the objection by distinguishing between penance before baptism, which requires remorse over sins, and penance after baptism, when there is remorse over mortal and venial sins.[30] We should note that this means that, to Aquinas, penance or *metanoia* plays a role both before and after baptism. Following the text, he then moves on to discuss what the kingdom of heaven is. He offers four interpretations and gives as the first that the kingdom is "Christ himself dwelling in us through grace... because the road of the heavenly kingdom is begun by grace dwelling in us" (*Commentary on Matthew*, c. 3 l. 1 n. 250). This interpretation is particularly important to this inquiry because Aquinas stresses that our turning toward the kingdom begins with grace.[31]

Aquinas has a number of things in common with present-day interpreters. He believes that the call to repentance is somehow linked to the teaching of the Sermon on the Mount. Doing penance is about the regret of past faults and it implies the beginning of something new, all of this in light of impending divine judgment. But when he reflects on the actors in the process of doing penance, he adds new tones to our palette of interpretations. He presents the kingdom that is proclaimed as a work of grace, as we already noted. Even when John preaches, it is Christ to whom penance leads since Christ "was speaking in John" (*Commentary on Matthew*, c. 3 l. 1 n. 253). In the preaching of John, we are not just called to turn to God; it is God himself who moves in our direction, as Aquinas beautifully comments: "One should know that we were so weak that we would not have been able to approach the Lord unless he came to us. And this is why John said above, 'the kingdom of heaven is at hand'; and this is, 'prepare'" (*Commentary on Matthew*, c. 3 l. 1 n. 254). In his commentary, Aquinas thus broadens the narrative from human *Umkehr* or turning-around to a divine inclination, namely God's turning to us first.

After John's arrest Christ begins to preach publicly. Aquinas assumes he preached privately to Peter, Andrew, Philip, and Nathaniel but "at first he did not wish to preach publicly, so as to give place to John's preaching; otherwise, it would have done no good, just as the light of a star is obscured by the light of the sun" (*Commentary on Matthew*, c. 4 l. 2 n. 360). Once Jesus begins to preach, he uses the same words as John so that "no one would scornfully refuse to preach words said by another," and "because John is the voice, but he is the

---

[30] In this edition of the commentary, John's preaching is said to pertain to penance *after* baptism. Both the context of the commentary and a reference to Acts 2:38 suggest this is a flaw in the manuscript tradition and that it should be taken to refer to penance *before* baptism.

[31] The three other interpretations of the kingdom are of less interest at this point. They are, respectively, Sacred Scripture, the present church militant, and the heavenly court.

Word. Now, the same thing is signified by the word and the voice because the word is expressive of the voice" (*Commentary on Matthew*, c. 4 l. 2 n. 360). This is a more theological elaboration of the earlier claim that Jesus speaks through John, inspired by the church fathers. Aquinas is relatively brief on the content of Christ's call to repentance, probably because he discussed the content of this call at length in relation to John. What is new is a distinction within the call to "do penance, for the kingdom of heaven is at hand." First, Christ urges to do penance because, despite previous admonitions "through the law of nature and the Scriptures," humans have transgressed (*Commentary on Matthew*, c. 4 l. 2 n. 361). Second, he makes a promise, namely that the kingdom of heaven is at hand. In discussing the kingdom, he again emphasizes that God approaches us while calling us to conversion to Him. After the transgressions of the past, Christ inaugurates a new pact between us and God, "and so he says, 'the kingdom of heaven is at hand,' namely eternal beatitude. And he says, 'is at hand,' because the one who was giving descended to us, since we were not able to ascend to God" (*Commentary on Matthew*, c. 4 l. 2 n. 362). Aquinas thus reminds us that conversion is not an end in itself but that it is ordered to the kingdom, which he interprets here as eternal happiness. The nearness of the kingdom in Christ is proclaimed at the beginning, and it becomes more visible throughout his ministry. Wherever the disciples of Christ preach, they urge their listeners to repentance with an eye to the promise of happiness and its fulfillment in Christ.[32]

We read the commentary to see what Aquinas brings to our understanding of *metanoia*. Initially, the translation *paenitentia* might seem to restrict its meaning and interpretation but we have seen that he adds a number of facets to the discussion. Aquinas takes up repentance with its connotations of regret but states more clearly that the regret is not just about missed opportunities in general but about transgressions toward God. The aim of conversion is to turn toward the kingdom of God, which is understood at least in part as the presence of God in the believer by grace. Ultimately, the call to repentance is Christ calling us to eternal happiness, something Aquinas repeats throughout his career in his teaching and preaching. In the *Summa theologiae*, he is most explicit about this, as Eric Luijten aptly summarized. Penance is aroused in the believer and this

> …gives an idea of how [Aquinas] understands the cause of the reorientation of the will. Not by force, nor by some form of magic, but by

---

[32] See ST III q. 85 a. 5 arg. 2; *Commentary on Matthew* c. 10 l. 1 n. 817, c. 16 l. 2 n. 1371, c. 24 l. 1 n. 1921, c. 26 l. 1 n. 2118; *Sermo* XX *Beata gens*, prothema, lines 11–15.

confronting the human soul with an act of love, which, in itself, is capable of re-directing the will, and igniting the fire of love.[33]

Key to understanding Aquinas is that he identifies the call to conversion itself as an instant of grace. The preaching indicates that God first comes to us before we turn to Him. Conversion therefore begins with the divine initiative, and we can understand the subsequent *Umkehr* as being contingent on this first movement of grace. This is why Aquinas can claim that repentance is a virtue because it springs forth from the grace of the Holy Spirit who moves the heart of the repentant sinner.[34] A full and total *metanoia* which excludes no domain of life and no part of one's being indeed requires the action of the Spirit.

CONVERSION AND GROWTH IN GRACE

From Lonergan we learned an appreciation for the complexity of the process of conversion. It is this appreciation for both the complexity, and of conversion as an ongoing process, that helped focus our reading of the New Testament and its interpretation by Thomas Aquinas. Looking at the Greek, we saw that *metanoia* means that one seizes an opportunity where it has been missed before. New Testament exegesis tells us that the connotations of regret are emphasized in Scripture, and that the *Umkehr* that John and Jesus call to is radical and complete. Thomas Aquinas adds an emphasis on grace as the principle of conversion and he reminds us of its finality: happiness. With these insights at hand, what can we say about their bearing on moral theology? We take this discipline here as Servais Pinckaers described it, namely as "the branch of theology that studies human acts so as to direct them to a loving vision of God seen as our true, complete happiness and our final end. This vision is attained by means of grace, the virtues, and the gifts, in the light of revelation and reason."[35]

We brought together considerations from Scripture, and with Lonergan briefly reflected on the human process of conversion. In the light of revelation and reason we thus considered conversion in general terms as a human act. But most of all we focused on how *metanoia* is directed to God. It is an invitation to turn or return to Him. The ultimate object of this turn is our true, complete happiness. What we could refine with regard to Pinckaers's definition is that this turn in itself takes place by means of grace. Already the virtuous movement of repentance is a result of God's turning to us first. We have used the terms *metanoia*, repentance, *Umkehr*, and conversion interchangeably to refer to that good action which signifies our response to God's call to a

---

[33] Eric Luijten, *Sacramental Forgiveness as a Gift of God: Thomas Aquinas on the Sacrament of Penance* (Leuven, Belgium: Peeters, 2003), 183.
[34] See ST III q. 85 a. 1 s.c.
[35] Pinckaers, *The Sources of Christian Ethics*, 8.

reorientation of our entire existence toward Him. Rather than fear of punishment or regret, its true motivation lies in the promise of true happiness.

Although our sources still tend to treat conversion as an initial movement of faith with which everything else begins, it is possible to broaden this understanding to include those forms of conversion of which Lonergan spoke. The first moment of *metanoia* is a moment of grace; God turns to us and invites us to turn to Him. We can think here of a passage of Scripture that Aquinas repeatedly quotes to explain conversion, which in the Vulgate version reads "Convert us, Lord, to you, and we shall be converted; renew our days as from the beginning" (Lamentations 5:21).[36] *Metanoia* is this dual conversion, in which God's turn to us is the principle of everything else. Conversion puts our life on the right track, namely toward the end for which we were made. Can anything else come after this initial grace? Aquinas can help us here because in the questions on merit at the end of the *prima secundae,* he posits the possibility of a growth in grace, following Augustine (ST I-II q. 114 a. 8 s.c.). In a similar vein, we could also speak of an ever-growing intensity of the human person's *Umkehr* or turning toward God. The New Testament scholarship in particular stressed that this is a full and total reorientation of life. This already implies that one cannot suffice with simply changing a few actions or switching to a limited number of beliefs. Lonergan's types of conversion help us to speak about how conversion can indeed touch on all that we choose to do, how we think and what we believe. Moving to this type of speech helps us to break down the all-encompassing call to *metanoia* and to make it practical. All of these domains need attention in our continuous process of conversion to God, and the more they are transformed by grace the more a person attains the wholeness for which he or she was made.

Theologically speaking, conversion stands at the beginning of everything. I would suggest that we reserve the term *initium fidei* to designate this fascinating yet mysterious prime moment of faith. This *metanoia* or conversion entails the reorientation of values toward the kingdom of God. This reorientation unfolds in moral, intellectual, and religious conversion. For some, this will follow the typical learning curve from slow beginning to steep acceleration and from there to an eventual plateau. For others it is a process of repeated fallbacks and renewed reorientation. A reflection of St. Francis de Sales offers a glimpse of what such a life of continual conversion might resemble: "when your heart wanders or suffers, carefully bring it back and place

---

[36] For a discussion see Michael A. Abril, "Lamentations 5:21 within the Development of Thomas Aquinas' Theology of the Grace of Conversion," *International Journal of Systematic Theology* 16, no.3 (2014): 251–272.

it gently in the presence of God. And even when you have done nothing in your life but bringing back your heart and placing it in the presence of God—even though it always ran off again—then you have lived your life well."[37] Conversion is thus much more than how we enter into the Christian life. A proper understanding of the term helps us to speak of how we can grow in that life, and how the grace of the Holy Spirit continually helps us turn to God so that we may eventually live with Him who is our true and complete happiness.

Fr. Anton ten Klooster studied theology in Utrecht, Fribourg, and Washington DC, and obtained his doctorate from Tilburg University in 2018 with the highest distinction, *cum laude*. He is the author of *Thomas Aquinas on the Beatitudes: Reading Matthew, Disputing Grace and Virtue, Preaching Happiness* (Leuven: Peeters, 2018). At present he is working on a postdoctoral project on conversion at the Tilburg School of Catholic Theology. Ten Klooster is a priest of the archdiocese of Utrecht, The Netherlands, and is rector of studies of the archdiocesan seminary Ariënsinstituut.

---

[37] Cited in German in Hildegard Aepli and Thomas Ruckstuhl, *Leben im Haus der Kirche: Zum 100-jährigen Bestehen des Salesianums* (Fribourg, Switzerland: Paulus Verlag, 2007), 100.

"Those He Predestined He Also Called" (Romans 8:30): Aquinas on the Liberating Grace of Conversion

Daria Spezzano

IN THE *SUMMA THEOLOGIAE*, THOMAS AQUINAS articulates his most developed understanding of both the absolute primacy of grace and the proper instrumental activity of the free will in the journey of the predestined rational creature to beatitude.[1] In the non-competitive causation of the creature's movement to supernatural perfection, God's grace causes the free will to use its freedom for excellence, participating in his plan of divine providence through a co-operative journey of progressive deification that constitutes the moral life. But what about the will that is *un*cooperative, turned away from God, and needing to be turned back to begin, or begin again, its journey to salvation? That is, what about every human will damaged by and in love with sin, before the healing and elevation of grace? In the beginning of the journey, Thomas thinks, the will seduced away from God by sin is moved by the divine help toward God's goodness without moving itself and with no preparation or merit on the part of the sinner. Yet even here, Thomas says, this extrinsic turning of the unwilling will is no case of divine coercion; rather, Thomas understands this as the liberating beginning of an ongoing process of conversion, in which the free will plays an increasingly significant role in meriting and ultimately enjoying the perfection of beatitude. Ongoing conversion is necessary because of the ever-present temptation of sin. Yet, those whom God predestines he also calls (Romans 8:30), again and again, away from the slavery of sin and back to the freedom to move towards himself as the truly good end. Thomas's thought on the ongoing conversion of the moral life of the predestined is shaped by many scripture texts. After outlining his teaching on the grace of conversion in the *Summa*, I draw from Thomas's biblical commentaries and other

---

[1] In the *Summa theologiae*, Thomas Aquinas frames the question of conversion within his larger picture of the human person's journey by grace to union with God in eternal life—the "advance of the rational creature to God" ST I q. 2 prol. All translations of ST are based on *S. Thomae Aquinatis Doctoris Angelici Opera Omnia Iussu impensaque Leonis XIII P. M. edita*, vols. 4–12 (Rome: Leonine Commission, 1888–1906). All translations from Latin are my own unless otherwise noted.

works to examine his use of a few scriptural texts that he often addresses together in discussions of conversion, from Lamentations 5:21, John 6:44, and Romans 6:23, 8:15 and 8:30. I argue that Thomas's reflection on these texts deeply informs his mature account of conversion as a progressive journey powered by grace from beginning to end, through moral struggle towards freedom and final beatitude for God's adopted children.

THE LIBERATION OF THE WILL BY GRACE (*SUMMA THEOLOGIAE* I-II, Q. 109)

Thomas touches on the question of conversion and the free will in the *Summa* in several places where he considers the work of grace, both as an infused habit and as the supernatural motion of divine *auxilium*. In ST I-II q. 109, he argues for the prevenience of grace at every stage of the moral life. The articles of this question sketch out the human person's continual need for grace, especially after original sin, in the journey to eternal life. In the movement of the predestined beginning with initial conversion away from sin, through the hurdles of repeated sin and further avoidance of sin, to final perseverance, the healing and elevation of grace is required to do supernatural and even, for fallen humans, most natural good.[2] Quoting Romans 6:23, "the grace of God is life everlasting," and the *Glossa Ordinaria* on that text, Thomas explains that without the gift of grace, one cannot perform works meritorious of eternal life (ST I-II q. 109 a. 5 *sed contra* and ad 2). Habitual grace prepares the will "to operate rightly and to enjoy God," perfecting one to the divine image by bestowing a participation in the divine nature; it therefore makes the free will the cooperating principle of supernaturally meritorious works (ST I-II q. 109 a. 6, q. 110 a. 4, q. 112 a. 2, q. 114 a. 3). In a. 6, Thomas argues further that one cannot even prepare oneself to receive habitual grace without another prevenient gift of grace, "a gratuitous gift of God who moves the soul inwardly or inspires the good wish." This gift of interior divine motion initially turns the will away from sin and towards God, preparing one to receive habitual grace. It is a special instance of God's helping grace, or *auxilium*, which Thomas associates in multiple places with the prompting or *instinctus* of the Holy Spirit, a gift that enables one to comply freely with God's will under the New Law of liberty.[3]

This grace of divine motion is necessary because we cannot prepare or turn ourselves on our own, Thomas insists in q. 109. In the *sed contra* of a. 6, he quotes John 6:44: "It is written, 'No one can come to me unless the Father, who has sent me, draw him'. But if one could

---

[2] On the last point, see ST I-II q. 109, a. 2.
[3] The life of the New Law can be called a life of liberty from the very beginning insofar as we "comply freely" with the interior *instinctus* of the Holy Spirit's grace. See ST I-II q. 108, a. 1 ad 2.

prepare himself, he would not need to be drawn by another. Hence one cannot prepare oneself without the help of grace" (ST I-II q. 109 a. 6). Therefore, as the first Mover, God prepares the soul to receive habitual grace by "a gratuitous help [*auxilium*] of God interiorly moving the soul, or inspiring the good intention." God

> converts just men to himself as to a special end, which they intend, and to which they desire to adhere, according to Psalm 72: "It is good for me to adhere to my God." And therefore, it cannot be that one is converted to God without God converting him. Now to prepare oneself for grace, is as it were to be converted to God, as he who has his eye converted away from the light of the sun, prepares himself to receive the sun's light by converting his eyes towards the sun. Whence it is clear that one cannot prepare oneself to receive the light of grace, except through the gratuitous help [*auxilium*] of God moving interiorly (ST I-II q. 109 a. 6).

In answer to objections that since we have free will, it seems that we can turn to God by our own power, he replies, "Man's turning to God is by free-will, and thus we are bidden to turn ourselves to God. But free-will can only be turned to God, when God turns it, according to Jeremiah 31:18: 'Convert me and I shall be converted,' and Lamentations 5:21: 'Convert us, O Lord, to you, and we shall be converted'" (ST I-II q. 109 a. 6 ad 1).

In this article, Thomas repudiates a common scholastic position he had held in his early *Scriptum* on Peter Lombard's *Sentences*, that *facienti quod in se est, Deus non deneget gratiam*: "to those who do what is in them"—that is, who take the first step towards God by doing their best—"God will not deny grace."[4] Through his reading of Augustine's later anti-Pelagian writings, quoted numerous times in q. 109, Thomas came to recognize this opinion as Pelagian, (or semi-Pelagian), developing an understanding of the all-encompassing and dynamic work of grace as an effect of predestination, both enabling (by habitual grace) and preveniently setting into motion (by auxiliary grace) supernaturally good human action throughout life's journey towards the end of beatitude.[5] Henri Bouillard notes that this shift takes place sometime before Thomas wrote the *Summa contra Gentiles*, where he rejects the *facienti quod* position as Pelagian.[6] From the time of the *Summa contra Gentiles*, too, Thomas makes use of a principle from Aristotle's *Eudemian Ethics* (known to him as the *Liber de bona fortuna*) that he employs in q. 109, that although the human will is free, there must be

---

[4] See Joseph Wawrykow, *The Westminster Handbook to Thomas Aquinas* (Louisville, KY: Westminster John Knox Press, 2005), 54–56.
[5] Henri Bouillard, *Conversion et grâce chez S. Thomas d'Aquin* (Paris: Aubier, 1944), 113–114.
[6] Bouillard, *Conversion et grâce*, 113–114.

a higher extrinsic principle (God) to move it into act in the first place, whether to do natural or supernatural good, especially in the state of fallen nature.[7] In response to an objection that "if one does what is in him God will not deny him grace," and that "what is in us, is what is in our power," Thomas answers that:

> One can do nothing unless moved by God, according to Jn. 15:5: "Without me, you can do nothing." Hence when one is said to do what is in him, this is said to be in his power insofar as he is moved by God (ST I-II q. 109 a. 6 ad 2).

In his commentary on John 15:5, Thomas says that by these words Christ "silences the mouths of the proud, especially of the Pelagians," who in "trying to assert our free will...really toppled it" (*Super Ioan.*, ch. 15, lect. 1).[8] This is so because we cannot even use our free will without the help of God. In his mature works, Thomas presents a carefully balanced picture of the absolute primacy of the divine initiative and the genuine, but secondary, causality of the human will in both natural and supernatural action.

If God's help is always needed to move the will to do good, that is even more the case for the will damaged by sin. Thomas takes seriously the enslavement of sin, that persists in its effects to some extent even after conversion and justification, exposing one to the attacks of temptation due to the weakness of the flesh. In q. 109 a. 9, Thomas argues that even after the gift of habitual grace, one always needs the help of God moving one to act righteously not only because the divine motion must precede every creaturely act but because of the condition of human nature after the fall, "For although healed by grace as to the mind, yet it remains corrupted and poisoned in the flesh, whereby it serves 'the law of sin' (Romans 7:25)." The darkness of ignorance also remains in the intellect, requiring the guidance and protection of God, "who knows and can do all things" (ST I-II q. 109 a. 9). God does not give us habitual grace so that we will no longer need his help; grace is not meant to make us self-sufficient. God gives us the dignity of acting as genuine secondary causes in the journey to salvation in order to free us from the slavery of sin so that we can live in the freedom of the children of God.

Therefore, Thomas is always careful to maintain in the *Summa* that, on the one hand, God's movement of the person cannot fail to turn them to himself to receive the gift of grace yet, on the other, that this is not coercion but liberation. In q. 112, he quotes Augustine *On the Predestination of the Saints* (14):

---

[7] Bouillard, *Conversion et grâce*, 123ff.
[8] All citations of the *Commentary on John* are based on *S. Thomae Aquinatis Super Evangelium S. Ioannis lectura*, ed. R. Cai, 6th ed. (Turin: Marietti, 1972).

Augustine says, "By God's good gifts, whoever is liberated, is most certainly liberated." Hence if God intends, while moving, that the one whose heart he moves should attain to grace, he will infallibly attain to it, according to John 6:45: "Everyone that has heard of the Father, and has learned, comes to me." (ST I-II q. 112 a. 3)

Without God's help, on the other hand, our free-will, wounded by sin, would fail to turn to God, would exercise its freedom wrongly to do evil, and so would be responsible for its own final loss of freedom, its eternal loss of God. Here, Thomas quotes Hosea 13:9: "Your destruction is your own, O Israel; your help is only in me" (ST I q. 23 a. 3; I-II q. 112 a. 3 ad 2). God's infallible foreknowledge of the ordination of the predestined to eternal life does not destroy their free will but enables it to act meritoriously under grace so as to reach the end (ST I q. 23 a. 5).[9]

Therefore, God's turning of the will to himself does not destroy but enables the will's freedom. If our free-will is bent towards evil, as we falsely think evil is good and are attracted to it, we simply cannot pick ourselves up by our own bootstraps and turn ourselves around; we are, in effect, trapped in a delusion. Thomas says elsewhere in the *Summa* that we still have *natural* liberty in this state—that is, we are free from external coercion to choose good or evil—but we have lost *true* freedom, "freedom from fault and unhappiness" (that is, the true freedom Adam enjoyed before the Fall) (ST I q. 83 a. 2., *corpus* and ad 3).[10] Only God, in his mercy, can pick us up and re-orient us towards the true good. This is why in initial conversion and justification, God alone is the mover of the will, re-directing it to the truly good end, and the will is simply moved without moving itself. This gift of divine motion is operating *auxilium*, which is at work "especially when the will, that hitherto willed evil, begins to will good" (ST I-II q. 111 a. 2).[11] On the other hand, with our wills re-oriented to the right end by

---

[9] See Thomas Joseph White, OP, "Catholic Predestination: The Omnipotence and Innocence of Divine Love," in *Thomism and Predestination: Principles and Disputations*, ed. Steven A. Long, Roger W. Nutt, Thomas Joseph White, OP (Ave Maria, FL: Sapientia Press, 2016), 115, where he expresses well how, in the graced free choice of the true good, the human person acts as "a finite creature dependent in all that it is qua free agent upon the transcendent creative gift of God, and as a creature stimulated in its inmost ontological core by God's wholly interior, nonviolent premotions."

[10] On the related notion of "freedom for excellence," see Servais Pinckaers, *The Sources of Christian Ethics*, trans. Mary Thomas Noble (Washington, DC: The Catholic University of America Press, 1995), 354–399.

[11] On the development of Thomas's teaching on operating and co-operating auxilium, see Bernard Lonergan, *Grace and Freedom: Operative Grace in the Thought of St. Thomas Aquinas*, ed. Frederick E. Crowe and Robert Doran (Toronto: University of Toronto Press, 2000, rpt., 2005), 404–438. Also see Joseph Wawrykow, *God's Grace and Human Action* (Notre Dame, IN: University of Notre Dame Press, 1995), 34–55,

God, we can actively cooperate in carrying out the good intention, though still with the help of God moving us. This moving grace is co-operating *auxilium*, in which the will is moved by God and also, as a secondary cause, moves itself. Thomas quotes Augustine again, who makes a similar distinction in his anti-Pelagian work *On Grace and Free Will*: "God operates that we may will; and when we will, he co-operates that we may perfect."[12] God helps us to will the good by operating grace and helps us to cooperate in freely assenting to and carrying out that good as well. This cooperation of our free-will, assisted by grace, allows us to truly merit eternal life.

SCRIPTURAL SOURCES

It is clear that Thomas's thought on these matters was deeply shaped by reflection on Scripture, as well as by Augustine's anti-Pelagian writings. So, I turn now to closer examination of a constellation of Scripture texts in the passages above that emerge with frequency in Thomas's teaching on conversion as liberation.

Lamentations 5:21

One significant scriptural text in Thomas's accounts of conversion is a verse from Lamentations 5:21: "Convert us, O Lord, to you, and we shall be converted," a text which does not appear at all in Thomas's early *Scriptum* on the *Sentences* but, like Augustine's anti-Pelagian works and the principle from the *Eudemian Ethics*, is seen with increasing frequency from the time of the *Summa contra Gentiles*. In his later works, he employs Lamentations 5:21 as an authority to exclude "Pelagian" errors.[13] In the *Summa*, in addition to the treatise on grace, he refers to it in ST I q. 23, a. 5 on predestination. Here, he argues that it is Pelagian to hold that our merits are in any way the cause of predestination, concluding that the effect of predestination not only includes the grace given to us after initial conversion, which enables us

---

266–273; Lawrence Feingold, "God's Movement of the Soul through Operative and Cooperative Grace," *Thomism and Predestination: Principles and Disputations*, eds. Steven A. Long, Roger W. Nutt, Thomas Joseph White, O.P. (Ave Maria, FL: Sapientia Press, 2016), 106–91.

[12] Augustine, *On Grace and Free Will*, 17.33.

[13] For instance, on 2 Timothy 2:4, he explains that one should be "modest in admonishing" false teachers because it is "God the Father [who] is able to lead them to repentance." Here, he says, "Pelagius's error is excluded, who said that the gifts of grace come from our works. But this is seen to be false, because even the beginning of good works, namely, repentance, is given by God: Lam 5:21: 'Convert us, O Lord, to you, and we shall be converted'" (*Super II Tim.*, ch. 2, lect. 4). All citations from Thomas's commentaries on the Pauline letters are based on *S. Thomae Aquinatis Super Epistolas S. Pauli lectura*, vols. 1–2, ed. R. Cai, 8th ed. (Turin: Marietti, 1953). In addition to the works discussed below, Lam 5:21 appears in *De veritate* q. 24 a. 15 ad 1; *Summa contra Gentiles*, 3.149.6; *Quodlibet* I q. 4 a. 2; I-II q. 109, a. 6 ad 1; *Super Matt.* [rep. Leodegarii Bissuntini], ch. 25, lect. 2; ch. 26, lect. 7.

to freely merit further grace and, ultimately, glory, but also includes preparation for the first grace itself, "For this does not happen without divine help either, according to the prophet Jeremiah (Lamentations 5:21): 'Convert us, O Lord, and we shall be converted.'" In an article on the virtue of penance, Thomas makes it clear that this verse refers to the initial movement of operating *auxilium*, which, turning us to God, makes it possible for us to cooperate with him. In the acts of penance, he says, "We cooperate with God operating, the first principle of which acts is the operation of God in turning the heart, according to Lamentations 5:21, 'Convert, us, O Lord,' etc." (ST III q. 85 a. 5). Thomas employs this verse from Lamentations to insist that God is always the first cause of salvation and that his predestinating plan encompasses the whole journey of the predestined to glory, from their preparation for initial conversion through sequential gifts of grace that empower them to cooperate meritoriously to the end with his will to bring them to eternal life.

Besides references in the *Summa*, Thomas also uses Lamentations 5:21 in his Scripture commentaries to underline that God's grace works the first movement of conversion. For instance, Lamentations 5:21 appears several times in his *Commentary on John*, notably in conjunction with texts from Romans, and here we see more clearly how Thomas understands the divine *auxilium* of conversion in the context of love, freedom, and divine adoption. In his discussion of John 1:12 ("He gave them power to be made the sons of God"), Thomas explains that only sanctifying grace can cause us to become sons of God by being made like God; here he quotes Romans 8:15: "You did not receive a spirit of slavery…but the spirit of adoption of sons." While justification requires the exercise of the free will's power in consent, the will,

> if it is to be moved to receive grace, needs the help [*auxilium*] of divine grace, not habitual grace, but moving grace. For this reason God gives power by moving the free will of man to consent to the reception of grace: "convert us, O Lord," that is, by moving our will to your love [*ad amorem tuum*], "and we will be converted" (Lam 5:21). And in this sense we speak of an interior call, of which it is said (Rom 8:30), "those whom he called" by interiorly instigating the will to consent to grace, "he justified," by infusing grace. (*Super Ioan.*, ch. 1, lect. 6, no. 154)

Here, with reference to Romans 8:30, Thomas adds to the notion of an initial motion of divine *auxilium* the idea that, in conversion, God calls the will of the predestined interiorly towards his love, giving the desire, and the power, to consent to his grace.

For Thomas, in fact, conversion, understood as "every movement of the will towards God," continues into beatitude. In a question on the grace of the angels, he describes a threefold conversion of the will to God:

> The first is by the perfect love of God; this belongs to the creature already enjoying God; and for this conversion, consummate grace is required. The second conversion is that which merits beatitude; and for this there is required habitual grace, which is the principle of merit. The third conversion is that by which anyone prepares himself to have grace; for this no habitual grace is required; but the operation of God, converting the soul towards himself, according to Lamentations 5:21: "Convert us, O Lord, to you, and we shall be converted." (ST I q. 62 a. 2 ad 3; cf., I q. 93 a. 4)

Lamentations 5:21 signifies for Thomas that in his plan of providence for the predestined, God never ceases to constantly and mercifully turn and draw the elect to himself, helping them with operating and cooperating grace from the moment of their initial conversion towards him through their perfect union with him in eternal life.

John 6:44

Another frequently cited text is John 6:44: "No one can come to me unless the Father, who sent me, draws him." In his commentary on this verse, Thomas reflects on how the divine motion of God in conversion involves not the compulsion of coercion but the freedom of attraction.

> The Father drawing us does not imply coercion, because there are some ways of being drawn that do not imply compulsion. Consequently the Father draws men to the Son in many ways, using the different ways we can be drawn without compulsion. (*Super Ioan.*, ch. 6, lect. 5, no. 935)

There is a difference between drawing and dragging. God turns our will to the good end by making us see that it *is* the true and good end. As in the commentary on John 1:12, Thomas distinguishes an exterior and interior call, the former involving external persuasion, and the latter, the hidden prompting of the will by grace.[14] The Father draws some externally by "persuading them with reason"; others, he draws by "attracting or captivating them," both by the paternal greatness and by "a wonderful joy and love of the truth, who is the very Son of God himself." Internally, the Father "draws many to the Son by the *instinctus* of a divine action, moving their heart from within to believe" (*Sup Ioan.* ch. 6, lect. 5, no. 935).[15]

---

[14] See *Quodlibet II* q. 4 a. 1 co.; *Super Gal.*, ch. 1, lect. 4.

[15] If this sounds rather Augustinian, it is not surprising. Thomas is drawing from Augustine's *Tractates on John* 26.4, on this same Gospel verse, where Augustine argues

Like Augustine, Thomas refers to John 6:44 very often in the context of discussions about the necessity, gratuity, and attraction of God's initial call for the predestined, to whom a share in divine sonship will be communicated. In his commentary on Romans 8:30 ("those he predestined, he also called"), Thomas refers to the same constellation of texts as he does in q. 109 a. 6 to underline the primacy of grace and again distinguishes between an external call, through preaching, and the interior call of God's *auxilium*, necessary to respond; the interior call is a motivating attraction,

> a certain *instinctus* of the mind by which man's heart is moved by God to assent to the things of faith or virtue....This call is necessary because our heart could not turn itself to God if God himself had not drawn us: "no one can come to me unless the Father who sent me draws him" (Jn 6:44) and "convert us to yourself, O Lord" (Lam 5:21). Furthermore, this call is efficacious in the predestined, because they assent to the call: "Everyone who has heard and has learned from the Father comes to me" (Jn 6:45). (*Super Rom.* ch. 8, lect. 6, no. 707)

The operative auxiliary grace of conversion moves by freely drawing, not dragging, one onwards; this is the beginning of a cooperative journey for the predestined, who are justified in the assent of their free will to grace, turning towards God's goodness and away from sin (See ST I-II q. 113 a. 3).[16]

Thomas's references to God's interior call as an *instinctus* in these texts underlines too the role of the Holy Spirit, who leads the children of God (Romans 8:14). Servais Pinckaers has shown the increasing significance of the notion of the Spirit's *instinctus* in Thomas's mature treatments of the moral life, especially to describe the Spirit's action in the operation of the gifts which assist every believer to live a life according to the Spirit by cooperating with God.[17] In his commentary

---

that if each is drawn by his own pleasure, "how much more strongly should we say that those whose delight is in the truth, whose delight is in happiness, whose delight is in justice, whose delight is in eternal life, are drawn to Christ, because each of those is Christ." Translation in *Homilies on the Gospel of John 1–40*, trans. Edmund Hill, OP (New York: New City Press, 2009), 452–453. Thomas included this text from Augustine in his *Catena on John*, ch. 6, lect. 6.

[16] In ST I-II q. 113, a. 3, Thomas again quotes John 6:45, to argue that learning requires assent to the teacher, so that "'no one comes to the Father' by justifying grace without a movement of the free will." Although justification is the effect of an initial operating grace instigating one to give up sin, it results in the cooperation of the free will with God (ST I-II q. 113, prol).

[17] Servais Pinckaers, "Morality and the Movement of the Holy Spirit: Aquinas's Doctrine of *Instinctus*," *The Pinckaers Reader: Renewing Thomistic Moral Theology*, ed. John Berkman and Craig Titus, trans. Sr. Mary Thomas Noble, Craig Titus, Michael Sherwin, and Hugh Connelly (Washington, DC: The Catholic University of America Press, 2005), 385–95. For an insightful discussion of the development of Thomas' use of the notion of *instinctus*, in relation to his doctrine on the gifts of the Holy Spirit,

on Romans, Thomas explains that to be "led by the Spirit of God" means to be "ruled by a leader and director" so that one is "not only instructed by the Holy Spirit about what to do, but his heart is also moved by the Holy Spirit." The inclination of the spiritual man to do good comes "not chiefly from his own will, but from the *instinctus* of the Holy Spirit" as director. Yet, this does not take away his freedom, for "the Holy Spirit causes the very movement of the will and of free choice" in him (*Super Rom.* ch. 8, lect. 3, no. 635).

Romans 6:23, 8:15, and 8:30

A third scriptural source central to Thomas's accounts of conversion is evidently Paul's Letter to the Romans, with its teaching on the freedom given to God's predestined adopted children, led by the grace of the Holy Spirit. Thomas makes so many references to Romans in this context that it is difficult to choose the most important. He refers numerous times in the *Summa*, as we have already seen, to Romans 6:23 ("The grace of God is life everlasting"), in connection with discussions of conversion and the cooperative attainment of eternal life, for which "God's mercy," he says, "is the first cause," and the merit won by our free-will the subsequent cause (ST I-II q. 114 a. 3 ad 2).[18] Romans 6:23 is the culminating verse of Paul's extended contrast of servitude to sin versus servitude to God. In Romans 6:22, Paul begins to bring this contrast to a head: "but now, being made free from sin and become servants to God, you have your fruit unto sanctification, and the end, everlasting life." On this verse, Thomas comments:

> Just as in the state of sin, one is a servant of sin which he obeys, so in the state of justice one is a servant of God and obeys him willingly...but this is true freedom and the best form of servitude, because by justice a human is inclined to what befits him [ie, as human], and is turned away from what is fitting to concupiscence, which is especially bestial. (*Super Rom.*, ch. 6, lect. 4, no. 513)

Service of God by willing obedience is the best kind of servitude because it makes one do what is especially human—properly using one's reason and will. This servitude, under the dominion of grace rather than of sin, is the true freedom given by the Son, who makes the children of God "free indeed" (John 8:36).[19]

---

but also to preparation for justification, see James Stroud, "*Instinctus* and the Gifts of the Holy Spirit: Explaining the Development in St. Thomas's Teaching on the Gifts of the Holy Spirit," *Journal of Moral Theology* 8, Special Issue No. 2 (2019): 60–79.

[18] See ST I q. 12, a. 4; q. 62, a. 2; I-II q. 109, a. 5; q. 114, a. 2; II-II q. 24, a. 2; III q. 52, a. 7; III q. 86, a. 3 ad 5.

[19] See *Super Ioan.* ch. 8, lect. 4, no. 1209.

At the very outset of his commentary on Romans, referring to Paul's introduction of himself as a servant (or subject) of God, Thomas says,

> It is praiseworthy for a person to be subjected to his salvation and the spiritual anointing of grace, because a thing is perfect to the extent that it is subjected to its perfection.... Yet this seems to conflict with John 15:15: "No longer do I call you servants but friends." But one should say that there are two kinds of servitude. One is the servitude of fear, which does not befit saints: "You did not receive the spirit of slavery to fall back into fear, but you have received the Spirit of the adoption of sons" (Rom 8:15). The other is the servitude of humility and love, which does befit saints. (*Super Rom.*, ch. 1, lect. 1, no. 21)

Thomas makes clear here with his reference to John 15:15 that the servitude of humility and love which is fitting to the adopted children of God is in the end the free and willing obedience of those whom Jesus calls "friends," those to whom he has "made known everything that he has heard from the Father" (John 15:15).[20] This servitude, Romans 8:15 tells us, is the glad self-offering of the child and of the lover of God, conformed to the Son by the Holy Spirit in knowledge and love of God.

In his commentary on Romans 8:15, following his argument that the Spirit's *instinctus* leads spiritual people in freedom, Thomas analyzes the difference between slaves and sons in the ongoing conversion of the moral life. The Holy Spirit produces two effects in us, fear and love, "but fear makes slaves; love does not" (*Super Rom.* ch 8, lect. 3, no. 638). Servile fear of punishment is not entirely unpraiseworthy; it is from the Holy Spirit but is defective. The newly converted most often have a mixed kind of fear, initial fear. They fear punishment but also separation from God, out of love. Initial fear and the more perfect filial or chaste fear are distinguished by the degree to which one loves God. Filial fear is the Spirit's gift of fear, flowing from charity, which Christ had in perfection. It makes one fear above all to be separated from God, so it helps one to be docile to the Spirit's

---

[20] In his commentary on John 15:15 (*Super Ioan.* ch. 15, lect. 3), Thomas repeats this idea and draws from Augustine's *Tractates on John* 85.3, where Augustine, himself referring to Romans 8:15, distinguishes between two kinds of fear and two kinds of servitude: "Because he gave us the power to become sons of God, let us be not servants, but sons, in order that in some way, marvelous and ineffable, but yet true, we are able to be servants that are not servants, servants of course because of the pure fear that belongs to the servant entering into the joy of his Lord, but not servants because of the fear that must be cast out, to which belongs the servant not remaining in the house forever. But let us know that the Lord makes it happen that we are [both] such servants [and yet] not servants." Translation in *Tractates on the Gospel of John 55–111* (Fathers of the Church Patristic Series), trans. John Rettig (Washington, DC: The Catholic University of America Press, 2014), 139.

prompting to gladly obey the Father.[21] Just as the fear of punishment makes slaves, "charity's love produces the freedom of sons" (*Super Rom.* ch 8, lect. 3, nos. 639–641). Beginners do not yet enjoy the full freedom of sons produced by a more perfect love of God but have begun on a journey of increasing freedom as Christ's joint heirs and friends. The more one advances in perfection in the moral life, under the Spirit's guidance, the more one becomes willing servant, child, and friend of God.

A final key text for Thomas's thought on conversion is Romans 8:30 ("those he predestined, he also called. And whom he called, he also justified. And whom he justified, he also glorified"). Thomas refers to this verse especially where he considers how God's predestination of the saints is carried out in time from the first call of grace to the final end of glorification. The execution of the divine plan to order some to salvation takes effect in them by their "calling and magnification," according to Romans 8:30 (ST I q. 23, a. 2). The predestined rational creature is directed towards eternal life like an arrow by an archer, and the effect of predestination includes all the grace that will call, transform, and move her on through a cooperative journey of good works to beatitude (ST I q. 23, a. 1, a. 2, a. 5).[22] In his commentary on Romans 8:30, Thomas outlines this sequence of predestination's effects in the saints in more detail. Predestination "begins to be carried out with the calling of the person," both externally by preaching and internally by the *instinctus* of grace, God converting and drawing us to himself efficaciously. Those whom God calls by an initial gift of interior motion, he justifies by the infusion of (habitual) grace; although justification can be frustrated in those who do not persevere, "in the predestined it is never frustrated." God magnifies or glorifies his chosen ones first by "growth in virtue and grace" and finally by "exaltation to glory" (*Super Rom.* ch. 8, lect. 6, no. 707–709). This scriptural exegesis complements and deepens Thomas's description in the *Summa* of the working of operating and cooperating grace on the journey to beatitude.

By placing Thomas's exegesis of this verse into its context in his Romans commentary, we gain an even richer view of his appreciation of the difficult but blessed nature of this journey, on account of which God's goodness should "stupefy us with astonishment" (*Super Rom.* ch. 8, lect. 6, no. 711).[23] In his *divisio* of verses 8:28–35, Thomas presents the text as an argument by Paul to demonstrate how the Holy

---

[21] See ST II-II q. 19; III q. 7, a. 6.
[22] See *Super Eph.* ch. 2, lect. 3 *Super Matt.* (rep. Petri de Andria), ch. 4, lect. 2; *Super Ioan.*, ch. 15, lect. 3; *Super I Cor.*, ch.1, lect. 1.
[23] In "Aquinas on Romans 8: Predestination in Context," in *Reading Romans with Thomas Aquinas*, ed. Matthew Levering and Michael Dauphinais (Washington, DC: The Catholic University of America Press, 2012), Matthew Levering provides a thorough examination of Aquinas's exegesis of Romans 8:30 within the context of his

Spirit "helps us with respect to external events, directing them to our good." First, Paul states his proposition about "the greatness of the benefit conferred on us by the Holy Spirit, namely, that 'all things work together for good'" for "those who love God" and who "according to his purpose are called to be saints" (8:28). Paul proves his argument in the verses from 8:29–8:34, beginning at "For whom he foreknew, he also predestined to be conformed to the image of his Son," drawing his conclusion when he says, "Who then will separate us from the love of Christ?" (8:35) (*Super Rom.* ch. 8, lect. 6, no. 695).

Predestination's effects described in Romans 8:30 are therefore an argument in support of the proposition that "all things work together for good" for the predestined. Discussing this proposition, Thomas gives a brief explanation of God's permission of evil in order to bring about the greater good especially of the just. Penal evils suffered help them to grow in virtue, but even their own sins "work together for their good," for this good

> consists not only in the amount of one's love but especially in perseverance until death.... Furthermore, because one has fallen, he rises more cautious and humble; hence, the Gloss adds that this makes them progress, "because they return to themselves more humble and wiser," for they have learned they should fear exulting about themselves, as if making any claim about themselves or trusting in their power to endure. (*Super Rom.* ch. 8, lect. 6, no. 698)

The sins of those called to be saints are not ultimately disastrous but encourage filial fear in them, becoming part of a holy history in which they rise by falling. Paul's proof of the claim that all things work together for the good of the saints is that "No one can harm those whom God moves forward [*promovet*; seemingly, a reference to the motion of divine auxilium]. But God moves forward the predestined who love him" (the minor premise). Therefore "nothing can harm them, but everything results in their good" (the major premise).

The minor premise that God moves the predestined forward is proved by considering first how God moves them from eternity by his foreknowledge and predestination, in 8:29 ("whom he foreknew he also predestined to be conformed to the image of his Son"), and then how God moves them in time, by predestination's effects in them, in 8:30 ("whom he predestined he also called," etc.) (*Super Rom.* ch. 8, lect. 6, no. 701). Predestination's effect is not only eternal life, Thomas

---

commentary on Romans 8, a context that Levering describes as "a rich portrait of human transformation through the missions of the Son and the Holy Spirit," which "makes clear that predestination is about God's eternal plan of deification" (208). The deification and ultimate glorification of the saints, in spite of their failures and sins along the way, is an astonishing manifestation of God's goodness.

explains, but "under predestination falls every benefit divinely prepared for man from eternity; hence...all the benefits bestowed on us in time have been prepared for us from eternity" (*Super Rom.* ch. 8, lect. 6, no. 703). The foremost effect of predestination, for the sake of which all grace is given, is to conform us to the image of the Son so that we might share in his sonship by adoption, his right to the eternal inheritance, and his splendor, "by the light of wisdom and grace" (*Super Rom.* ch. 8, lect. 6, no. 704). It is for this that we are called, justified, and glorified (8:30).

The major premise that "nothing can harm those moved forward by God" (*Super Rom.* ch. 8, lect. 6, no. 710) is clarified when Paul says, "What then shall we say? If God is for us, who can be against us?" (8:31). Nothing can nullify God's gifts to his elect, Thomas argues: "'What then shall we say?' For in considering these things, we should be stupefied with astonishment ... what could we return to God for such great blessings?" (*Super Rom.* ch. 8, lect. 6, no. 711). The predestined cannot be harmed by persecution, or the removal of their goods, for "God did not even spare his own Son" from tribulation, "but delivered him up for us all" (Rom 8:32), giving us all things along with him, "the highest things, namely, the divine persons to enjoy, rational spirits to live with, all lower things to use, not only prosperity but adversity as well" (*Super Rom.* ch. 8, lect. 6, no. 714). Thomas nuances this Augustinian explanation with the thought that, for those whom God calls, even adversity is a gift to be used in order to reach God who alone can be enjoyed. Paul's conclusion is that in every trial we conquer because nothing "can separate us from the love of God in Christ Jesus our Lord"; here, he is speaking "in the person of all the predestined" about the certainty of predestination, which is "caused by the power of charity" (*Super Rom.* ch. 8, lect. 7, no. 734). Indeed, Thomas says, God bestows such great benefits on his saints that "when we consider them, such love of Christ burns in our hearts that nothing can extinguish it" (*Super Rom.* ch. 8, lect. 6, no. 722). For Thomas, then, Paul's description of the journey of the predestined in Romans 8:30 is a central argument for the Apostle's proposition that all things work together for the good of those who love God and are called to be saints, despite the difficulties posed by evil, even the evil of one's own sin, along the way. Nothing in the end can frustrate God's plan for the predestined and their final victory, even their own weakness, because of the power of grace.

In his sermon *Beatus Vir*, preached on the feast of St. Martin, Thomas demonstrates the fruits of this exegesis. He gives as his theme our need, like St. Martin, for divine help (*auxilium divinum*) in order "to arrive at the glory of highness" (*Beatus Vir*, 1). Thomas employs the three parts of Romans 8:30 to illustrate the "triple help" that God gives us to attain beatitude through successive stages in the progress to holiness. First, "that God chastises us is a way to beatitude." God calls us from afar when we are in sin:

> The Apostle shows us the blessing of that calling when he says, "The ones he predestined he also called" (Rom 8:30). And St. Martin was called by the Lord and chastised; that is, removed from original sin and preserved from actual sin. (*Beatus Vir*, 2)

God's chastisement, by inspiring fear, forgiving sins, and drawing us away from sin, is all accomplished by grace, and "is a sign of his love" (*Beatus Vir*, 2). His second help is to teach us, raising up our intellect and affections: "Someone who subjects his heart to divine inspiration learns; this pertains to justification. The Apostle says in Rom 8:30, 'Those whom he called, he also justified'" (*Beatus Vir*, 2). God's third help is that he "raises us up": "This action of raising someone up pertains to the third blessing of God, namely, magnification. The Apostle says in Rom 8:30, 'Those whom he justified, he also magnified.'" God magnified St. Martin by the holiness of his works, his miracles, and his fame (*Beatus Vir*, 2), the source of all St. Martin's happiness in his ascent "from the low state of misery to a high state" (*Beatus Vir*, 3) was God's help, described from beginning to end in Romans 8:30.

CONCLUSION: THE PRIMACY OF GRACE AND THE HOPE OF SALVATION

Thomas's account of the ongoing conversion of the moral life is shaped by a catena of scriptural texts from the Old and New Testaments, from the Gospel and the Pauline letters, all of which, for him, underline the primacy of God's grace and our need for divine help to attain the true freedom of salvation. The moral life of the predestined is a journey of conversion towards final happiness, not without struggle, but with certain hope of God's gracious assistance for those who love him. The "grace of God is life everlasting" (Romans 6:23) because the initial gift of conversion, for the predestined, is just the beginning of the growth in freedom of the children of God, in a loving servitude that perseveres with filial fear against temptation, allowing hope even during moral and physical evil, as one presses on with increasing joy to victory in eternal life. This should cause us to burn with love for Christ and be astonished at God's goodness.

Is Thomas's vision of conversion as liberation still relevant today? The documents of Vatican II and the writings of recent popes underscore the way in which false understandings of the human person, and of human freedom, conspire to contribute to secularism and atheism in contemporary culture; these, along with a prevailing cryptopelagianism, undermine the proclamation of the Gospel. Yet the documents also underline the unquenchable desire for God and true freedom written into the human heart.[24] Thomas provides a positive counterargument to modern misconceptions of freedom and human destiny. His teaching has ongoing relevance because it speaks profoundly to the human condition, God's mercy, the primacy of grace despite sin, the dignity of human freedom, and the hope of our salvation.

With this in mind, I give the last word—perhaps unexpectedly—not to Thomas but to the Renaissance poet and preacher John Donne, who was influenced by Thomas's teaching. Donne admired Thomas and knew his works, which still shaped the intellectual climate of Europe.[25] At the same time, the rise of skepticism and Donne's own conflicted relationship with Calvinism left him hesitant and inconsistent about the role of human reason and free will in salvation.[26] This tension appears in his Holy Sonnets, so there is some dispute as to whether they express despair or assurance about reason's role in salvation by grace.[27] I conclude with a speculative proposal about Thomas's possible influence on Donne: perhaps, at the end of Donne's famous Holy Sonnet XIV, we can read him as expressing not despair of reason but a Thomist confidence in the power of the grace of conversion to make wounded reason truly free again:

> Batter my heart, three-personed God; for, you
> As yet but knock, breathe, shine, and seek to mend;
> That I may rise, and stand, o'erthrow me, and bend
> Your force to break, blow, burn, and make me new.
> I, like an usurped town, to another due,
> Labour to admit you, but oh, to no end,
> Reason, your viceroy in me, me should defend,
> But is captived, and proves weak or untrue,
> Yet dearly I love you, and would be loved fain,
> But am betrothed unto your enemy,
> Divorce me, untie or break that knot again,
> Take me to you, imprison me, for I
> Except you enthral me, never shall be free,
> Nor ever chaste, except you ravish me.[28]

---

[24] For example, *Gaudium et Spes*, nos. 1–10, 17; *Fides et Ratio*, nos. 1–5; Cardinal Joseph Ratzinger, "Truth and Freedom," *Communio* 23, no. 1 (1996): 17–35; *Caritas in Veritate*, nos. 1–4, 70.

[25] John Carey, *John Donne: Life, Mind and Art* (London: Faber and Faber, 2008, repr. 2011), 232.

[26] Carey, *John Donne*, 231–262.

[27] Robert Young, *Doctrine and Devotion in Seventeenth-Century Poetry: Studies in Donne, Herbert, Crashaw, and Vaughan* (Rochester, NY: Brewer, 2000), 16–17; Paul Cefalu, "Godly Fear, Sanctification, and Calvinist Theology in the Sermons and 'Holy Sonnets' of John Donne," *Studies in Philology* 100, no. 1 (2003): 71–86; John Stachniewski, "John Donne: The Despair of the 'Holy Sonnets,'" *ELH* 48, no. 4 (1981): 677–705; Lucio P. Ruotolo, "The Trinitarian Framework of Donne's Holy Sonnet XIV," *Journal of the History of Ideas* 27, no. 3 (1966): 445–446.

[28] John Donne, "Holy Sonnet 14," in *John Donne: The Complete English Poems*, ed., A.J. Smith (London: Penguin Books, 1971, repr. 1996), 314–315.

Dr. Daria Spezzano is an associate professor of Theology at Providence College in Providence, Rhode Island. She holds a PhD in Theology from the University of Notre Dame, and a Master's in Liturgical Studies from The Liturgical Institute. Her book, *The Glory of God's Grace: Deification according to St. Thomas Aquinas*, was published by Sapientia Press in 2015. Recent publications include articles in *Nova et Vetera*, *Cistercian Studies* and *Antiphon*, and chapters in several edited volumes, including *Thomas Aquinas, Biblical Theologian* (Emmaus Academic Press, 2021), *Reading Job with St. Thomas Aquinas* (CUA Press, 2020) and *Aquinas on Initiation and Mystagogy* (Peeters, 2019).

Almsgiving as a Formative Practice of Repentance for Christian Discipleship: The Gospel of Luke and Daniel 4:24

James W. Stroud

IN LUKE 3:7–9, JOHN THE BAPTIST WARNS THOSE coming to him for the baptism of forgiveness to be fruitful trees that provide evidence of a change of heart instead of the trees that bear no good fruit and thus exhibit no repentance.

> He [John the Baptist] said to the crowds who came out to be baptized by him, "You brood of vipers! Who warned you to flee from the coming wrath? Produce good fruits as evidence of your repentance [*metanoias*]; and do not begin to say to yourselves, 'We have Abraham as our father,' for I tell you, God can raise up children to Abraham from these stones. Even now the ax lies at the root of the trees. Therefore every tree that does not produce good fruit will be cut down and thrown into the fire."[1]

According to Frank Matera, the use of *metanoia* emphasizes "the need for a radically new way of thinking about reality that involves a profound change of mind."[2] And this change of mind is evidenced through specific action. "Bearing fruits authenticates and renders visible the change in thinking involved in repentance."[3] Repentance involves a changed mentality which is made visible through concrete actions.

---

[1] New American Bible Revised Edition (NABRE). All biblical texts are taken from the NABRE unless otherwise noted. For a detailed examination of the role of John the Baptist and conversion in the Gospel of Luke, see Joel B. Green, *Conversion in Luke-Acts: Divine Action, Human Cognition, and the People of God* (Grand Rapids, MI: Baker Academic, 2015), 53–86.

[2] Frank J. Matera, *New Testament Ethics: The Legacies of Jesus and Paul* (Louisville, KY: Westminster John Knox Press, 1996), 69. According to Fitzmyer, in Luke-Acts, the noun *metanoia* appears 11 times; the verb *metanoein* appears 14 times. Joseph A. Fitzmyer, *The Gospel According to Luke I–XI* (New York: Doubleday, 1970), 237. For a detailed consideration of the usage of *metanoia* in the literary milieu prior to Luke-Acts and contemporaneous with it, see Nave, *The Role and Function of Repentance in Luke-Acts*, 39–144.

[3] Nave, *The Role and Function of Repentance in Luke-Acts*, 149.

What kinds of fruit (or concrete actions) should those seeking repentance bring about? In his reply, John the Baptist urges the crowds to share their possessions and food with those who do not have clothing and food, the tax collectors to be honest in their collecting, and the soldiers to avoid extorting money, to stop falsely accusing others, and to be satisfied with their income.[4] Fitzmyer comments that what John the Baptist describes "is not tied up with sacrificial offerings for sins or ascetic practices, such as the use of sackcloth and ashes, or even a flight into the solitude of the desert, such as his own withdrawal had been."[5] Instead, John the Baptist commends concrete actions involving possessions, money, and honesty and the like for those coming to his baptism of repentance within the larger community. Indeed, "It is by translating into concrete actions one's God-orientation or the repentance-baptism within the framework of the human community that one proves one's identity as part of the covenant people."[6] These concrete actions are to be the signs of their changes of heart as proof of undergoing *metanoia*.[7] Matera, commenting on this passage in the Gospel of Luke, states, "Repentance from sins…is necessary for faith in Christ."[8] Additionally, in repenting of one's sins, a person comes to know one's status before God. "To enter this kingdom [of God and the age of salvation] and be exalted by God, one must humble oneself."[9] What can one do to enter the kingdom of God? John the Baptist, in his reply to the crowds, has already provided one way to do this: to seek repentance through almsgiving.[10]

In this paper, I will be treating an idea that is articulated by St. Thomas Aquinas in his *Super Evangelium S. Matthaei Lectura* on almsgiving. St. Thomas, in his discussion of the Our Father prayer in Matthew 6, in response to the question raised "[b]ut what is to be said of those who do not wish to forgive and nevertheless say Our Father?" writes: "It should be said that he does not sin by saying Our Father,

---

[4] "Here John's ethical teaching foreshadows a major theme of Jesus's preaching: the correct use of possessions." Matera, *New Testament Ethics*, 69. See also Kiyoshi Mineshige, *Besitzverzicht und Almosen bei Lukas: Wesen und Forderung des lukanischen Vermögensethos* (Tübingen, Germany: J.C.B. Mohr, 2003), 170.
[5] Fitzmyer, *The Gospel According to Luke I–XI*, 469.
[6] Thomas Malipurathu, "'Produce Fruits in Keeping with Repentance!' (Lk 3:8): Following Up the Biblical Trail towards the Ideal of a Poor Church," *Jeevadhara* 44 (2014): 123.
[7] Matera points out that Luke 7:29–30 notes "the people and tax collectors accepted John's baptism of repentance while the Pharisees and lawyers did not." Matera, *New Testament Ethics*, 70.
[8] Matera, *New Testament Ethics*, 70.
[9] Matera, *New Testament Ethics*, 70.
[10] "In other words, the sensitivity to the needs of others, which therefore deliberately eschews all expressions of wanton luxury, is *part of the fundamental convictions linked to the living of the Christian vocation*." Malipurathu, "'Produce Fruits in Keeping with Repentance!'" 124. Emphasis added.

however much he may be in rancor and grave sin, for such people should do whatever they can of good, both alms and prayers and such things that dispose one to the recovery of grace."[11] St. Thomas in this passage argues that a person even in a grave sin can dispose oneself to the recovery of grace through almsgiving.

Following St. Thomas's insight, I argue that almsgiving is not simply a work of charity or justice but serves as an important formative practice of repentance for the Christian disciple that leads the disciple to place one's faith in God, to seek repentance for one's sins, and subsequently to dispose oneself to the reception of grace. For the initial scriptural foundations of this argument, I focus on the biblical text of Daniel 4:24, which presents almsgiving as a way of repentance. This is ultimately because in giving to the poor one performs an act of faith in God, a turning to God in seeking the redemption of one's sins. After a review of Daniel 4:24 and its context in Daniel, I examine how the Gospel of Luke sheds light on the practice of almsgiving in Jesus's encounters with the Pharisees, his teachings and parables, and his encounters with the rich ruler and Zacchaeus. These different stories in the Gospel of Luke further my argument concerning almsgiving as a formative practice of repentance for Christian discipleship. The Gospel of Luke, in particular, emphasizes the need to bear good fruits worthy of repentance to encounter salvation in Christ whereby in almsgiving a sinner develops an important practice for placing one's faith in God, in seeking repentance and ultimately salvation. Accordingly, almsgiving as a practice of repentance aims to dispose the disciple to the recovery of grace.

DANIEL 4 AND ALMSGIVING

In this section, I focus on Daniel 4:1–24, which includes Daniel's interpretation of Nebuchadnezzar's dream and Daniel's subsequent advice, which focuses on almsgiving. I chose this text because of the position that Gary Anderson has articulated regarding the importance of Daniel 4 for understanding the forgiveness of sins in Jewish and Christian thought. As Anderson states, "In the Old Testament, the book of Daniel contains the first fruits of an idea that will come to full harvest in later rabbinic and patristic thought. Indeed, much of both

---

[11] *Super Evangelium S. Matthaei Lectura* Chapter 6, Lecture. 3, #597 (Aquinas Institute translation, Vol. 33). For Aquinas' mature treatment on almsgiving, see ST II-II, q. 32. For a recent discussion bringing together Aquinas' teaching on merit and almsgiving in Dan 4:24, see Matthew Levering, *Jesus and the Demise of Death: Resurrection, Afterlife, and the Fate of the Christian* (Waco: Baylor University Press, 2012), 89–95. For a modern scholarly consideration of Aquinas' treatment of almsgiving, see Stephen J. Pope, "Thomas Aquinas on Almsgiving, Justice, and Charity: An Interpretation and Assessment," *Heythrop Journal* 32 (1991): 167–91.

Jews' and Christians' understanding of the forgiveness of sins will follow from that text."[12] Daniel 4 establishes the importance of almsgiving as a practice of repentance in which the sinner through almsgiving turns to God and repents of his previous way of life. Therefore, Daniel 4 has a special role in helping us understand the relationship between repentance and almsgiving.

Daniel 4 starts with King Nebuchadnezzar recounting his dream.[13] King Nebuchadnezzar "reigned in Babylon from 605 to 562 BC. He was a powerful and cruel monarch who defeated Assyria and Egypt; in 597 BC he captured Jerusalem" and later "destroyed the Temple and took many of the people to Babylon (586 BC)."[14]

> I, Nebuchadnezzar, was at home in my palace, content and prosperous. I had a terrifying dream as I lay in bed, and the images and my visions frightened me.... "These were the visions I saw while in bed: I saw a tree of great height at the center of the earth. It was large and strong, with its top touching the heavens, and it could be seen to the ends of the earth. Its leaves were beautiful, its fruit abundant, providing food for all. Under it the wild beasts found shade, in its branches the birds of the air nested; all flesh ate of it. In the vision I saw while in bed, a holy watcher came down from heaven and cried aloud in these words: 'Cut down the tree and lop off its branches, strip off its leaves and scatter its fruit; Let the beasts flee from beneath it, and the birds from its branches, but leave its stump in the earth. Bound with iron and bronze, let him be fed with the grass of the field and bathed with the dew of heaven; let his lot be with the beasts in the grass of the earth. Let his mind be changed from a human one; let the mind of a beast be given him, till seven years pass over him. By decree of the watchers is this proclamation, by order of the holy ones, this sentence; That all who live may know that the Most High is sovereign over human kingship, giving it to whom he wills, and setting it over the lowliest of mortals.' This is the dream that I, King Nebuchadnezzar, had. Now, Belteshazzar, tell me its meaning. None of the wise men in my kingdom can tell me the meaning, but you can, because the spirit of the holy gods is in you." Then Daniel, whose name was Belteshazzar, was appalled for a time, dismayed by his thoughts. "Belteshazzar," the king said to him, "do not let the dream or its meaning dismay you."

---

[12] Gary Anderson, *Sin: A History* (New Haven, CT: Yale University Press, 2009), 137.
[13] "That an author in the second century would choose a sixth-century exilic setting to tell his story about how Israel will be restored is significant. It confirms the fact that the exile was thought to be still in effect, despite the efforts of prophets such as Zechariah." Anderson, *Sin*, 82. For the manuscript and textual history surrounding chapter 4, see Carol Newsom and Brennan Breed, *Daniel: A Commentary* (Louisville, KY: Westminster John Knox Press, 2014), 127–134.
[14] "Nebuchadnezzar," *A Dictionary of the Bible*, www.oxfordbiblicalstudies.com.shsst.ezproxy.switchinc.org/article/opr/t94/e1320.

"My lord," Belteshazzar replied, "may this dream be for your enemies, and its meaning for your foes. The tree that you saw, large and strong, its top touching the heavens, that could be seen by the whole earth, its leaves beautiful, its fruit abundant, providing food for all, under which the wild beasts lived, and in whose branches the birds of the air dwelt—you are that tree, O king, large and strong! Your majesty has become so great as to touch the heavens, and your rule reaches to the ends of the earth. As for the king's vision of a holy watcher, who came down from heaven and proclaimed: 'Cut down the tree and destroy it but leave its stump in the earth. Bound with iron and bronze, let him be fed with the grass of the field, and bathed with the dew of heaven; let his lot be with wild beasts till seven years pass over him'—here is its meaning, O king, here is the sentence that the Most High has passed upon my lord king: You shall be cast out from human society and dwell with wild beasts; you shall be given grass to eat like an ox and be bathed with the dew of heaven; seven years shall pass over you, until you know that the Most High is sovereign over human kingship and gives it to whom he will. The command that the stump of the tree is to be left means that your kingdom shall be preserved for you, once you have learned that heaven is sovereign. Therefore, O King, may my advice be acceptable to you: Redeem your sins by almsgiving [*ṣidqâ*ʿ] and your iniquities by generosity to the poor [*mihanʿănāyîn*]; then your serenity may be extended" (Daniel 4 1–2, 7–24).[15]

The narration of a dream by a powerful non-Jewish leader in the Old Testament parallels the dream of Pharaoh in Genesis (41:1–24). Pharaoh's dream and Nebuchadnezzar's dream "warn of terrible days ahead…and both require a righteous Israelite…to interpret them."[16] Yet the dream accounts differ. Pharaoh had two dreams revealing the same famine. According to Joseph's interpretation, "That Pharaoh had the same dream twice means that the matter has been confirmed by God and that God will soon bring it about (Genesis 4:32)."[17] Nebuchadnezzar, on the other hand, had only one dream. His dream involves a great and mighty tree being cut down and its stump being reduced to a near animal state. This "led Daniel to conclude that this dream could not possess the same degree of certainty as to its fulfillment. In other words, there must be a way to avert or at least ameliorate what was coming."[18] In order to prevent the looming punishment of God, Daniel tells Nebuchadnezzar: "Redeem your sins by almsgiving [*ṣidqâ*ʿ] and your iniquities by generosity to the poor [*mihan*

---

[15] NABRE with the exception of verse 24 which is the translation of Anderson, *Sin*, 138. Newsom and Breed also translate *ṣidqâ*ʿ as almsgiving (verse 27 in their translation) and note this is how the Original Greek and the Theodotion Greek texts of Daniel translate *ṣidqâ*ʿ in that verse. Newsom and Breed, *Daniel*, 126 and 145.
[16] Anderson, *Sin*, 138. See also Newsom and Breed, *Daniel*, 135–136.
[17] Anderson, *Sin*, 138.
[18] Anderson, *Sin*, 138.

'ănāyîn]; then your serenity may be extended."[19] Daniel advises almsgiving as a way to prevent the outcome of the dream, thereby instructing Nebuchadnezzar to atone for his sins through acts of mercy.

But how do almsgiving and generosity to the poor enable a person to have one's sins and iniquities redeemed? To answer this question requires that one understand the nature of sin as a debt. Gary Anderson has argued persuasively that the notion of sin in the Old Testament shifted from viewing sin as a "weight" to sin as a "debt." This first arose due to the influence of Aramaic, as the language of the Persian empire during 538–333 BC.[20] It was the vocabulary of Aramaic that understood sin as "debt," and this influenced Jews who were bilingual in Hebrew and Aramaic.[21] Additionally, during the development of the Israelite language in the Persian period, the Israelites "were also experiencing exile and enslavement."[22] This centered around the punishment of being sold into slavery for Israel's sinfulness. Physical punishment served as a way to pay the debt of sin. This idea of paying for sins is encapsulated well in Isaiah 40 (dating to the sixth century BC): "Comfort, comfort my people says your God. Speak tenderly to Jerusalem, and cry to her that her penal service is ended, that her sin has been paid off, that she has received from the Lord's hand double for all her sins (Isaiah 40 1–2)."[23] The idea of using physical punishment

---

[19] In the scholarly literature, there is a debate as to whether Daniel 4:24 (or 27) is referring to almsgiving. ṣidqâ' normally is translated as "righteousness." See "Justice, Justification, and Righteousness," *The Oxford Encyclopedia of the Bible and Theology*, www.oxfordbiblicalstudies.com.shsst.ezproxy.switchinc.org/article/opr/t467/e132. Most English translations of this text render the term as "doing good deeds" or "doing righteousness." Additionally, most scholars agree that the term ṣidqâ' means "generosity" or "almsgiving" in rabbinical literature. See "Righteousness," *The Oxford Companion to the Bible*, www.oxfordbiblicalstudies.com.shsst.ezproxy.switchinc.org/article/opr/t120/e0629. What did ṣidqâ' mean when the Book of Daniel was composed? I follow Anderson's view as outlined in *Sin*, 139, which argues that ṣidqâ should be translated as almsgiving. For opposition to Anderson's view, see David J. Downs, *Alms: Charity, Reward, and Atonement in Early Christianity* (Waco, TX: Baylor University Press, 2016), 50–56, in which Downs disagrees with Anderson's argument concerning Dan 4 and prefers to translate ṣidqâ' and eleēmosynē as acts of mercy and not specifically almsgiving. Additionally, Christopher Hays argues that the use of Daniel 4 as a text for redemptive almsgiving "could be seen as misguided." See Christopher M. Hays, "By Almsgiving and Faith Sins Are Purged? The Theological Underpinnings of Early Christian Care for the Poor," in *Engaging Economics: New Testament Scenarios and Early Christian Reception*, ed. Bruce W. Longenecker and Kelly D. Liebengood (Grand Rapids, MI: William B. Eerdmans Publishing Company, 2009), 273.
[20] Anderson, *Sin*, 7.
[21] Anderson, *Sin*, 8.
[22] Anderson, *Sin*, 8.
[23] (Anderson's translation); *Sin*, 8. Also, Anderson makes the point of how significant the imagery of God redeeming Israel from slavery is. "For our purposes, however, it is important to understand the typological interpretation Second Isaiah has given to Israel's experience of captivity. For this prophet, Israel's exile in Babylon called to

as a form to pay one's debt "comes directly from the experience of debt-slavery.... In this tradition, anyone unable to repay a loan could work as a debt-slave for the creditor until the loan was paid off. Similarly, if a sinner committed a serious error and so incurred a 'great debt,' the penalty imposed upon him was thought to 'raise currency' in order to pay down what was owed."[24]

Once the nature of sin as "debt" appeared, its natural opposite appears – a "credit." As Anderson notes:

> The very idiom of rabbinic Hebrew supports this, because the antonym for the term ḥôb (debt) is zekût (credit). No such antinomy existed in the First Temple period—the idiom of 'bearing the weight of one's sin' did not have a natural opposite.... [I]n Second Temple Jewish texts, it becomes common to speak of persons whose moral virtuosity was so remarkable that they were able to deposit the proceeds of their good deeds in a heavenly bank.[25]

An example of storing up treasure (in the heavenly storehouse) appears in the Book of Tobit (dated to the third or second century BC). Tobit tells his son Tobias:

> Give alms from your possessions. Do not turn your face away from any of the poor, so that God's face will not be turned away from you. Give in proportion to what you own. If you have great wealth, give alms out of your abundance; if you have but little, do not be afraid to give alms even of that little. You will be storing up a goodly treasure for yourself against the day of adversity. For almsgiving delivers from death and keeps one from entering into Darkness (Tobit 4:7–10).[26]

Anderson acknowledges this development of "credit" as "a doctrine of merit" which "leads to an increased role for the agency of human beings in counteracting the ravages of sin."[27] This development of a doctrine of merit does not go unrecognized in rabbinical writings. For

---

mind the slavery Israel had experienced in Egypt many centuries before." This point is made time and again by the writer when he declares that God's saving act should be characterized as an act of redemption (gĕ'ullâh), that is, a release of individuals from their bondage in slavery. Indeed, this word in its nominal and verbal forms occurs some twenty-two times within the book. Anderson, *Sin*, 46.

[24] Anderson, *Sin*, 8. Leviticus 25 describes well this concern of debt and debt-slaves and how one or one's family member can redeem a debt-slave.

[25] Anderson, *Sin*, 9.

[26] This Tobit text, according to Anderson, is an interpretation of Proverbs 10:2 and 11:4. See Anderson, *Sin*, 145–6. For a lengthier examination of the Book of Tobit and almsgiving, see Gary Anderson, *Charity: The Place of the Poor in the Biblical Tradition* (New Haven, CT: Yale University Press, 2013), 70–103. See also Roman Garrison, *Redemptive Almsgiving in Early Christianity* (New York: Bloomsbury Academic, 1993), 53–54.

[27] Anderson, *Sin*, 10.

example, in Exodus 32, after the golden calf incident, Moses appeals to God to change his mind about the punishment of the Israelites by saying: "Remember your servants Abraham, Isaac, and Israel, and how you swore to them by your own self, saying, 'I will make your descendants as numerous as the stars in the sky; and all this land that I promised, I will give your descendants as their perpetual heritage'" (Exodus 32:13). In commenting on this text, rabbinical writings did not focus on what God had promised. "[R]ather, Moses asks God to remember *what* these men had done. By this was meant the great acts of piety they had once accomplished that generated a vast surplus of credit in heaven, credit that was more than sufficient to counterbalance the debt Israel now owed."[28] Thus, human agents through particular acts could generate credit towards the debt of sin.

Having considered sin as debt and the possibility of human merit as credit, one final etymological consideration is necessary. This concerns the term for "redeem," which in Aramaic is *praq*.[29] The Aramaic term originally meant "to buy oneself out of slavery."[30] In Hebrew the word for "redeem" is *gā'al*. This term appears in Leviticus 25 when discussing how a person can become a debt-slave.[31] "When your kindred, having been so reduced to poverty, sell themselves to a resident alien who has become wealthy or to descendants of a resident alien's family, even after having sold themselves, they still may be redeemed by one of their kindred, by an uncle or cousin, or by some other relative from their family; or, having acquired the means, they may pay the redemption price themselves" (Leviticus 25:47–49). The English words "redeemed" and "redemption" are translated from the Hebrew root *gā'al*.[32] Leviticus 25 provides an understanding of how one "redeems" oneself, through one's own means or the means from one's family, from being a debt-slave.

This last etymological consideration provides the final clue to reading Daniel 4:24 as an instruction of almsgiving for the redemption of one's sins. Analogous to the debt slave of Leviticus 25, King Nebuchadnezzar's "horrible sins" have "turned him into a debt-slave in the eyes of God. One way out of debt is physical punishment [as the dream portends], but Daniel informs us that there is a second option: giving away one's money to the poor."[33] There is no "get out of jail free card," but there are two ways to repay a debt: to offer sacrifice voluntarily or

---

[28] Anderson, *Sin*, 10.
[29] Anderson, *Sin*, 143.
[30] Anderson, *Sin*, 10.
[31] See Matthew 18:23ff for Jesus's use of the debt-slave imagery in a parable. For a detailed historical consideration of debt slavery and release, see David L. Baker, *Tight Fists or Open Hands? Wealth and Poverty in the Old Testament Law* (Grand Rapids, MI: William B. Eerdmans Publishing Company, 2009), 161–174, 275–285.
[32] Anderson, *Sin*, 143.
[33] Anderson, *Sin*, 10.

to suffer punishment forcibly. As Anderson notes, "In rabbinic Judaism and early Christianity, Daniel's advice will become commonplace. Repentance without the giving of alms, in some sources, is unimaginable."[34] Almsgiving becomes a kind of "spiritual currency," to use the phrase of Anderson.[35] Thus, Daniel's advice to King Nebuchadnezzar finally can be appreciated. King Nebuchadnezzar is in the debt of sin and to redeem himself (to buy himself out of slavery to debt-sin) he either has to endure the physical punishment that will come about as predicted in the dream, similar to Israel's experience of exile and physical punishment for its sinfulness, or he can redeem his sins through almsgiving to the poor. By giving alms, King Nebuchadnezzar gains a kind of spiritual currency to pay down his sin-debts. Additionally, by turning to and caring for the poor "God's face will not be turned away from" King Nebuchadnezzar. This story from the book of Daniel points to almsgiving as a practice of repentance, in that a sinner has accumulated a debt due to sin and in order for the sinner to alleviate this sin-debt one must practice almsgiving. In this understanding, almsgiving serves as a powerful way for a sinner to turn towards God and away from sin.

ALMSGIVING, THE REDEMPTION OF SINS, AND DISCIPLESHIP IN THE GOSPEL OF LUKE

In returning to the opening passage of this paper, Luke 3, John the Baptist's instruction to the crowds coming to him for the baptism of repentance describes one concrete practice that leads to salvation and the redemption of one's sins: almsgiving. John the Baptist's recommendation of almsgiving for the atonement of one's sins does not prove to be shocking considering the examination of Daniel 4 since Second Temple Judaism practices offer ways for understanding salvation through the mercy of God through specific activity like almsgiving. This focus on almsgiving in Luke's Gospel is due to the Lukan focus on salvation and the requisite repentance and turning away from sin in concrete practices that is necessary for the Christian disciple. "In the wider context of Luke's narratives, the human response to divine mercy can be best described as μετάνοια (ἐπιστρέφω). This is not an abstract concept but is expressed in transformative and practical

---

[34] Anderson, *Sin*, 143.
[35] Anderson, *Sin*, 143.

deeds in interpersonal relations, namely showing mercy and doing justice."[36] And as Anthony Giambrone notes, "Luke unoriginally envisions charity as an act of atoning repentance, somehow critical for fulfilling Israel's covenantal destiny."[37]

In the following discussion, I examine several key Lukan Gospel texts that argue the importance of almsgiving for the redemption of sins as a pathway towards discipleship in Christ.[38] In particular, these texts underscore the role of almsgiving as a sign of repentance and a pathway of turning to God and investing one's faith in God so that one can find salvation in Christ.[39] To put it another way, "Almsgiving…represents a concrete manifestation of repentance (*metanoia*), so that to live a life of almsgiving, or to divest oneself and give to the poor in conjunction with following Jesus, is a holistic participation in God's ways."[40] Indeed, almsgiving is not simply a practice of charitable giving for those in need of material goods but serves as a concrete sign of repentance for the almsgiver on the journey of salvation in Christ.

Before turning to specific Lukan texts that treat almsgiving, it is important briefly to link the Gospel of Luke with the sin-debt metaphor that is central to understanding Daniel 4 and the use of almsgiving as a practice of repentance. In *Sacramental Charity, Creditor Christology, and the Economy of Salvation in Luke's Gospel*, Anthony Giambrone has argued that the Gospel of Luke maintains and utilizes the sin as debt understanding and that the Lukan Gospel develops an

---

[36] MiJa Wi, *The Path to Salvation in Luke's Gospel: What Must We Do?* (New York: T&T Clark, 2019), 63.

[37] Anthony Giambrone, O.P., "'Friends in Heavenly Habitations' (Luke 16:9): Charity, Repentance, and Luke's Resurrection Reversal," *Revue Biblique* 120, no. 4 (2013): 535.

[38] In my selection of Lukan texts, my study complements other relevant Lukan studies on related topics. For example, Anthony Giambrone, OP, *Sacramental Charity, Creditor Christology, and the Economy of Salvation in Luke's Gospel* (Tübingen, Germany: Mohr Siebeck, 2017); Zacharias Mattam, "The Cost of Discipleship: Lk 14:25–35," *Bible Bhashyam* 25 (1999): 104–116; Timothy W. Reardon, "Cleansing Through Almsgiving in Luke-Acts: Purity, Cornelius, and the Translation of Acts 15:9," *The Catholic Biblical Quarterly* 78 (2016): 463–482. There are other monographs that touch on related themes which only limitedly apply to the scope of my own project. For example, see Kyoung-Jin Kim, *Stewardship and Almsgiving in Luke's Theology* (Sheffield, England: Sheffield Academic Press, 1998). Kim uses the idea of stewardship as the guiding thread to understanding almsgiving in Luke and thus does not touch on key themes I elaborate in this section of the paper. Lastly, for a monograph dedicated to discipleship in Luke-Acts, see Holly Beers, *The Followers of Jesus as the 'Servant': Luke's Model from Isaiah for the Disciples in Luke-Acts* (New York: Bloomsbury T&T Clark, 2015).

[39] See Giambrone's "'Friends in Heavenly Habitations' (Luke 16:9)," 536–538 for broader consideration of this purity-almsgiving thread in Luke-Acts.

[40] Reardon, "Cleansing Through Almsgiving in Luke-Acts: Purity, Cornelius, and the Translation of Acts 15:9," 477.

image of Christ as Israel's creditor. The sin-debt metaphor can be found in an examination of the Our Father in Luke's Gospel, in the distinction of human beings seeking God's forgiveness of sins and human beings seeking forgiveness of debts from others.[41] In addition, Giambrone examines in detail the story of the sinful woman in the house of the Pharisee (Luke 7:36–50) such that Giambrone argues in a rather novel way that the story of the sinful woman represents Christ rewarding her charity (her generous love) by forgiving her sins.[42] Similarly, MiJa Wi agrees that

> [t]he parable in Lk. 7:36–50 juxtaposes the moneylender's gracious act of cancelling debts (χαρίζομαι) with Jesus' forgiving (ἀφίημι) sins. It sheds further light on the response which is described as tangible acts of love (ἀγαπάω). Hence Luke's juxtaposition of ἄφεσις of sin and debt strengthens the mutual relationship of religious and economic matters while debt retains its financial meaning. *All of these points elaborate the sin-debt metaphor with the Gospel of Luke.*[43]

With an understanding of the sin-debt metaphor in the background of the Gospel of Luke, one then can see in Luke 11 a consideration of an almsgiving-repentance connection in Jesus's encounter with the Pharisees.

Near the end of Luke 11, a Pharisee invites Jesus to eat a meal at the house of the Pharisee.[44] The Pharisee is scandalized that Jesus did not perform the ritual washing prior to eating.[45] Jesus responds to the Pharisee's sense of scandal: "The Lord said to him, 'Oh you Pharisees! Although you cleanse the outside of the cup and the dish, inside you are filled with plunder and evil. You fools! Did not the maker of the outside also make the inside? But as to what is within, give alms, and behold, everything will be clean for you'" (Luke 11:39–41).[46] This response of Jesus begins a series of chastising statements of Pharisaic

---

[41] See Giambrone, *Sacramental Charity*, 66–126.
[42] See Giambrone, *Sacramental Charity*, 95–126.
[43] Wi, *The Path to Salvation in Luke's Gospel*, 63. Emphasis added.
[44] For a discussion of the role of the Pharisees in Luke, see Halvor Moxnes, *The Economy of the Kingdom: Social Conflict and Economic Relations in Luke's Gospel* (Philadelphia, PA: Fortress Press, 1988), 1–21.
[45] This is the second of two Pharisee meal incidents that turn on being clean. In the first, Luke 7:36–50, it is the sinful woman who bathes Jesus's feet with tears and provides him with hospitality because of the neglect of the Pharisee host.
[46] This is paralleled in Matthew 23:25–26 without a reference to almsgiving. For a brief discussion of the Matthean parallel, see Nathan Eubank, *Wages of Cross-Bearing and Debt of Sin: The Economy of Heaven in Matthew's Gospel* (Boston, MA: de Gruyter, 2013), 63–70. Giambrone contrasts Luke 11:42 with 1 Enoch 95:4 and 98:10, which speaks of the impossibility of the wealthy being saved. Giambrone, *Sacramental Charity*, 261. Jesus leaves open a path for the atonement of sin, where 1 Enoch has no such path.

behavior. Jesus accuses the Pharisees of being concerned with cleaning the outside of the body (the outside of the cup and dish) by ritual washings but inside the body (in the heart of the person) there is greed (*harpagēs*) and evil.[47] Jesus calls the Pharisees fools or unwise (*aphrones*) for behaving in a way that ignores the fact that it is God who made both the outside and the inside of the body and that there is a correlation between what is inside the person and what is outside the person. Having ritual exterior purity and interior sinfulness cannot be a coherent position for someone who understands the God who makes all things. Jesus addressed this incoherency earlier in the Lukan Gospel during the Sermon on the Plain.

In the Sermon on the Plain in Luke 6:43–45, Jesus says, "A good tree does not bear rotten fruit, nor does a rotten tree bear good fruit. For every tree is known by its own fruit. For people do not pick figs from thorn bushes, nor do they gather grapes from brambles. A good person out of the store of goodness in his heart produces good, but an evil person out of a store of evil produces evil; for from the fullness of the heart the mouth speaks."[48] Bovon notes that sin "springs up from inside."[49] In using this terminology, Jesus explains that the exteriority of the body does not produce the evil; rather the evil is stored inside the person and then produces such evil fruits with the exterior of the body. So ritual purity or impurity would not coincide with interior purity. How, then, does one make pure the interiority of the body if it is impure or evil?

Returning to the end of Luke 11 with Jesus's eating with the Pharisee, verse 41 provides Jesus's answer for rectifying the interior impurity of the Pharisees. They are told to "give alms (*eleēmosynēn*)" and "everything will be clean for you." One should note the initiative required here on the part of the Pharisees to be made clean in their hearts from the greed and evil that exist there. Jesus instructs the Pharisees to give alms and through giving alms, "everything" will be made clean, both the interior and the exterior of the body. In this encounter, almsgiving acts as a concrete practice of repentance for those seeking

---

[47] The term *harpagēs* can mean plundering but in this context the term is singular feminine genitive, and referring to one's inside being full of plunder does not make much sense. The term in this context makes better sense as the inside being full of or filled with greed.

[48] "Fruit as a figure for deeds, good or bad, is used in the OT (Hos 10:13; Isa 3:10, Jer 17:10; 21:14)." Fitzmyer, *The Gospel According to Luke I–XI*, 643. In Luke 7:33–35, Jesus raises the concern about exterior things when discussing John the Baptist and himself. People focused on John's lack of eating and drinking as John being possessed by a demon and then focused on Jesus's eating and drinking with sinners and Jesus is accused of being a glutton and a drunk. Exterior behaviors can only reveal so much. Thus, the need to be attentive to the fruits that such actions bear.

[49] François Bovon, Donald S. Deer, and Helmut Koester, *Luke 2: A Commentary on the Gospel of Luke 9:51–19:27* (Minneapolis, MN: Fortress Press, 2013), 299.

interior purity. "It would be a mistake, however, to see this [almsgiving] as emphasizing exterior works over inner faith. That would only reinforce the bifurcation of inner and outer. Almsgiving is a representation of the whole self. One's actions are part of one's being, so that almsgiving embodies one's existence, not simply exterior works."[50] By giving alms as Jesus instructed, the Pharisees produce good fruit by this act of repentance for the sin-debt they have accrued, and thereby they are made clean. This instruction of Jesus to the Pharisees is reminiscent of Daniel's advice to Nebuchadnezzar in which Daniel instructs Nebuchadnezzar to redeem his sins through almsgiving and of John the Baptist's admonition to bear fruits worthy of repentance by caring for the poor. This intersection of repentance, greed, and caring for the poor gets put into the specific context of discipleship in Jesus's encounter with the rich ruler in Luke 18:18–23:

> And a ruler asked him, "Good Teacher, what shall I do to inherit eternal life?" And Jesus said to him, "Why do you call me good? No one is good but God alone. You know the commandments: Do not commit adultery, Do not kill, Do not steal, Do not bear false witness, Honor your father and mother." And he said, "All these I have observed from my youth." And when Jesus heard it, he said to him, "One thing you still lack. Sell all that you have and distribute it to the poor, and you will have treasure in heaven; and come, follow me." But when he heard this he became sad, for he was very rich.[51]

In this story, a rich ruler has come to Jesus seeking what the rich ruler must do to inherit eternal life, or, in other words, salvation.[52] Jesus, in response, notes that the rich ruler knows the "commandments (*entolas*)". And Jesus proceeds to list many of the commandments that belong to the second tablet of the ten commandments that concern proper behavior toward one's neighbor. The rich ruler responds that he has observed all of these commandments from his youth. Then Jesus tells the rich ruler that the rich ruler lacks one thing and that he should sell *all* of his possessions and give the proceeds to the poor for treasure in heaven, and to follow after Jesus. Instead of following Jesus, the rich ruler leaves sad because he was "very rich." This passage and its parallels in Mark and Matthew have elicited much commentary. What exactly is lacking in the rich ruler? What will be the reward for the rich ruler if he follows through with Jesus's instruction? And does this encounter provide a way to understanding an integral link between

---

[50] Reardon, "Cleansing Through Almsgiving in Luke-Acts: Purity, Cornelius, and the Translation of Acts 15:9," 474.
[51] Text taken from the Ignatius Catholic Study Bible New Testament, Second Catholic Edition (RSV).
[52] This story contains the common refrain again from St. Luke, "What shall I/we do?"

almsgiving and Christian discipleship? Each of these questions deserves a response.

What is lacking in the rich ruler is a detachment from material wealth that shows a lack of interior purity. He suffers from what ails the Pharisees in Luke's Gospel: the debt of sin due to greed. As a privileged and wealthy person among the Israelites, he is too attached to his own wealth to follow through with Jesus's instruction by emptying himself of his possessions and using the proceeds for the poor. This story should make one recall what Jesus said in Luke 16:13: "No servant can serve two masters. He will either hate one and love the other or be devoted to one and despise the other. You cannot serve God and mammon." The rich ruler can only serve one master and has chosen to put his faith in wealth instead of in Christ. There is at least one silver lining here in the rich ruler's reaction. One should feel at least pity for the rich ruler since he went away sad instead of sneering at what Jesus said concerning mammon like the Pharisees in Luke 16:14. If the rich ruler had been able to let go of his possessions through his act of repentance, he would have gained three rewards: interior purity and release from the sin-debt of greed and attachment to material things; a treasure in heaven, a kind spiritual credit/currency set aside in heaven; and becoming a disciple/follower at Jesus's invitation. These connections are noteworthy because of this parable's concerns regarding the use of possessions/wealth with notions of bearing/harvesting fruit and the storing of treasures.

In the parable of Luke 12, the rich man has an abundant fruitful harvest. In an interior monologue, he asks himself: "What shall I do…?" He replies to himself that he will tear down his old barns and build new and larger barns to store his harvest and goods so that he can "have so many good things stored up for many years, rest, eat, drink, be merry!" And yet God, speaking to the rich man in Luke 12, says, "You fool (*Aphrōn*), this night your life will be demanded of you; and the things you have prepared, to whom will they belong?" Jesus ends the parable saying, "Thus will it be for the one who stores up treasure for himself but is not rich in God."[53] The unwise or foolish rich man has placed his faith and future in the things of the earth and when death comes upon him, what good will these earthly treasures have for him? These earthly treasures (or credits) will not matter when one is in the debt of sin because of the rich man's faith in the power of wealth and possessions. He will not be rich in God but only rich in himself with no heavenly treasures available to him in his time of need.

Three minor features of this story are worth attending to because of their repetition in the Lukan Gospel. First, the land of the rich man

---

[53] I have modified the NABRE translation to conform to Bovon's translation which is a more literal rendering of the text.

has produced an abundant/fruitful harvest. This should remind one of John the Baptist in Luke 3 and his discussion of producing good fruit and the saying from the Sermon on the Plain about where good fruit comes from. Second, the rich man asking himself, "What shall I do?" echoes the crowds in Luke 3:10: "What then shall we do?"[54] To which John the Baptist urged the crowd to share their possessions. And third, this desire for more and larger barns expresses the deep-seated greed and impurity present in the Pharisees of Luke 11 and how such greed makes them "fools" and "unclean" from within. The earthly wealth sought for by the rich barn owner and the Pharisees represents an earthly credit for which there is no heavenly return when they live lives filled with greed and impurity. For Bovon, "The failure of the human project [of the rich man] confirms the guilty intention" in that the rich man's life will be taken away and his desire for new larger storehouses was not only misguided but sinful. The rich man, in this parable, "symbolizes the attitude that should not be adopted ... he should have been making donations to others rather than hoarding. God gave, but this person refused to share."[55] Jesus's concern for greed, impurity, and misplaced faith does not end in verse 21.

In Luke 12:22–34, Jesus launches into an explanation that the disciples need to be dependent on God who provides all things in the right manner for each person and not be anxious about material/earthly things.[56] The disciples must place their belief and faith in God first and foremost above all things. And it should be noted that Jesus's instruction to the disciples is not limited to those who are wealthy but also to those who are poor.[57] Sin and impurity affect both the rich and poor alike, thus causing the need for repentance, a turning away from sin and a turning towards God. Jesus concludes his explanation with the following verses: "Sell your belongings and give alms (*eleēmosynēn*). Provide money bags for yourselves that do not wear out, an inexhaustible treasure in heaven that no thief can reach nor moth destroy. For where your treasure is, there also will your heart (*kardia*) be." Instead of building newer and bigger earthly barns for themselves to store up earthly treasures which have no real credit in the Kingdom of God, the disciples are urged to store the inexhaustible treasure and credit in heaven that will not decay or be stolen in the moneybags of those who need alms, like the poor, the widows, and the orphans. And Jesus's

---

[54] Bovon notes the connection of Luke 12:16 with the parable of the sower in Luke 8:14–15. Bovon, *Luke 2*, 199.

[55] Bovon, *Luke 2*, 200. Bovon rightly calls attention to how the text refers to "my crops," "my goods", "my grain," and "my soul."

[56] For an argument that explores the plan of God that underlies all things as the central guide for reading Luke, see Nave, *The Role and Function of Repentance in Luke-Acts*, 11–29.

[57] See Mineshige, *Besitzverzicht und Almosen bei Lukas: Wesen und Forderung des lukanischen Vermögensethos*, 167–168.

final sentence in this explanation highlights the placement of one's treasure and the placement of one's heart, which indicates the center of one's existence. Is one's heart filled with the sin of greed and ultimately evil and impurity? Is one's heart concerned with one's own fruit? One's own earthly treasures? Then one's treasure is earthly-bound and will not bear good fruit in what really matters – eternal life and heavenly treasure.[58] Is one's heart rich in God? Is one's heart filled with care for the poor?[59] Then one's treasure is a heavenly inheritance that cannot be destroyed or stolen, and one's treasure will bear good fruit. And with a heavenly treasury, one finds a purity of the heart that cannot be found in exterior things and that can only be found in a lasting faith in the mercy of God. As Jesus reminded his disciples: "Be merciful, just as [also] your Father is merciful" (Luke 6:36). The mercy one bestows on others is the measure of the mercy one will receive from God.

Having dealt with the heavenly inheritance in giving alms, the last question remains for this encounter with the rich ruler in Luke 18: does this encounter provide a way to understanding a link between almsgiving and Christian discipleship? I argue the rich ruler story in Luke 18 helps illuminate a concern that the Lukan Gospel raises concerning the sin of greed and subsequent impurity as destructive of the pathway to discipleship because the sin of greed fosters one's faith in material wealth and possessions. This kind of faith is misplaced since these earthly treasures will not provide salvation. For some on the way to following Jesus, the demands of Luke 18 to give away everything in almsgiving will be necessary because of the way in which a person has faith in mammon over God. The corrective to such a wrong-headed impurity is through almsgiving-repentance, placing one's faith in God, and then following Christ. For others on the way to following Jesus, one does not need to sell all of one's possessions to gain repentance and purity and to follow after Christ.[60] This latter approach is typified in the encounter of Jesus with the tax collector Zacchaeus.

---

[58] "[Wealth] tends to foster in the rich a feeling of self-sufficiency incompatible with the trust in him alone which God asks of us." Wilfrid Harrington, OP, "Property and Wealth in the New Testament," *Scripture in Church* 20 (1990): 236.

[59] In this story, one finds the heart of Luke's ethics which encompasses love of God (being rich in God) and love of neighbor (giving to the poor). Christopher Hays, *Renounce Everything: Money and Discipleship in Luke* (New York: Paulist Press, 2016), 26–27.

[60] The view I have articulated here finds resonance in other scholars. See for example Peter Liu, "Did the Lucan Jesus Desire Voluntary Poverty of his Followers?" *Evangelical Quarterly* 64 (1992): 291–317. See also Luke Timothy Johnson, *Sharing Possessions: What Faith Demands*, 2nd ed. (Grand Rapids, MI: Eerdmans, 2011), 11–28, in which Johnson unpacks the complicated picture regarding the use of possessions especially in Luke-Acts. Johnson, though, would differentiate radical dispossession and almsgiving where I would find continuity between the two acts depending upon the individuals involved. See *Prophetic Jesus, Prophetic Church: The Challenge of*

Luke 19 begins with the story of Zacchaeus, a very wealthy chief tax-collector in Jericho, who wants to see Jesus passing along the way but is unable to see Jesus along with the crowds due to his short stature. Zacchaeus climbs a tree to see Jesus and when Jesus sees Zacchaeus, Jesus invites himself to Zacchaeus's house. Filled with joy, Zacchaeus climbs down to greet Jesus. The grumbling of the crowd commences about Jesus visiting the house of a sinner. "But Zacchaeus stood there and said to the Lord, 'Behold, half of my possessions, Lord, I shall give to the poor, and if I have extorted anything from anyone, I shall repay it four times over.' And Jesus said to him, 'Today salvation has come to this house because this man too is a descendant of Abraham. For the Son of Man has come to seek and to save what was lost'" (Luke 19:8–10).[61] Zacchaeus, like the rich ruler, comes in search of Jesus. The reader is not told why Zacchaeus has come to look for Jesus, nor does Zacchaeus ask Jesus "what shall I do?" The short Zacchaeus climbs a tree to encounter Jesus. Jesus takes note of Zacchaeus and calls upon the hospitality of Zacchaeus and his house. And in return, Zacchaeus receives Jesus with joy, not sadness like the rich ruler. Spontaneously, Zacchaeus promises acts of almsgiving from his wealth and restitution for his extortion. He does not wait for any instruction from Jesus. In his joy, Zacchaeus manifests fruits worthy of repentance through almsgiving and restitution and thereby shows the interiority of his body, his heart. Zacchaeus places his faith in Jesus and finds his heavenly treasury.

Zacchaeus's response is indeed a response of repentance considering John's instructions (and ultimately Jesus's to the rich ruler). Zacchaeus pledges to give half of his possessions to the poor. John advises the crowds to give a tunic if one has two—so half of one's possessions. Zacchaeus also pledges to repay any extortion four times over. John advises tax-collectors to stop collecting more tax than necessary. This pledge of repayment goes beyond John's instructions. And in light of these pledges, Jesus announces that "salvation has come to this house." Jesus has brokered the return of Zacchaeus who comes to salvation through his pledge to assist the poor and repay the victims of extortion. Indeed, Zacchaeus becomes a new disciple who has recognized his need for redemption, repentance, and purity, and he enacts almsgiving and restitution to turn to God and to follow Christ. Zacchaeus's story represents the culmination of one thread in the Gospel of Luke of how to find purity through repentance and almsgiving. In

---

Luke-Acts to Contemporary Christians (Grand Rapids, MI: William B. Eerdmans Publishing Company, 2011), 99.

[61] The translation of verse 8 is not without controversy. Bovon notes how the verbs can be futuristic, iterative, or durative presents. Bovon translates the terms as futuristic presents along with other scholars, like the NABRE version of the text, due to verses 9 and 10 suggesting that Zacchaeus was lost and needed to be saved. See Bovon, *Luke 2*, 598–599.

doing so, Zaccheaus models a disciple who, though sinful due to greed and extortion, now bears good fruit of repentance through concrete acts of almsgiving and restitution.[62]

The stories in the Gospel of Luke centered around almsgiving, wealth, and repentance build a case for understanding the importance of almsgiving as a practice for the Christian disciple. Almsgiving for the sinner becomes a way of repentance whereby the sinner turns to God and away from his faith in his own wealth and possessions. In this turning to God, the sinner places his faith in God and repents for his sin-debt that he has accrued due to his misplaced concern for wealth and possessions. And subsequently, the sinner finds salvation in Christ and thereby accrues a heavenly treasure. The sinner who was once lost has been found: "For the Son of Man has come to seek and to save what was lost" (Luke 19:10).

CONCLUSION

I have argued in this paper that almsgiving is an important formative practice of repentance for the Christian disciple in that the disciple turns away from sin and from faith in one's wealth and possessions and turns instead toward God. With a new faith in God, the disciple thereby finds salvation and a heavenly treasury. And it is in this turning towards God that the Christian disciple disposes oneself to the recovery/reception of grace.

Daniel 4 provides a substantial Jewish point of reference to late Second Temple Judaism that begins to see sin as a debt and the need to exercise a credit to be released from such a debt. Almsgiving acts as the means of credit for the wiping away of sins. Daniel advises King Nebuchadnezzar to use almsgiving as a way of redeeming one's sins. In the Book of Daniel, almsgiving serves as the *metanoia* whereby the king is instructed to place his faith in God and not in his wealth and possessions and find salvation in God.

The Gospel of Luke, using the sin-debt theology of Second Temple Judaism, likewise counsels almsgiving as a practice of repentance. This emphasis on almsgiving finds its first articulation in the words of John the Baptist's preaching to the crowds that they need to bear wor-

---

[62] "Zacchaeus, who, both welcoming and welcomed, bore the fruit of repentance, that is, showed by what he did that he had repented. In this way, the Gospel writer confirmed what he had John the Baptist say: 'Bear fruits worthy of repentance.'" Bovon, *Luke 2*, 600. See how this culmination was anticipated in the description of John the Baptist and his ministry: Luke 1:76–77 ("And you, child, will be called prophet of the Most High, for you will go before the Lord to prepare his ways, to give his people knowledge of *salvation* through the forgiveness of their sins") and Luke 3:5–6 ("Every valley shall be filled and every mountain and hill shall be made low. The winding roads shall be made straight, and the rough ways made smooth, and all flesh shall see the *salvation* of God"). Emphasis added.

thy fruits of repentance through almsgiving. By this practice of almsgiving, those seeking repentance can find salvation. The Gospel of Luke describes this mission of John the Baptist and in a certain way the mission of Jesus Christ using the words of Isaiah: "The winding roads shall be made straight, and the rough ways made smooth, and all flesh shall see the salvation of God" (Luke 3:5–6 which refers to Isaiah 40:4–5). This focus on almsgiving as an important practice of repentance is further elaborated through several key Lukan texts, including the Pharisees, the rich ruler, the disciples, and Zacchaeus. These different texts relate almsgiving as an act of repentance in which the Christian disciple is urged to turn away from sin and from faith in material possessions and instead put one's faith in God through almsgiving. As Bovon argues, "The Gospel [of Luke] proposes a lifestyle in which happiness is lived out in relationships, and in which giving, usually counted as a loss, becomes the best way to succeed and to be on the receiving end of things. Any possessions we might have at our disposal do not, in the last resort, belong to us."[63] The giving sought after in the Lukan Gospel is almsgiving as a way of repenting of one's sins and turning towards God.

One finds a high point of the Lukan Gospel in the story of Zacchaeus, a chief tax collector, who upon Jesus's invitation to dine at Zacchaeus's house, freely vows to give alms and make restitution for his extortion. He has performed acts that bring about the good fruit of repentance. He has placed his faith in God, and indeed, salvation has come to his house. Almsgiving then represents an important practice of repentance for the Christian disciple. Sometimes it may be demanded that one be like the rich ruler and give away all of one's possessions for the poor. Other times it may be like the story of Zacchaeus in which one gives away a good portion of one's possessions for the poor. These stories in the Gospel of Luke lead one to ask: does sin cause one to place one's trust in wealth and possessions? If so, then these earthly treasures will rot and pass away. Instead of placing one's faith in material things, the Christian disciple is urged to give alms as a way of repenting of one's sins and as a way of turning to and placing one's faith in God. The instruction to give alms for repentance is meant for both wealthy and poor alike since the attachment to wealth and possessions indicates what is in the heart of the person.[64] Both the Book of Daniel and Gospel of Luke remind us that it is only in God

---

[63] Bovon, *Luke 2*, 206. "The response of the believer is to share what has been received as a gift with those who are deprived of such benefits." John Gillman, *Possessions and the Life of Faith: A Reading of Luke-Acts* (Collegeville, MN: Liturgical Press, 1991), 95.

[64] Johnson, *Prophetic Jesus, Prophetic Church*, 114: "Consistent with the Gospel narrative, Luke uses a character's disposition of possessions as a character indicator." For other examples, see Luke 7:5; Acts 9:36 and 10:2.

whereby one finds salvation from sin. And it is in this turning [*metanoia*] to God in almsgiving whereby the disciple is disposed to the recovery of grace. As the words of Tobit remind us:

> Give alms from your possessions. Do not turn your face away from any of the poor, so that God's face will not be turned away from you. Give in proportion to what you own. If you have great wealth, give alms out of your abundance; if you have but little, do not be afraid to give alms even of that little. You will be storing up a goodly treasure for yourself against the day of adversity. *For almsgiving delivers from death and keeps one from entering into Darkness. Almsgiving is a worthy offering in the sight of the Most High for all who practice it* (Tobit 4:7–11).

James W. Stroud is an associate professor of Moral Theology at Sacred Heart Seminary and School of Theology in Hales Corners, Wisconsin. He has interests in the moral theology of St. Thomas Aquinas, biomedical ethics, the role of Sacred Scripture in moral theology, and the intersection of science and moral theology.

A Defense of the Command/Counsel Distinction Based on Matthew 19 and 1 Corinthians 7

John Meinert

PRIOR TO VATICAN II, the command/counsel distinction was ubiquitous and unquestioned in Catholic moral theology.[1] Post Vatican II saw a serious decline in its use. Undoubtedly, the historical connection between the command/counsel distinction and two-tiered ethics is the reason for the decline. As David Cloutier and William Mattison write, "[There has been a] near total abandonment of any sort of two-level ethic within the Church."[2] A two-tiered ethic was rejected because it "helps create a *de facto* higher class of Christians."[3] As a two-tiered ethic is typically articulated, all Christians are required to live the commandments, but only some live the counsels. As a result, a kind of minimalistic ethic grows up around the laity, whereas religious (those who vow the counsels) are called to a higher holiness. After Vatican II and the clearer proclamation of the universal call to holiness, two-tiered ethics no longer makes sense, and, as a result, moral theologians do not speak of commands and counsels. In fact, some moral theologians are openly critical of the distinction.[4] To use the command/counsel distinction would seem to bring back two-tiered ethics and all that is assumed to be bad about pre-Vatican II ethics.

The purpose of this paper is to defend the command/counsel distinction. It is based on solid biblical sources. Making this case is the purpose of section one. The second section aims to meet some objections to the distinction, principally that by adopting it a two-tiered ethic follows. In that section, I argue that, though the rise of two-tiered

---

[1] One can find the distinction in almost all manuals of moral theology, especially in the sections on vows, the new law, or the virtue of charity.
[2] David Cloutier and William Mattison III, "Method in Catholic Moral Theology," *Journal of Moral Theology* 1, no. 1 (2012): 176–178. For an exception see Kent Lasnoski, *Vocation to Virtue* (Washington, DC: The Catholic University of America Press, 2014).
[3] James Bretzke, *Handbook of Roman Catholic Moral Terms* (Washington DC: Georgetown University Press, 2013), 247.
[4] Charles Curran, *A New Look at Christian Morality* (Notre Dame: Fides Publishers, 1970), 9.

ethics is related to the use of the command/counsel distinction historically, the connection is only true if one assumes a morality of obligation.

THE SCRIPTURAL SOURCES OF THE COMMAND/COUNSEL DISTINCTION

The Scriptural roots of the command/counsel distinction are found in two texts: Matthew 19 and 1 Corinthians 7. Sustained attention to both, even with the critical eye of modern biblical exegesis, leaves one with only one option: some actions are not required but are recommended as more fitting ways of reaching the shared goal of Christian life. This is the substance of the command/counsel distinction.

Matthew 19:3–12: Eunuchs for the Sake of the Kingdom
The first passage which is typically invoked in favor of the command/counsel is Matthew 19:3–12 (cf. Mark 10:2–12). In this passage, Jesus responds to the Pharisees concerning the legitimate grounds for divorce. In his response, Jesus returns to the logic of creation: "Male and female he created them, and on account of this a man will leave his father and mother and will be joined to his wife and the two shall become one flesh." The Pharisees respond: "Then why did Moses command us to give a bill of divorce and dismiss her?" Jesus responds that Moses tolerated divorce, but it was not so from the beginning. He then utters the famous line: "I say to you that whoever divorces his wife and marries another, not concerning *porneia*, is committing adultery." Ignoring the exception clause, the disciples respond flabbergasted: "If it is so with the cause of a man and his wife, then it is not fitting to marry." Jesus's response is ambiguous: "Not all can accept this word, but only those to whom it is given." Jesus then follows this with the eunuch saying and an exhortation: "There are [some] eunuchs who were born so from the womb of their mother, [some] who were made so by man, and [some] who make themselves eunuchs for the kingdom of God. The one who is able to do this should do it" (Matthew 19:1–12).[5]

The classical interpretation of this passage sees it as a straightforward source of the command/counsel distinction. There is a command: avoid divorce and remarriage; this is adultery.[6] To avoid transgressing this commandment, one can enter a marriage and remain or avoid the marital state entirely (celibacy). One of these ways is more fitting/profitable (*sumpheron*).[7] Yet the command itself does not require one to take the more profitable way. It must be a calling from God,

---

[5] All translations, unless noted, are my own.
[6] John Meier, *A Marginal Jew: Rethinking the Historical Jesus, Volume IV: Law and Love* (New York: Yale University Press, 2009), 106.
[7] The verb used here is *sumphero* – used impersonally.

which is implied by the theological passive: "only those to whom it is given." Those who are given this gift, "make themselves eunuchs on account of the kingdom." In other words, it seems that Jesus is partly admitting the disciples' objection but qualifying it that only those to whom it is given can live a celibate life. Nevertheless, the commandment binds all: nobody should divorce and remarry.

Although the above interpretation seems cogent, there is a powerful alternative interpretation, which claims that Jesus's response ("not all can accept this word") refers not to the disciples' response but to the prohibition of divorce and remarriage.[8] In this interpretation, Jesus is correcting the disciples' erroneous interpretation. To marry is part of the kingdom, and absolute fidelity is its sign. If you separate from your spouse, you must live as a eunuch—one (morally) incapable of sexual acts. This is a requirement of the kingdom, and those who are Christian can live by this command. Christians are those "to whom it is given." In other words, according to this interpretation, we are not here dealing with a command and a counsel, but an absolute command addressed to all (no divorce and remarriage). If one separates from one's spouse (e.g., on account of him or her abandoning the Christian way of life) then the power of the kingdom enables celibacy.[9]

The pivotal issue separating these two interpretations is the ambiguity of Jesus's response. Does "this saying [*ton logon*]" refer to the disciples' reaction or to Jesus's divorce saying? If it refers to the disciples' reaction, then the first interpretation is more likely. Jesus is admitting their reaction that celibacy is better, considering the prohibition of divorce, but qualifying it to say that celibacy is a gift. If it refers to Jesus's prohibition of divorce and remarriage then the second interpretation is more likely. The celibacy being referenced is to avoid a second marriage and God's grace enables this. Each interpretation has strengths and weaknesses.[10] Nevertheless, solving this convoluted debate is, in a substantial sense, beside the point for the command/counsel distinction.

---

[8] Quentin Quesnell, "Made Themselves Eunuchs for the Sake of the Kingdom," *The Catholic Biblical Quarterly* 30, no. 3 (1968): 335–358. See also Nil Guillemette, "Is Celibacy Better?" *Landas* 10 (1996): 3–38.

[9] Francis Moloney, *A Life of Promise: Poverty, Chastity, Obedience* (Eugene, OR: Wipf and Stock Publishers, 2001), 96ff.

[10] For a defense of the second interpretation see Moloney, *A Life of Promise*, 88ff. There are problems with the second interpretation Moloney does not note, though. First, it implies that faithfulness in marriage is a gift, a grace, and cannot be accepted by all humans. This would be problematic to the claim that marriage is a natural institution (though one could claim that without grace nature is wounded and incapable). Second, it does not fit the grammar of the passage as well as the first. Third, it seems to imply (based on the final exhortation) that some are not able to live chastely after separation (and that they are not exhorted to do so). For a defense of the first see Daniel Harrington, *The Gospel of Matthew* (Collegeville, MN: Liturgical Press, 2007), 273ff.

This passage supports the distinction either directly or indirectly. It supports the distinction directly if one takes the first interpretation. Here we find Jesus straightforwardly giving a command, do not divorce and remarry, and counseling the disciples on a more fitting way to avoid breaking the command, celibacy. Yet, one could avoid breaking the commandment by remaining faithful to marriage as well. If that is not the case, then the passage only supports the command/counsel distinction indirectly by supporting the option of living either celibately or in marriage as a follower of Christ. The scholars who defend this interpretation still recognize that there were those who lived celibate lives in the early Christian community: Jesus, John the Baptist, possibly some of the disciples.[11] Yet, none of those scholars would claim that either celibacy or marriage would be required to avoid divorce and remarriage. In other words, there are still multiple ways of fulfilling Jesus's command. Granted, the command/counsel distinction requires more than this, namely that one of the ways be more fitting than the other. Yet that can easily be supplied by Jesus's own example or the link between celibacy and the resurrected state.[12] In other words, though one could make a strong argument that this passage does not recommend one of the two ways as more fitting, it would be hard to deny it based on other passages.[13]

Matthew 19:16–30: Poverty and the Kingdom

The second passage (Cf. Luke 18:18–30, Mark 10:17–31) typically invoked to support the command/counsel distinction concerns wealth. In this passage a rich young man approaches Jesus and asks, "Teacher, what should I do to obtain eternal life?" Jesus responds, "If you wish to obtain eternal life keep the commandments." The youth responds, "Which ones?" Jesus responds with commandments from the second tablet of the Decalogue. The youth responds, "I have kept all these. What do I still lack?" Jesus responds with the famous line: "If you wish to be perfect/whole (*teleios*) sell all your possessions and give [them] to the poor, and you will have treasure in heaven, and then follow me." The young man is saddened by this, for he has many possessions. Jesus then explains the encounter to his disciples, "Entering the kingdom of heaven is difficult (*duskolōs*) for the rich." The disciples are surprised by this and respond, "Who then can be saved?" Jesus responds, "For humans this is not possible, but for God all [things] are possible" (Matthew 19:16–26).

One of the oldest interpretations of this passage comes from Jerome and sees this passage as a straightforward presentation of the

---

[11] Quesnell, "Made Themselves Eunuchs for the Sake of the Kingdom," 337, n. 9.

[12] For more on Jesus's example of celibacy, see Moloney, *A Life of Promise,* 103ff.

[13] Cornelia Horn and John Martens, *Let the Little Children Come to Me: Childhood and Children in Early Christianity* (Washington DC The Catholic University of America Press, 2009), 88ff.

command/counsel distinction and the call to monastic life.[14] The youth has kept the commandments but still lacks something, still lacks the possibility of perfection made possible by the counsels. Jerome says that "whoever wants to be perfect ought to sell what he has and sell not merely a part of it, as Ananias and Sapphira did, but sell everything." Though this does not automatically render someone perfect, "Many who abandon wealth do not follow the Lord,"[15] says Jerome. It does, however, give the possibility of perfection. In other words, it is impossible to retain possessions and reach perfection. St. Jerome calls retaining possessions (i.e., following the commandments), a "lesser way" and those who follow it have a "second degree of virtue."[16] Those who give up all their possessions follow the counsel of Christ and can reach perfection. Though this is not the only pre-modern interpretation of this passage, it is a dominant one.[17]

An alternative interpretation is found in the *Oxford Biblical Commentary*, which is drawing, in part, from John Calvin. The *OBC* reads this passage as a recommendation of obedience to Christ through a story of failed obedience (cf. 4:18–20, 8:18–20, and 9:9). In other words, this interpretation claims that the passage is not about wealth or about two levels of Christians. The details of the story are not universalizable, just as "leave the dead to bury the dead" is not. Jesus is speaking to the young man in front of him, not to all Christians. Because of this, there is not a commandment and a counsel here, nor an implication that there are two levels of Christians. What some have read as a counsel is really a command to this individual. As evidence of this, the *OBC* cites the loss of the kingdom by the rich young man, not the loss of perfection, when he goes away sad.[18] If there were two levels, one would expect the loss of perfection and not the loss of the kingdom, full stop. In other words, perfection in this passage is "perfect obedience" and is required of anyone who will reach the kingdom.

What is lacking in both these interpretations is any substantial connection to the Sermon on the Mount. Neither interpretation uses Matthew 5:48 to interpret what perfection/wholeness means in this passage.[19] This not only takes Matthew 19 out of the proper context of the whole Gospel of Matthew but also ignores the clear references from

---

[14] Moloney, *A Life of Promise*, 56ff.
[15] Jerome, *Commentary on Matthew*, trans. Thomas Scheck (Washington, DC: The Catholic University of America Press, 2008), 220.
[16] Benoit Matougues, *Œuvres de Saint Jerome* (Paris: Rue Neuve-Des-Petits-Champs, 1838), 79. "second degré de la vertu."
[17] For Aquinas's interpretation, see Thomas Aquinas, *Commentary on the Gospel of Matthew, Chapters 13–28* (Lander, WY: The Aquinas Institute, 2013), 1589ff.
[18] John Barton and John Muddiman, eds., *The Oxford Bible Commentary* (New York: Oxford University Press, 2013), 869–870.
[19] Moloney, *A Life of Promise*, 63ff.

Matthew 19 to the Sermon.[20] Three pieces of evidence make this clear. The first is the grammatical parallel between Matthew 5:48 and Matthew 19:21. In each, there is a call to perfection. This is Matthew's addition to the story of the rich young man and so naturally brings the reader's attention back to the Sermon. Second, in Matthew 5, Jesus is explaining the place of the moral precepts of the Mosaic Law in the life of Christians. Jesus says he has not come to abolish the law but to fulfill it. This fulfillment is a greater righteousness. Jesus is approached by a young man who is observing the law but lacks the deeper righteousness of the Sermon, the perfection/wholeness. In other words, "*exactly* the same argument is being pursued through the narrative of the rich young man [as the Sermon]."[21] Finally, the injunction to give alms and store up treasure in heaven is also straight out of the Sermon (Matthew 6:2–4, 19, 24). The grammatical and structural parallels are undeniable.

So, what does the Sermon add to our understanding of Mt 19? In the Sermon, Jesus says that one's righteousness must surpass that of the scribes and the Pharisees. Jesus is not setting aside the law but bringing it to completion/fullness.[22] It is the observance of the moral law in its fullness that brings the believer to perfection/wholeness. This perfection/wholeness, as recently argued by both Mattison and Pennington, is the deeper righteousness of interiorizing the commandments; it is virtue.[23] This is the correct explanation of what perfection means, and this is precisely what the youth lacks. He may keep the commandments exteriorly (and love his neighbor exteriorly), but he is still attached to riches and is thus divided; virtue is not only concerned with actions but also desires. This means the issue of riches is not one of prohibition but of disposition ("he left sad"), luxury, and excess (Matthew 5:1, 6:24, 6:33; Luke 7:25, Luke 19:1–10; 1 Timothy 6:6–19; 2 Peter 2:13).[24] This makes sense given Jesus's explanation to the disciples after the youth leaves. He gives an explanation based on disposition: "It is hard for the rich to attain the kingdom…but all things are possible with God" (Matthew 19:23, 26). He does not say it is impossible but is difficult. Why? Because the goal is the wholeness/perfection of the Sermon, and it is hard to remain detached from riches. In addition, the connection to the Sermon also makes sense of why Jesus only asks the youth about the commandments on the second tablet (while still recognizing that the reference to Leviticus was meant

---

[20] Moloney, *A Life of Promise,* 63.
[21] Moloney, *A Life of Promise,* 64.
[22] William Mattison III, *The Sermon on the Mount and Moral Theology* (New York: Oxford University Press, 2017), 64ff. Jonathan Pennington, *The Sermon on the Mount and Human Flourishing* (Grand Rapids: Baker Academic, 2018), 174ff.
[23] Pennington, *The Sermon,* 298f.
[24] See also Tzvi Novick, "Wages from God: The Dynamics of a Biblical Metaphor," *The Catholic Biblical Quarterly* 73, no. 4 (2011)*:* 708–722.

to summarize the whole law): the invitation to perfection/wholeness is an invitation to follow Christ, as is clear in the Sermon. Indeed, the entire Sermon is a portrait of Christ.[25] In Matthew 19, Jesus references the second tablet because he is inserting himself in place of the first three commandments. This makes sense of why some commentators read this as a conversion story.[26]

What the two former interpretations lack comes from attention to the Sermon on the Mount. According to the first, this passage is a straightforward recommendation of the higher way of religious life. Yet, the Sermon calls all people to the greater righteousness which is perfection. The first interpretation is only sustainable by calling some Christians to perfection. The Sermon belies this option. The second interpretation cannot be correct either. Though the *OBC* denies that the same kind of perfection/wholeness is in question in Matthew 5 and Matthew 19, it offers no evidence. The conceptual and grammatical references seem undeniable, and I see no reason why Matthew 19 would be referencing the "completeness of obedience" and Matthew 5:48 the "completeness of love."[27] Jesus follows the encounter with a general point about riches. To undercut a two-tiered reading of the passage, the *OBC* particularizes the story so much that Jesus's explanation makes no sense. Why make a general point about riches if the story is in no way universalizable? Why make a point about riches if the whole point is obedience? It is by recognizing the connection to the Sermon on the Mount, an instruction dedicated to all disciples, that two-tiered ethics is undercut. There are not two standards or two calls, but one call to wholehearted devotion to God. It is in this context that Jesus warns all his disciples against riches. The reason the youth loses the kingdom is because he refuses to part with what is keeping him from the perfection/wholeness of the kingdom.

But what of the command/counsel distinction? Connecting the passage to Matthew 5:48 does not seem directly to support the command/counsel distinction. In fact, it seems to undermine it. In the Sermon, there are not two grades of believers or two standards—one living the commandments and one living the counsels. All believers are called to the greater righteousness of the Sermon; all are called to one goal of perfection/wholeness. Nevertheless, it is in connection to the Sermon that the command/counsel distinction reasserts itself in another form.[28] The greater righteousness of the Sermon, the singular goal of the Christian life, is possible both to those who possess riches

---

[25] Servais Pinckaers, *The Pinckaers Reader,* eds. John Berkman and Craig Steven Titus (Washington, DC: The Catholic University of America Press, 2005), 383.

[26] Harrington, *The Gospel of Matthew,* 281.

[27] Barton, ed., *Oxford Biblical Commentary,* 869–870.

[28] I think a strong case can also be made for reading the antitheses through the distinction as well. See Mattison, *The Sermon on the Mount and Moral Theology,* 68–90.

and those who do not. It is not an issue of two standards or merely keeping the commandments versus observing the counsels of perfection but an issue of difficulty and obstacles. The rich can attain the wholehearted devotion and detachment necessary for greater righteousness, but it is more difficult. This is why Jesus uses the adverb to say that it is only "with difficulty" that the rich will enter the kingdom. In other words, poverty removes a major obstacle to the holiness of a Christian, yet one does not have to be poor to be whole/perfect. For example, some claim that Mary Magdalene was very wealthy and traveled with Jesus and provided for him out of her means (Luke 8:3).[29] Yet Jesus is saying that this is the harder way. It is difficult to be rich and not be attached to one's riches, "For where one's treasure is, there is one's heart also" (Matthew 6:21). The advice is clear. Poverty is the more fitting, but not the only possible way, of achieving wholehearted love of God and neighbor (Matthew 22:35–40). This is the command/counsel distinction. There are multiple ways, and one is more fitting.[30]

1 Corinthians 7: Paul's Preference for Virginity

This passage has been the subject of massive amounts of scholarship. Most biblical exegetes go to great lengths to argue that Paul is not claiming that celibacy is superior to marriage or that later Pauline literature developed this point.[31] Both of these debates are beyond the purview of this essay. What concerns me is that this passage explicitly contains the command/counsel distinction. Paul is recommending celibacy, but it is not necessary. Celibacy is not a commandment of the Lord but rather Paul's counsel. It is a more fitting means toward a certain common goal of the Christian life.

The provenance of this passage is a series of questions concerning marriage, celibacy, and virginity Paul receives from the Corinthians.[32] Paul finds himself in an interesting position, caught between extreme ascetics who claim that sex, even within marriage, should be avoided and his own desire to recommend celibacy. Against the extreme ascetics (7:1), Paul defends the goodness of marriage and even calls it a charism: "[Though] I wish that all were as I am, each one has a particular gift [*charisma*] from God, one of one kind and one of another" (1 Corinthians 7:7). One can see the foreshadowing of 1 Corinthians 12 and a vision of a unified body with each contributing, both married

---

[29] Likewise, wealthy and influential people were often named by their hometown.
[30] Even the *Oxford Biblical Commentary* implicitly admits that riches make it harder to attain the kingdom. If obedience is the goal, then poverty would be the safer/more fitting way. Riches make it harder to be obedient. See Barton, ed., *Oxford Biblical Commentary*, 870.
[31] The developed position, whether Paul's or not, would be found in Ephesians 5.
[32] For a division of this chapter see Joseph Fitzmyer, *First Corinthians* (New York: Yale University Press, 2008).

and celibate. In other words, against the extreme ascetics, Paul teaches that sex and marriage are not sinful and, on the contrary, contribute to the one body of the Church. On the other hand, Paul still wants to recommend celibacy and not simply because of an eschatological crisis. Put more bluntly, celibacy is not simply an interim ethic. Paul wants people to be free of "worldly troubles" and "anxieties" so that they may give "undivided devotion" to the Lord.[33] This is true regardless of the timing of Christ's return. In every age, celibacy has a certain advantage for prioritizing the Lord and "the Lord's affairs" (1 Corinthians 7:32).[34]

In recommending celibacy, Paul utilizes the command/counsel distinction explicitly. As he says, he is offering his *gnome* (1 Corinthians 7:25). This word means more than opinion. It is closer to a judgment on the matter.[35] Paul says explicitly that he does not lay a restriction (*brochon*) or have a commandment (*epitage*) in this regard. Paul is immediately making clear this is not an issue of necessity. Celibacy is not required for the fulfillment of the moral law, as some Corinthian ascetics seem to be suggesting. Those who marry do not sin (1 Corinthians 7:28). Rather, he wishes that all be dedicated to the Lord, *aperispastos*: without distraction, living in the world as if not living in it, and free from anxieties.[36] In Paul's judgment, both marriage and virginity are good, yet certain goals render celibacy preferable. These are goals that all Christians share. As Paul says, "I am saying this for what is advantageous/fitting (*sumphoron*) to you" (1 Corinthians 7:35).

Paul's use of the command/counsel distinction could not be more explicit. The central proposition in this passage is not the avoidance of *porneia* or divorce (though those are necessary also) but living in this world truthfully, "for the shape of this world is passing away" (1 Corinthians 7:31). Certain things are required for all: to avoid *porneia*, to shun divorce, and to live in the world as though not in the world (i.e., as Paul says—"keeping the commandments") (1 Corinthians 7:19). Paul is not recommending that those who have undertaken marriage abandon it but rather live "as though they had none" (1 Corinthians 7:29). By this he does not mean to argue sex or marriage is sinful; that would admit the position of the extreme ascetics. His point is that marriage draws you into this world and causes anxieties, making it harder to have undivided devotion. Likewise, he is not saying you should never be involved in the affairs of the world or be married, but

---

[33] These are the goals whether the world is ending soon or not, married or celibate. See verses 7:7 and 32ff.

[34] See Fitzmyer, *First Corinthians*, 316ff.

[35] Rollin Ramsaran, "More Than an Opinion: Paul's Rhetorical Maxim in 1 Corinthians 7:25–26," *The Catholic Biblical Quarterly* 57, no. 3 (1995): 531–541.

[36] What does Paul mean by dedication to the Lord? He means what most scholars think of as prayer, presence in cultic or church assemblies, charitable works, even preaching. These things are harder to do consistently if you are married.

that concern for the things of the Lord must take priority, and this is harder when you are married.[37] He is also not claiming that marriage is not more advantageous in other ways. Paul counsels marriage for those who struggle with sexual desire. If one's goal is to avoid adultery and one struggles with sexual desire, marriage is more fitting. When it comes to the affairs of the Lord and pleasing the Lord, celibacy is more fitting. Which is the more fitting way depends on the person and the goal in mind, but what is clear is that the commandments are distinct from what Paul counsels. This is the command/counsel distinction.

The major points of debate among scholars concerning this passage are irrelevant to this claim about the command/counsel distinction. Some scholars say that Paul is proposing his opinion here and not exercising apostolic authority. This would seem to be wrong since Paul invokes his authority by saying he is trustworthy and has the Spirit. Nevertheless, with what authority Paul recommends celibacy (or marriage) is not really a concern. Either way the structure of the command/counsel distinction is there. Other scholars say that Paul only prefers celibacy because he thinks that the *Parousia* is immanent (and is mistaken). Once he (or later Pauline literature) realizes the truth, he abandons his preference for celibacy and goes back to the equality of the callings (Ephesians 5). In some sense, this objection too is beside the point. Paul recommends celibacy for reasons other than the end of the world: undivided attention, concern for the affairs of the Lord, etc. These ought to mark every Christian life. Furthermore, even if Paul is wrong about the circumstances in which celibacy might be preferred (i.e., those goals or the poignancy he gives them are only on account of a mistaken belief in the immediate *Parousia*), he clearly admits as a method of reasoning that the commands are required and there are more or less fitting ways to fulfill them.[38] In other words, the command/counsel distinction would still be present even if the particular circumstances in which it is applied are mistaken. Likewise, some scholars claim that Paul does not claim celibacy is a higher calling.[39] While this claim seems hard to support, it is still irrelevant. What Paul counsels (marriage or celibacy, hierarchically arranged or not) is not necessary to fulfill the moral commandments, and so the commands and counsels are distinct. Paul is still distinguishing the commandment from the counsel, even if there is no absolute hierarchy among the ways of fulfilling the command. Finally, the long and detailed debates

---

[37] Vincent L. Wimbush, *Paul: The Worldly Ascetic* (Macon, GA: Mercer University Press, 1987), 96: "Thus, the relativizing argument (ὡς μὴ ἀμέριμνος) is not used for debunking, but for accepting involvement in, the structure of the world, with the provison that concern for 'the things of the Lord' take priority."

[38] Furthermore, there are tribulations in every generation, and one must always engage with the world as if it is passing away.

[39] Guillemette, "Is Celibacy Better?" 16ff; Fitzmyer, *First Corinthians,* 275f.

concerning 7:35ff and the precise meaning of *parthenos* are irrelevant.[40] In Paul's advice he indicates again that it is not a sin to marry, but that the preservation of virginity in this case is better vis-à-vis the positive goal of Christian life. This, again, implicitly involves the command/counsel distinction.

DOES THE COMMAND/COUNSEL DISTINCTION ENTAIL TWO-TIERED ETHICS?

These three Biblical passages, especially the latter two, present a picture of a shared goal of Christian life (perfection/wholeness/focus on the Lord) and certain activities which are required to reach it (e.g., love) or are necessarily contrary to this goal (e.g., adultery). Yet these passages also recognize fitting ways of reaching the goal of holiness.[41] As these passages present them, counsels are recommendations of the more fitting way. Jesus thinks that riches are an obstacle to the goal of perfection/wholeness, but they are not *ipso facto* contrary to perfection/wholeness. Likewise, Paul clearly thinks that marriage makes it more difficult to live in the world as if it is passing away and to devote more attention to the things of the Lord, yet marriage is not contrary to the Christian life and has its own gifts to bring to the body.

In some ways this is clear, and in other ways it raises more questions than it answers. It is still unclear whether a counsel is itself a greater participation in the goal or simply removes obstacles to the goal (or both), how vows should be understood in relation to counsels, whether all Christians are called to live the counsels, and whether the command/counsel distinction gives rise to two-tiered ethics (as some have contended it does). Given space limitations, I cannot answer all these questions satisfactorily. I wish to address the last question only. Nevertheless, answering this final question will allow me to cursorily touch the others.

The Command/Counsel Distinction Understood in a Morality of Happiness

The key issue for how to understand the relation between the command/counsel distinction and two-tiered ethics is freedom. Following Servais Pinckaers, one can distinguish two major conceptions of freedom: a freedom of indifference and a freedom for excellence. The first conceives of freedom as the "power to choose between contraries" whereas the second is "the power to act freely with excellence and perfection."[42] These two concepts of freedom in turn "produce two

---

[40] The three options are virgin daughter, betrothed virgin, or a cohabitating virgin committed to preserving virginity. See Fitzmyer, *First Corinthians*, 322ff.
[41] See footnote 60.
[42] Servais Pinckaers, *The Sources of Christian Ethics*, trans. Sr. Mary Thomas Noble (Washington, DC: The Catholic University of America Press, 1995), 375.

concepts of morality...[and] of happiness."[43] A freedom of indifference generates a moral vision which excludes nature, has no room for growth, tries to maximize choices, requires the choice of evil as a possibility, and pits the individual's freedom against others, faith, tradition, law, natural inclinations, and community. Put differently, because freedom is primarily conceived non-teleologically and negatively, any influence on the individual is inimical. Hence, commands are essentially coercive and unrelated to what an individual truly desires. In its Christian form, this ethic focuses on law, conscience, and obligation. Morality is an obligation imposed by God and received/applied in conscience. What is necessary is what God's will deems is necessary. Where God's law is silent, conscience is left with only indifferent matters.[44] The central question is: What does God's will compel me to do? If there is no law, then there is no obligation, and an individual is free to do whatever he pleases. Morality, in this conception, is the lesser of two evils (hell being the worse), but not what one wants or what fulfills.

In fact, it is a morality of obligation, and the nominalism that intellectually undergirds it,[45] which uses the command/counsel distinction to generate two-tiered ethics. One can easily see why this is the case. In a morality of obligation, law represents a minimum imposed by a higher authority under threat of punishment. One could go beyond the law, but it is not one's duty. What are the counsels, then? They become optional extras undertaken beyond the commands and represent the desire of the individual to pursue a higher way. The only connection between these two ways is the supererogatory will of the individual willing to undertake the more difficult path. Having bound oneself to the higher road (i.e., undertaken a life of the counsels), one is now subject to different requirements than those merely living the commandments. Commands and counsels constitute two competing ways of showing obedience and are related only inasmuch as both are from God. One can see why, in this conception, the command/counsel distinction can be tied to the states of life in the Church. Since the goals of the commands and counsels are diverse, the command/counsel distinction can be correlated with states of life in the Church. The laity are those who merely live the commands. Religious are those who vow and live the counsels.

In a morality of happiness, on the other hand, the command/counsel distinction is understood differently. Since commands are ordered toward the mind and direct people to an end or prohibit what is necessarily contrary to that end (ST I-II q. 90, a. 2, co.), the end toward

---

[43] Pinckaers, *The Sources of Christian Ethics*, 465–466.
[44] Viktoria Deak, *Consilia Sapientis Amici* (Rome: Editrice Pontificia Universita Gregoriana, 2014), 34–43.
[45] Pinckaers, *The Sources of Christian Ethics*, 240ff.

which commandments and counsels point is one and the same: virtue, another name for the biblical perfection/wholeness (ST II-II q. 184, a. 1, co).[46] This is the shared goal of all Christians. It is within and toward this shared goal that commandments are distinguished from counsels. According to a morality of happiness, commands and counsels differ in their type of necessity for reaching an end, the absolutely necessary versus the fittingly necessary.[47] In the analogous metaphysics which undergirds a morality of happiness, there are more or less fitting ways to reach an end.[48] Fitting necessity does not require a particular action but merely recommends it as the more fitting way. The less fitting way can still reach the goal, though. This is precisely the distinction between counsel and command (ST I-II q. 108, a. 4, co). Commandments concern those actions which are necessarily contrary to the end or necessary to reach the end of virtue.[49] In those acts not concerning necessity, counsels are the recommendation of a more fitting acts *ad finem* or the recommendation to avoid certain obstacles to the end.[50] The counsels are not ordered toward a different end than the commands.[51] Both are ordered to holiness and virtue.[52] Put differently, no counsel is necessary because there is more than one way of being virtuous. This is precisely the historical and biblical teaching on the commands and counsels: all are called to perfection/wholeness; there are not two

---

[46] "unumquodque dicitur esse perfectum inquantum attingit proprium finem."

[47] See John Meinert, *The Love of God Poured Out: Grace and the Gifts of the Holy Spirit in St. Thomas Aquinas* (Steubenville, OH: Emmaus Academic, 2018), 116ff.

[48] This also makes sense of what are called "near occasions of sin," which amount to counsels of avoidance.

[49] One should also notice the asymmetry between positive and negative commands (inasmuch as they relate to virtue). Negative commandments, those that move an individual to act not, inform an individual of what is contrary to an end, contrary to a virtue. Positive commandments, those that move an individual to act, inform the individual of actions that do belong to a virtue. Positive commands are absolute only in general. One must be wholeheartedly devoted to God, but this end can be reached many ways. In other words, reaching the goal of a positive command is circumstantial and actions *ad finem* are fitting. The command/counsel distinction with respect to positive commands has to do with the general and necessary (command) vs. the acts toward that end (counsel). A negative command is different. Negative commands are absolute in particular. They tell you what not to do. The command/counsel distinction in relation to negative commands is different. Here commands tell you what is necessarily contrary to virtue and counsels what is a fitting way of avoiding doing the vicious behavior (e.g., avoid near occasions of sin).

[50] Acts *ad finem* are those ordered toward and end and participating in it, but not yet fully realizing it. Aquinas, ST I-II q. 108 and ST II-II q. 186. Aquinas, ST I-II q. 108, a. 4, co.: "*Sed expeditius perveniet totaliter bona huius mundi abdicando. Et ideo de hoc dantur consilia Evangelii.*"

[51] Louis Bouyer, *Introduction to the Spiritual Life* (Notre Dame, IN: Christian Classics, 2013), 241ff.

[52] Thomas Aquinas, *Quodlibetal Questions*, trans. by Nevitt and Davies (New York: Oxford University Press, 2019), IV, q. 12, a. 2, co.: "The commandments are given for acts of virtue."

standards or tiers (Matthew 5 & 19). Yet, this does not mean that all ways are equal. Some ways are more fitting ways to reach the shared goal.[53]

Implications of a Morality of Happiness for the Command/Counsel Distinction

Given a morality of happiness, which follows from the biblical witness, four things are implied about counsels: there are positive and negative counsels; the number of counsels is potentially infinite; all are required to live the counsels in some sense; and one could live the counsels without vowing them. First, there are both positive and negative counsels. Positive counsels are a fuller good and a greater participation in the end. Positive counsels should not be conceived of as purely instrumental. The acts recommended by a positive counsel are themselves a greater participation in the end.[54] Negative counsels recommend the removal of obstacles to the end. The negative counsels are purely instrumental and are not, ipso facto, a greater participation in the end. Simply because one does not have junk food in the house does not make one healthier, for example. The evangelical counsels seem to be negative counsels. Simply avoiding marriage or money does not make one more virtuous. On the other hand, both positive and negative counsels can be called a more fitting way to pursue an end. A positive counsel is more fitting because performing acts which are a greater participation in the end is more fitting than performing those with a lesser participation. A negative counsel is more fitting because to pursue an end without obstacles is more fitting than to pursue it with obstacles.

Second, the number of counsels in a morality of happiness are potentially infinite, and this follows from the diversity and plurality of proximate ends. Anytime there is a more fitting way to reach an end

---

[53] Historically, the Church has consistently rejected any movement that claimed the counsels are required, effectively/in fact (Foulechat) to be virtuous or that one could progress beyond the necessity of the commandments (Quietism). See Heinrich Denzinger and Helmut Hoping, *Compendium of Creeds, Definitions, and Declarations on Matters of Faith and Morals,* 47th edition (San Francisco: Ignatius Press, 2012), 250, 866, 1087, 2181–2192, 2201–2269.

[54] Aquinas claims that the counsels (and he has the evangelical in mind) are ordained to the interior acts of virtue as an end but to the exterior act of virtue as the removal of obstacles. See Aquinas, *Quodlibetal Questions,* IV, q. 12, a. 2, co.: "Sic ergo patet quod consilia ordinantur sicut ad finem ad praecepta, prout sunt de interioribus actibus virtutum; sed ad praecepta, secundum quod sunt de exterioribus actibus, ordinantur consilia ad hoc quod tutius et firmius conserventur per modum removentis prohibens." I think this is right in relation to the evangelical counsels, which are negative counsels and so concern avoiding obstacles, but if you take counsel in a broader sense then it would seem to be possible to have positive counsels ordered toward exterior acts of virtue which are greater participations in a good.

or to avoid obstacles to that same end, it is a counsel.[55] Hence, a diversity of ends will yield a diversity of counsels, both positive and negative. For example, there are better and worse ways to eat vis-à-vis the end of health. The more fitting way, a better diet for example, is a greater good. To undertake eating in a worse way (e.g., keeping junk food in the house or adequate but not fully healthy meals) is not necessarily to commit acts of gluttony or insensibility. In other words, there are more counsels than just the evangelical counsels (poverty, chastity, and obedience); there are positive and negative counsels relative to each virtue.[56]

Third, all Christians are required to live the counsels in some sense since all persons are ordered to virtue. The historical distinction between the affective and effective living helps to explain this.[57] The affective living (disposition) of the counsel is simply to have the virtue, to have the purpose of the counsel. The effective living of the counsel is to live the counsel in fact (to avoid possible obstacles to acquiring the virtue or to act in a more virtuous way). Not all are called to the second (especially inasmuch as it is a negative counsel), nor is it a sin to fail to live a counsel in fact/effectively.[58] This is precisely what we see in Vatican II and subsequent magisterial teaching, especially *Lumen Gentium*, *Perfectae Caritatis*, and *Vita Consecrata*.[59] These documents, following Matthew 19 and 1 Corinthians 7, recognize the command/counsel distinction, reject ethical minimalism, and claim that all are called to holiness and to the counsels. An easy way to make sense of this claim is that the counsels are necessary for holiness, not in fact (effectively) but in disposition (affectively).[60] One does not have to be poor in fact, but one must be poor in spirit.

Fourth, a morality of happiness implies that one could live a counsel effectively/in fact by vow or not. The Benedictines vow stability, which removes the obstacle to which the Gyrovagues had fallen prone,

---

[55] See Merkelbach's discussion of restitution, which can be done in better or worse ways. See Benedictus Merkelbach, *Summa Theologiae Moralis: Tomus Secundus* (Desclee de Brouwer et Cie, 1946), 287ff.

[56] This, likewise, makes sense of how some counsels can be a fuller participation in the end and others are not. A negative and instrumental counsel is not a fuller participation in the end. A positive counsel, the choice of a fuller good, is a fuller participation in the end.

[57] Catherine of Siena, *The Dialogue,* trans. Susanne Nofke (New Jersey: Paulist Press, 1980), 309–310; 318f.

[58] Sara Butler, "*Perfectae Caritatis,*" in *The Reception of Vatican II*, ed. Matthew Lamb and Matthew Levering (New York: Oxford University Press, 2017), 221.

[59] Matthew Lamb and Matthew Levering, eds., *Vatican II: Renewal within Tradition* (New York: Oxford University Press, 2008).

[60] This seems to be what Aquinas means by the "internal acts of virtue toward which the commandments are aimed." See Aquinas, *Quodlibetal Questions,* IV, q. 12, a. 2, co.

instability and its attendant dangers.[61] Benedictines live the counsel of stability under a vow. Yet it is possible to be stable without vowing stability (an effective living of a counsel without a vow). One could be voluntarily poor without vowing to be so. One could choose to avoid obstacles (negative counsel) or choose the fuller good (positive counsel) in relation to almost any virtue without vowing to do so.[62]

Given this understanding of the command/counsel distinction, the negative elements associated with the command/counsel distinction by a morality of obligation are undercut. There is no implication that marriage itself, the sexual act, wealth, or lacking an immediate superior to whom one owes obedience (to use the evangelical counsels) are evil.[63] They are not. This is because these are negative counsels, removing obstacles. In fact, the obstacles in this case are good things and acts ordered to the ultimate end (presupposing charity). Nevertheless, it is precisely their proximate goodness that can prove distracting. We are particularly tempted to greed, worldliness, pleasure, and pride. Hence, it is more fitting, given the end of full attention to and love of God, that these goods are not pursued. Can they be pursued virtuously? Of course. Are you more likely to be distracted by them or pursue them in a disordered way if you pursue them in the first place? Yes. Could you still be distracted by them, even if you vow not to pursue them? Sure. Could you fail to live a counsel effectively even if you vow it? Certainly. Could you live counsel more effectively but not vow it? Absolutely.[64] There are not two different standards or tiers.[65] There is one fundamental Christian vocation and fitting acts *ad finem*.

---

[61] Benedicta Ward, ed., *The Desert Fathers: Sayings of the Early Christian Monks* (New York: Penguin Books, 2003), chapter 1.

[62] To grow, one wills the fuller good or the less full good with (more) intensity. Yet this is not required. You do not always have to choose the more fitting means to an end. Likewise, we need less fitting ways to reach an end so that we can pursue a higher end without rejecting the lower. Think of the interior and exterior purgations of the tradition. You can still reach the end of health without eating very healthy food. You can reach the goal of health without eating for long periods of time. This is obviously a less fitting way to reach the good of health than eating very healthy food regularly, but you have not acted contrary to that good.

[63] In the third and fourth centuries, when virginity and monasticism became much more popular, there were those authors who suggested that sexual acts within marriage were sinful (thereby implying that to be fully virtuous you had to be celibate). On the other hand, it seems the more predominant concern of these writers is not sexual activity itself but the desire (*epithumia/concupiscentia*) that accompanies sexual activity. The Stoic influence is unmistakable. See also Antonio Marin, *The Theology of Christian Perfection,* trans. Jordan Aumann (Eugene, Oregon: Wipf & Stock, 2018), 142ff.

[64] This seems to be what Pope Francis is recognizing in *Amoris Laetitia*, no. 162.

[65] In a morality of happiness there are still two tiers. There are those who effectively live the counsels of a virtue and those who do not. You cannot undertake, effectively, all more fitting acts. You cannot always choose the greater good in each situation, if

Finally, one can also see that in a morality of happiness the command/counsel distinction does not give rise to different states of life. It is not living the counsels that separates states of life in the Church but a vow to live them. In *Vita Consecrata,* John Paul II confirms this interpretation.

> In fact, all those reborn in Christ are called to live out, with the strength which is the Spirit's gift, the chastity appropriate to their state of life, obedience to God and to the Church, and a reasonable detachment from material possessions: for all are called to holiness, which consists in the perfection of love. But Baptism in itself does not include the call to celibacy or virginity, the renunciation of possessions or obedience to a superior, in the form proper to the evangelical counsels. The profession of the evangelical counsels thus presupposes a particular gift of God not given to everyone. (John Paul II, *Vita Consecrata*, no. 30)

Those without religious vows are called to live the counsels affectively (part of the goal inasmuch as they are positive) or effectively (e.g., poverty—to avoid attachment), but not to do so under a vow. A morality of happiness requires the counsels (in some form) of all individuals. It is a vow that generates religious life, not living the counsels (negative, positive, evangelical, or otherwise).[66] Neither does vowing the more fitting way (negative or positive) imply that one will necessarily reach the end or that the vow is somehow, in itself, a greater participation in the end.[67] Those who vow the counsels are not *ipso*

---

only because choosing the greater good often means reaching a lower good in a less than optimal way or forgoing another more fitting way to reach another good.

[66] Code of Canon Law, c. 573, § 2, in *New Commentary on the Code of Canon Law,* ed. John P. Beal, James A. Coriden, and Thomas J. Greene (New York: Paulist Press, 2000), 744. See *Lumen Gentium* 44 also: "*Per vota aut alia sacra ligamina.*"

[67] Deak, *Consilia Sapientis Amici,* 364. She notes a tension in the account of Aquinas between two visions of the counsels. She notes that Aquinas develops on this point, since the perfection of bishops could not depend on poverty. I think that given the teaching of Vatican II and the magisterium of John Paul II and Francis, we should go wholly with the instrumental account concerning negative counsels. This would allow the Church to recognize marriage as a state of perfection (i.e., a state of life that trains one in virtue). This does not require us to elide the superiority of vowing the (negative) counsels, for instruments which tend to the same end are of differing efficacy. Yet, all are still instruments. See Lasnoski, *Vocation to Virtue,* for an extended defense of this account of marriage. Likewise, this also does not require us to abandon the sense that there are some counsels which are a fuller participation. It simply depends on what type of counsel is in question. The evangelical counsels do seem to be instrumental, though. The tradition has consistently talked of them as avoiding certain obstacles: self-will, pleasure, wealth.

facto holier.⁶⁸ In a morality of happiness, the command/counsel distinction has nothing to do with two-tiered ethics.

IS RELIGIOUS LIFE SUPERIOR TO NON-RELIGIOUS LIFE?

Traditionally, the religious life (a life characterized by vows of a greater good) is thought to be superior to one not characterized by vows. This is usually spoken of as an "objective superiority."⁶⁹ Does jettisoning a morality of obligation and two-tiered ethics require that we reject this traditional claim in favor of religious life? If the counsels are simply more fitting ways to pursue an end, then how is the religious life universally superior (vs. circumstantially superior—i.e., for this or that person)?⁷⁰

In order to answer this question, one must recall the distinctions between counsels (positive and negative), evangelical counsels, and living of those counsels (affectively, effectively, and vowing). It is the vowing of the counsels that is objectively superior. Why? In a morality of obligation, it would be because you are binding your freedom (which is equally ordered to good and evil, and so needs binding) and doing what is more difficult.⁷¹ This is not the case in a morality of

---

⁶⁸ On the other hand, it does imply that those vowing the more fitting way should, given the lack of obstacles, reach the end in a fuller way and are more blamable if they do not.

⁶⁹ Butler, "*Perfectae Caritatis,*" 209.

⁷⁰ Another possible objection would be that it loses the connection between the evangelical counsels and the life of Jesus. If the evangelical counsels are simply more fitting ways (by removing obstacles) to the love of God, then how can they be a greater participation in the life of our Lord? Indeed, the early Church discerned the Evangelical Counsel of obedience by a deeper reflection on the life of our Lord (Moloney, *A Life of Promise*, 119ff.). Seeing the counsels as a greater participation in the life of Jesus seems to give them value in themselves and not as instruments. Though a full answer to this objection is not possible here, two things should be noted. First, a negation cannot be good in itself. At least two, and probably all three, of the evangelical counsels, are a lack of goods. That is why I characterized them as negative counsels. They counsel the avoidance of something that is good. A lack of a lower good can open us up more fully to a higher good, but that is precisely what it means to be instrumental. Second, we should not forget the pedagogical function of the Lord's life (Butler, "Perfectae Caritatis," 212). Every action is an example for us. Did he undertake a life of poverty, chastity, and obedience because he needed training in virtue or did he avoid those goods for his mission and to give us an example? Only the second is an option. Yet in the second option, the evangelical counsels are still instrumental. Put simply, to see the Evangelical counsels as a greater imitation of the life of Jesus and to see them as removing obstacles are not mutually exclusive.

⁷¹ Aquinas does leave a place for difficulty concerning the commandments and counsels. The counsels are the fastest and easiest way to achieve the perfect observance of the commands. Likewise, he says that the counsels are more difficult in their external acts than the commands, but the commands are more difficult in their internal acts than the exterior acts of the counsels. See Aquinas, *Quodlibetal Questions,* IV, q. 12, a. 2, ad 3 & 9.

happiness. Vowing the evangelical counsels is not the binding of freedom but its permanent training. It makes sure (as much as that is possible) that you are committed to practice the virtue or effectively remove the obstacles to a greater practice of virtue (Aquinas, *Quodlibetal Questions,* IV, q. 12, a. 1, co.).[72] This makes sense in a virtue perspective because it is repeated and consistent action that produces character change which is the goal. The vow puts you in a state of perfection, i.e., the permanent training of perfection (ST II-II, q. 184, a. 2, co.).[73] This is what, as John Paul II teaches, has "an objective superiority" (*Vita Consecrata,* no. 32). It also makes sense of how those who do not vow a counsel can still live it – effectively or affectively. One can be poor without vowing to be poor, which is an effective living of the counsel (provided it is voluntary and for God). One could have wealth but remain unattached to it and use it always for the common good, an affective living of the counsel (and a possibility of living of other virtues – munificence, for example).[74] Put simply, vowing the counsels is objectively superior because it creates the conditions for a more consistent practice (ST II-II q. 186, a. 1, ad 3). I think this is a sufficient answer to show the real, but limited, teleological superiority of vowing a counsel.[75]

CONCLUSION

The command/counsel distinction is solidly biblical. One finds clear support of it in Matthew 19 and 1 Corinthians 7. There is no need to jettison the distinction to get rid of two-tiered ethics. Understanding commands as necessary acts and counsels as more fitting acts will do that. The Lord does not give two standards but calls all people to holiness. This does not, however, require the effective living or vowing of the counsels. Yet, they remain advantageous toward that same end.

The recovery and wider use of this distinction also inoculates moral theology against serious errors and contributes to current debates. Those who avoid this distinction are apt to confuse commands and counsels. Christian perfection is a matter of command, not counsel. The commandments are not mere recommendations but are necessary.

---

[72] "Hence, it is much better for their will to be set on doing so [*eorum voluntas sit ad hoc firmata*], which is done by taking an oath or vow."

[73] "omne illud quod impedit ne affectus mentis totaliter dirigatur ad Deum."

[74] Aquinas recognizes that to reach the end despite obstacles is a sign of "great virtue." ST II-II q. 186, a. 4, ad 2. For an excellent treatment of what it means to use wealth for the common good see David Cloutier, *The Vice of Luxury* (Washington DC: The Catholic University of America Press, 2015).

[75] Putting it positively, vowing the evangelical counsels makes it more likely you will love God in act (given the lack of obstacles) vs. habitually, i.e., referencing your love of other things (spouse/children/work, etc.) to God through the habitual reference of charity. If one thinks of a different end (virtue), then I think it is clear that other states of life are superior. This seems to be what Pope Francis is teaching in *Amoris Laetitia,* nos. 159–160.

Nevertheless, the acts by which we reach perfection are a matter of fittingness. To treat what is advantageous as required or what is required as simply advantageous is a serious problem. Likewise, without this distinction certain debates flounder. The debate between pacifists and just war theorists could be a debate between those who want to undertake a counsel (pacifists) and those who defend the possibility of fulfilling the commands in a less fitting, but still good, way. Similar things could be said about accompaniment, solidarity with the poor, ownership and communal living, almsgiving, reconciliation, restitution, sexual activity, dieting, and many other topics. Without the command/counsel distinction, writing on these topics will undoubtedly tend to rigorism (requiring the counsels) or treating the commands as mere recommendations. Both are serious errors. M

John Meinert, PhD, is an associate professor of Theology at Franciscan Missionaries of Our Lady University in Baton Rouge, LA.

Newness of Life and Grace-Enabled Recovery from Addiction: Walking the Road to Recovery With Romans 7[1]

Andrew Kim

IN HIS LETTER TO THE CHRISTIANS IN ROME, St. Paul says that he does not do the good he wants to do but does the evil he does not want to do (Romans 7:19).[2] This statement is enormously problematic for several reasons but primarily because of questions it raises regarding the relationship of God's grace to human sinfulness. Why has God's grace not fully freed Paul from his sin? Moreover, if the Apostle is, as Aquinas thinks, above the "common lot of Christian believers, not merely in terms of authority but also in terms of moral exemplarity," then what are the implications of Paul's ongoing struggle for the rest of us?[3]

More specifically, questions arise regarding the compatibility of grace and sin in one's life. Can a person who is actively engaging in sin simultaneously be in a state of grace? Is there a degree of sinfulness that can share space with grace in the soul but upon exceeding that degree expels grace? Precisely how much sin in the soul can grace

---

[1] I would like to thank Caitlin Kim, William C. Mattison III, and Matthew Levering for their encouragement and support in helping me to write this essay.

[2] I draw from the New American Catholic Bible translation throughout. There is, of course, a vast debate among biblical scholars as to whether Paul is speaking in the voice of Saul or as the Christian Paul. For more on this topic and related debates among Pauline Scholars on Romans 7 more broadly, see N. T. Wright, Paul J. Sampley, and Robert W. Wall, *The New Interpreter's Bible: Acts; Introduction to Epistolary Literature; Romans; 1 Corinthians*, vol. 10 (Nashville: Abingdon, 2002). See also Joseph A. Fitzmyer, *Romans: A New Translation with Introduction and Commentary* (New York: Doubleday, 1993); James D. G. Dunn, *The Theology of Paul the Apostle* (Cambridge: Eerdmans, 1998).

[3] Charles Raith II, "Portraits of Paul: Aquinas and Calvin on Romans 7:14–25," in *Reading Romans with St. Thomas Aquinas*, ed. Matthew Levering and Michael Dauphinais (Washington, DC: Catholic University of America Press, 2012), 258. For more on this topic, see Michael Sherwin, OP, *On Love and Virtue: Theological Essays* (Steubenville, OH: Emmaus Academic, 2018). See also Nicholas Austin, SJ, *Aquinas on Virtue: A Casual Reading* (Washington, DC: Georgetown University Press, 2017).

abide? My purpose in this essay is not to attempt to resolve any of these questions but rather to consider them anew from the standpoint of addiction. My question is: how does God's grace unfold in the life of the addict? Responding to this question, I maintain that God's grace is sufficient to heal a person from addiction and examine four stages in which this healing may occur.[4]

The arguments of this essay are developed in two sections. The first section considers and moves beyond a disease model of addiction that prescinds the role of volition and thus marginalizes or entirely excludes addiction as a subject for moral analysis. Instead, I endorse a theological model for understanding addiction as in some ways analogous with disease but not reducible to it.[5] With this understanding in place, the second section draws from Augustine's and Aquinas's respective interpretations of Romans 7:14–25 in order to elucidate four stages in grace-enabled recovery from addiction. I conclude by revisiting the question of grace's relationship to sin on the basis of the analysis and arguments put forward in this essay and, drawing from Romans 1 and select passages in James, propose a way of assisting addicts through the stages of recovery.

ADDICTION: SIN OR DISEASE?

The purpose of this section is to consider whether addiction is best understood as sinful or as a disease. I begin by making rival cases for addiction as either sin or disease. Based upon this analysis, I argue that addiction is best understood as sinful even though it is analogous to disease in several ways.

There are several good and noble motivations for conceptualizing and treating addiction as disease. The most basic motivation, perhaps, is one that desires to help the addict and recognizes austere moralizing as contrary to that end. James Keenan puts the criticism in concise form:

> People with compulsions have never benefited, however, by the longstanding traditional (though not rooted in the Scriptures) identification of wrong action with personal badness or sin. On the contrary, that identification has caused, over the centuries, hurt, consternation

---

[4] I am not arguing that it happens in the same way for everyone or even that healing grace is reserved only for those with explicit faith. For more on this topic, see William McDonough, "*Caritas* as the *Prae-Ambulum* of All Virtue: Eberhard Schokenhoff on the Theological-Anthropological Significance and the Contemporary Interreligious Relevance of Thomas Aquinas's Teaching on the *Virtutes Morales Infusae*," *Journal of the Society of Christian Ethics* 27, no. 2 (2007): 97–126.

[5] See Timothy McMahan King, *Addiction Nation: What the Opioid Crisis Reveals About Us* (Harrisonburg, VA: Herald Press, 2019), 36, where he argues that "we need to appreciate what [the disease model of addiction] illuminates and to be aware of what it might cover up."

and frustration. In light of that history, moral theology needs to recognize the damage of telling people that each time they capitulate to a compulsion they sin. The capitulation produces substantial confusion and destructive self-understanding. Those negative obstacles to rightly-ordered living are only reinforced when moral theology adds shame and guilt to the repertoire.[6]

I agree with Keenan both that the purpose of moral theology ought not to be the manufacture of shame and that shame is often more harmful than helpful in the life of the addict. The issue is really the source of that shame. It could very well be an inability or even refusal on the part of the addict (influenced perhaps by misguided moral theologians) to disassociate the good person he truly is deep down from the harmful and destructive actions he keeps on doing. However, it is also possible that in some cases his shame is much more the result of the harmful effects that he sees the addiction causing in his own life and in the lives of those he loves. There is even a kind of shame that results merely from feeling unable to control one's own behavior to the extent one wants.

Now, it is uncontroversial that a person can suffer from a misplaced sense of shame. For example, a mother with chronic kidney disease may be ashamed of the great burden it places on all of those around her as well as her increasing inability to contribute to her family's well-being in all of the ways she would like. Such shame is clearly misplaced because the person has done nothing wrong. The disease reflects nothing bad or disordered in her being of which she needs to repent. In fact, allowing herself to be a burden to those she loves along with the recognition that this, too, is a part of loving may, for the hypothetical mother, be an occasion for moral growth. But is the situation the same for addicts? If they are indeed striving "out of love to do the right" but continually capitulating to a compulsion to sin, is it better for them to "regret" the "wrongdoing" than to repent? Keenan argues that "a person who strives out of love to do the right but fails has no reason to repent, since there is no sin."[7] Is the shame that follows

---

[6] James F. Keenan, SJ, "The Problem with Thomas Aquinas's Concept of Sin," *Heythrop Journal* 35, no. 4 (1994): 416. Keenan isn't arguing that addiction is a disease. At the risk of oversimplification, Keenan's argument is that Aquinas's view of morality does not make space for the good person who continually does wrong things. Put another way, Aquinas does not allow for the good person with good motivations who nevertheless consistently fails to effectively enact those motivations in a manner that comports with objective moral standards. For more on the broader topic of addiction and the disease model, see Kent Dunnington, *Addiction and Virtue: Beyond the Models of Disease and Choice* (Downers Grove, IL: InterVaristy Press, 2011). See also Christopher C. H. Cook, *Alcohol, Addiction, and Christian Ethics* (Cambridge: Cambridge University Press 2008).

[7] Keenan, "The Problem with Thomas Aquinas's Concept of Sin," 415.

compulsive wrongdoing comparable to the hypothetical mother's misplaced shame linked to her physical disease?

The answer appears to hinge on the extent to which the addict, unlike the hypothetical mother with chronic kidney failure, is or is not responsible for his condition. There are two interrelated but importantly distinct questions here. First, is he responsible for acquiring his addiction? Second, is he responsible for persisting in it? If he is indeed responsible for one or both, then some kind of sin model, and corresponding call to repentance, would seem appropriate. If he is not responsible for either, then a disease model is more fitting. Before analyzing these questions, however, it is helpful to consider one possible explanation for how the disease model gradually replaced the sin model in modern thought.

While the secularization thesis is not the only story to tell about modernity, it may serve as a useful tool for thinking about sin and addiction. While some may regard secularization as involving a mere demolition of previously held "religious" views, another perspective is that what actually happens is more subtle. According to this latter view, religious ideas and concepts reappear in secular or modern thought serving similar functions but divorced from the religious context in which they were originally nested. The philosopher Simon May argues, against Nietzsche, that God did not really die but rather was translated into a rather robust vision of human love that surreptitiously smuggled in divine attributes. As Ian Claussen has observed, "True love now looked rather curiously familiar: unconditional, disinterested, impartial, universal, and perfect in every way that once distinguished the Christian God."[8] God is love morphed into the rather different idea that love is God.

Christian ethicists have often critiqued a similar morphing with respect to sin and addiction. The critique is stated poignantly by the Catholic philosopher Charles Taylor: "We have transferred so many issues which used to be considered moral into a therapeutic register. What was formerly sin is often now seen as sickness. This seems…to involve an enhancement of human dignity, but can actually end up abasing it."[9] Christian ethicist Linda Mercadante has even gone so far as to posit the emergence of "biological determinism" in the shift away from traditional understandings of sin to the modern view of sin as sickness.[10] At issue, then, is not only "contemporary Western culture's

---

[8] Ian Claussen, *On Love, Confession, Surrender, and the Moral Self* (New York: Bloomsbury, 2018), 24.

[9] Charles Taylor, *A Secular Age* (Cambridge, MA: Harvard University Press, 2007), 618.

[10] Linda Mercadante, *Victims & Sinners: Spiritual Roots of Addiction and Recovery* (Louisville, KY: Westminster John Knox Press, 1994), 141.

tendency to replace the theological language of sin with the therapeutic language of addiction" but also the value of this transition.[11] I argue that the movement is good only if addiction can be reduced to a disease but bad if addiction admits of moral responsibility in a manner that disease as commonly understood does not.

Let us begin with a consideration of hard biological determinism. Is it good to understand addiction as biologically determined to such a degree that religious or metaphysical views of the role of the intellective will both in acquiring and persisting in the addiction are removed from consideration? The answer, in my view, depends on whether addiction truly is biologically determined. If it is, then lecturing addicts about their responsibility for their addiction is just as silly as lecturing them about their height. What would you like them to do about the matter? On the other hand, telling addicts that they are merely victims of bad biology is wrong if they are indeed more than their biology. How strong, then, is the case for biologically determined addiction?[12]

Neurobiologists and psychiatric geneticists agree that there are complex pathways from genes to psychiatric disorders, including addiction. While Mendelian disorders, such as sickle-cell anemia or cystic fibrosis, are directly determined insofar as there is a clear path from the mutation of a single gene to the disease, the pathway from genes to addiction is more complex and less understood. At issue, for our purposes here, is one's ability or inability to influence those very pathways. Since Mendelian disorders are, in a sense, buffered from the intellect and will of the individual who suffers from them, as of yet futuristic methods of gene therapy are likely the only way that human agency can alter the genetic pathways. However, the variegated pathways from genes to addiction may be more porous in relation to the intellective will than is the case with direct and determined genetic pathways.

Obviously, no one is claiming that mere human agency can directly will away a genetic pathway to an addiction. However, there is evidence to suggest that human beings can indirectly alter their genetic pathways. K. S. Kendler, for example, argues against an overly rigid model of gene action in which genes are "conceptualized as working through silent physiological pathways in the bowels of our biology far

---

[11] William McDonough, "Sin and Addiction: Alcoholics Anonymous and the Soul of Christian Sin-Talk," *Journal of the Society of Christian Ethics* 32, no. 1 (2012): 39.

[12] While my focus here is on a deterministic variant of the disease model emphasizing genetic predispositions to addiction, I think the argument holds even for those versions of the disease model that emphasize other factors. King argues in *Addiction Nation*, for instance, that "thinking you have a disease can lead some people to believe that the responsibility of a cure, of healing, belongs to a doctor or medical professional. This is a problem with treating not just addiction but other diseases, like type 2 diabetes and heart disease, as well" (35).

from the influences of human thoughts, feelings, or desires." In contrast, Kendler maintains that at the "individual, family, and societal level, humans can intervene in causal pathways from genes to behavior." Unlike the "uncontroversial and deterministic" pathways involved in Mendelian disorders, the pathways from genes to behavior admit of greater complexity as well as susceptibility to human agency.[13]

Kendler makes his case through an examination of alcoholism. He acknowledges that there is strong evidence for a genetic pathway to alcoholism that involves factors such as "alcohol metabolism in the liver and neuro-transmitter systems that may mediate some of the psychoactive effects of alcohol."[14] Thus, genes can indeed place one at greater risk for developing alcohol dependency particularly when one adds to the calculation the likelihood of children witnessing alcoholism in their parents in cases where both share similar genetic predispositions. However, as Kendler notes, the data reveals that "offspring of families with high rates of alcohol problems, who are at an elevated genetic risk for [alcohol dependency], also have an increased probability of being teetotalers."[15] Drawing on this and other qualitative and quantitative studies, Kendler concludes that human decision-making can influence genetic pathways to addiction and other psychiatric disorders to a much greater degree than is often supposed.

This, then, is one argument against reducing addiction to disease. The concept of disease tends to wipe away any sense of moral responsibility (no one would blame someone for having sickle-cell anemia). Yet, the data indicates that the interaction of decision-making and genetic pathways to addiction is in the very least significantly more complex than those involved in other kinds of brain disorders. While one can certainly be at an increased genetic risk for certain kinds of addiction, such as alcoholism, the data does not support a thesis of hard biological determinism.

Even if people are not biologically predetermined to suffer from addiction, there remains the question of whether, once having acquired the addiction, there is a line beyond which the person is no longer responsible for participating in the addiction because the compulsive behaviors are now buffered from decision-making. This question brings us back to Keenan's view that a person who "*strives* out of love or out of duty to realize right living...is good notwithstanding the fact that

---

[13] K. S. Kendler, "Decision Making in the Pathway from Genes to Psychiatric and Substance Use Disorders," *Molecular Psychiatry* 18, no. 6 (2013): 640.
[14] Kendler, "Decision Making in the Pathway from Genes to Psychiatric and Substance Use Disorders," 640.
[15] Kendler, "Decision Making in the Pathway from Genes to Psychiatric and Substance Use Disorders," 640.

the actual realization might be right or wrong."[16] Thus, Keenan continues, "If out of love one tries to overcome compulsive behavior, angry outbursts, lack of self-confidence, narrow-mindedness, depression or suspicion, and still fails to attain the aim sought, then despite that wrongness, one is good."[17] It follows, then, that the addict, or person with compulsions, in Keenan's language, who cannot overcome the compulsions but is striving out of love to act rightly has cause for regret but not for repentance.[18] Thus, Keenan appears to regard the move away from a sin model of addiction, which he links to Aquinas, to a contemporary disease model as a positive development:

> Aquinas's treatise is theologically unsound both by contemporary standards and in the context of his own writings. But these theological liabilities become personally harmful when applied pastorally. Today psychology teaches how well-disposed people are to wrong behaviour despite their strongest desires otherwise. For instance, various "twelve-step" programmes describe just how inclined people are to compulsions, whether in eating, smoking, drinking, sex, even work. As the programmes admit, these compulsions are wrong behaviour; through a variety of methods—counselling, narrative, peer support, self-disclosure, transference—their members seek to avoid engaging these disordered compulsions.[19]

The basic claim is that a disease model is better equipped to treat addiction than a sin model because the latter does not understand the

---

[16] Keenan, "The Problem with Thomas Aquinas's Concept of Sin," 411 (italics in original). In Keenan's view, "Goodness is the striving out of love, charity, or duty for the right. But rightness, whether it focuses on particular act, a class of rules or values, or even habitual character traits or virtues, measures not whether we strive, but whether we attain those standards" (412).

[17] Keenan, "The Problem with Thomas Aquinas's Concept of Sin," 412–413.

[18] Keenan, "The Problem with Thomas Aquinas's Concept of Sin," 415; "A person who strives out of love to do the right but fails has no reason to repent, since there is no sin. But having sought unsuccessfully the right, the person regrets the failure."

[19] Keenan, "The Problem with Thomas Aquinas's Concept of Sin," 415. There are two distinct questions here. First, is the expression of genetic inclination subject to change based on factors including the person's agency and environment (epigenetics)? Second, even granting a stable inclination toward dependency, is one predetermined to comply with that inclination? Put another way, is there a direct line from inclination to compulsion? Indeed, one of the issues with the disease model applied to addiction is the kind of disease it implies. There are, of course, different kinds of diseases. Some diseases are merely inherited such that the decisions and actions of the person with the disease do not meaningfully contribute to its bettering or worsening. Other diseases, like certain forms of heart disease, are both inherited but also bettered or worsened by one's decisions, choices, and environment (diet, stress, access to healthy food, access to health care, etc.).

nature of compulsions and therefore is capable only of adding guilt and shame to an already bad situation, thereby making it worse.[20]

While Keenan is certainly not a determinist, there does appear to be a kind of soft determinism informing much of his presentation that adds an additional layer to our previous discussion of hard biological determinism. Kendler's focus was on genetic pathways to becoming an addict. He argues that, though pathways exist, they are not deterministic because our decisions are able to interrupt and redirect them. Keenan, on the other hand, is considering persons who, by whatever means, have already been compromised by the addiction. Telling them that they had the ability to avoid the addiction had they made better decisions may be as useful as telling a man at the bottom of a well that he could have avoided falling in had he been more cautious. Even if true, it is not very helpful at the present moment.

The question that arises, then, is whether the addict is responsible for persisting in her addiction at every level of the addiction or whether there is some point at which the behavior becomes compulsive and therefore no longer blameworthy. To reiterate, at issue is not the usefulness or value of blame attributions but whether the transition from a sin model to a disease model of addiction was a step in the right direction. I am arguing that the movement is good only if addiction is reducible to disease but needs to be rethought if addiction is more than a disease.[21]

In the clinical literature, there are two main arguments, based on two empirical factors, made in favor of the view that the compulsions of the addict lead to non-voluntary behavior. The first is "biological evidence of changes to the normal operation of the brain caused by regular consumption of drugs." The second is "observational evidence of addicts' repetitive self-destructive behavior...accompanied by strong ambivalence: the addict expresses a desire not to consume drugs prior to, after, or even during the drug intake."[22] Both are commonly used to underwrite the view that addiction is a neurobiological disease.

However, the just-mentioned evidence has been heavily criticized in much of the same literature as ambiguous at best. While it is

---

[20] King attributes the "moral" or "sin" model, at least in the twentieth century, to the work of Dr. Lawrence Kolb. See King, *Addiction Nation*, 33, as well as Caroline Jean Acker, *Creating the American Junkie: Addiction Research in the Classic Era of Narcotic Control* (Baltimore: John Hopkins University Press, 2002).

[21] My argument here is similar to King's. The argument is not that the disease model should be "thrown out entirely" but simply that it is limited. I am arguing against a view, which I don't attribute to Keenan, that regards the disease model as the only or best way to think about addiction; see King, *Addiction Nation*, 36.

[22] Edmund Henden, Hans Olav Melberg, and Ole Jørgen Røgeberg, "Addiction: Choice or Compulsion?" *Frontiers in Psychiatry* 4, no. 17 (2013): 1.

acknowledged that repeated drug use does indeed lead to dopaminergic changes in brain chemistry, critics note that such changes are "common to most forms of pleasurable experience."[23] Advocates of the disease model, according to their critics, too easily conflate an intensely strong desire with an irresistible desire or compulsion. This is an important distinction, because if what are commonly referred to as compulsions are in fact strong but resistible desires, then the individual is still responsible for acting on them: "There is nothing pathological about strong desires."[24] As for the addict's self-report of his lack of volition, critics of the disease model hold that the empirical evidence "shows both that addicts can be persuaded to exercise their capacity for self-control if they are given what appear to them to be sufficiently good reasons, and that statements regarding loss of control are—at least to some extent—factually inaccurate and motivated by a desire to shift attribution of behavior from choices to circumstances."[25] It would seem, then, that compulsions may diminish but do not entirely remove moral responsibility insofar as the addict is still acting voluntarily.

Nevertheless, the addict need not be overcome by genetically predetermined, irresistible compulsions in order for Keenan's argument to stand. Rather, Keenan's argument still holds for the addict who is striving to stop a compulsive behavior but is prohibited by desires stronger than those involved in the striving (or obstacles to the actualization of that striving) that the addict simply cannot will away. Keenan acknowledges that the addict may on occasion also possess bad motivations that are more blameworthy than his wrong actions.[26] In this way, Keenan's critique is not so much of the sin model itself but of a "domesticated and trivialized" understanding of sin that focuses more on actions than underlying motivations.[27] What is needed, then, is not so much a shift into a responsibility-free disease model of addiction but rather an adequate theological model for understanding the sinful motivations that often underlie addiction. Aquinas's account of sin, I argue, can be of assistance in the formulation of such a model. Interestingly, much of the foundational literature of Alcoholics Anonymous (AA) seems to agree.

---

[23] Henden, Melberg, and Røgeberg, "Addiction: Choice or Compulsion?" 1.
[24] Henden, Melberg, and Røgeberg, "Addiction: Choice or Compulsion?" 1.
[25] Henden, Melberg, and Røgeberg, "Addiction: Choice or Compulsion?" 1.
[26] See Keenan, "The Problem with Thomas Aquinas's Concept of Sin," 416: "Certainly, not all wrongdoing is the result of good-meaning attempts to control one's compulsions."
[27] John Mahoney, *The Making of Moral Theology* (Oxford: Clarendon Press, 1987), 32.

AA does indeed claim that "alcoholism isn't a sin."²⁸ However, as William McDonough observes, this "claim is often misunderstood."²⁹ A more accurate understanding is that alcoholism is a symptom of a more deeply rooted sinfulness within the soul. Thus, focusing on each compulsive act without attending to the underlying causes is like examining rotten pieces of fruit with no attention to the bend in the tree producing them. And what is wrong with the tree? One way of examining this question is through the seven capital (deadly) sins.

Desert monks were among the first to offer a sustained focus on the inner states of being that close the human heart in on itself. According to the monks, sin begins, in some sense, in the world of thought. They saw it as obvious that one should carefully examine the substance of his own thoughts: "The arch-enemy of the soul is in the practice of a certain kind of thought, for which the monks used the word *logismoi*...a train of thought which engages the mind, so that bit by bit one drifts away from what one is supposed to be doing into a world of fantasy."³⁰ These harmful trains of thought, *logismoi*, are understood later by Aquinas as the wellspring of all kinds of sin. They are "deadly" in that they are radically contrary to God's love and "capital" in that they produce a vast array of sinful dispositions and corresponding actions.

Aquinas provides a list of seven capital sins all rooted in pride. Excessive self-love or pride does not want to need anyone, even God, to be happy. It wants absolute power to provide for its own happiness and avoid all suffering. Thus, it tempts one to turn away from God, which is "the beginning of every evil" (ST I-II q. 84, a. 2).³¹ If this pride is the tyrant, then the seven capital sins are its henchmen. Vainglory demands praise and honor from others as confirmation of the tyrant's absurdly exaggerated sense of greatness. Lust and gluttony seek to produce any variety of pleasurable experience at the tyrant's whim and sloth to avoid anything that is good but may involve suffering. Envy and covetousness want to be superior to everyone in every possible respect and thus view the good of others as a "hindrance to one's own excellence" (ST I-II q. 84, a. 4).³² Finally, anger or wrath is perhaps best understood as the tyrant's constant, outwardly-directed frustration and resentment at the obvious futility and unreality of his

---

²⁸ Alcoholics Anonymous: *The Story of How Many Thousands of Men and Women Have Recovered from Alcoholism* (New York: AA World Services, 2002), 344.
²⁹ McDonough, "Sin and Addiction: Alcoholics Anonymous and the Soul of Christian Sin-Talk," 40.
³⁰ Simon Tugwell, OP, *Ways of Imperfection: An Exploration of Christian Spirituality* (Springfield, IL: Templegate Publications, 1985), 15.
³¹ I draw from the 1948 Benziger Brothers translation throughout; this edition contains the translation by the Fathers of the English Dominican Province.
³² For more this topic, see Rebecca DeYoung's *Glittering Vices: A New Look at the Seven Deadly Sins and Their Remedies* (Grand Rapids, MI: Brazos Press, 2009).

entire project. Thus, the *logismoi* are seemingly innocent little fantasies of pleasure, superiority, and total control that gradually shape the individual in a way of life patterned on absolute rejection of God.

In this view, alcoholism, or whatever other addiction, is a symptom of something far deeper and far more difficult to treat. Indeed, AA co-founder Bill Wilson predicates the fourth step—make a searching and fearless moral inventory—on the seven deadly sins. However, much like how Aquinas modified the list given by Gregory the Great who adapted the list from the desert monks, Wilson, too, presents his own modified version: "Anger, resentments, jealousy, envy, self-pity, [and] hurt pride" are the culprits in his view.[33] While Aquinas may not be as comfortable as Wilson in dismissing the sinfulness of the symptoms, he has no problem with the project of looking deeper to their root causes. However, there is another mesh point between Aquinas's understanding of sin and AA's understanding of addiction that may be even more important.

It is obvious and excellent sense that in order for sin to qualify as sin, sinners must be blameworthy. Put simply, sinners must have known what they were doing was wrong or in the very least had the ability to know, and they must have had sufficient freedom not to do it. If either of these conditions are lacking, then blaming people for their bad actions may itself be blameworthy on the part of the blamer depending on the very same conditions. In much the same way, even if our hypothetical addict is consumed by self-pity, resentments, hurt pride and the like, this in and of itself really does not tell us much about the level of cooperation in becoming such a person. After all, people may be consumed by self-pity because they just unexpectedly and tragically lost a spouse, while others because their favorite football team keeps losing. People may be resentful at the world for failing to confirm their exaggerated sense of their own greatness while others are resentful because they have found themselves in an occupation where they are continually punished for their virtues. Finally, hurt pride might be the result of an overly inflated ego in one person but in another it may be the result of long and sustained attempts by others, even those close to them, to viciously remind them of their own worthlessness. Indeed, an addict may not have been self-pitying and resentful but then underwent some serious trauma that pushed them in that direction. In cases of addictive abuse of prescription drugs, perhaps even family and friends and well-meaning doctors unwittingly conspired in leading people down a wrong path. Thus, in certain cases, lectures about the seven deadly sins may be in the same category as the moralizing of Job's friends. They simply don't understand the subject about which they keep on talking.

---

[33] *Twelve Steps and Twelve Traditions* (New York: AA World Services, 2002), 8.

Blame, then, often misses the mark, but even when it does not miss it entirely, it is still not the only or even the main point about sin, including the sinfulness that underlies addiction. The point rather is that sin is a drastic impediment even to the imperfect happiness possible in the present life (ST I-II q. 5, a. 3). Resentment, self-pity, and destructive behaviors make already bad situations more hellish than they already were. Thus, addiction, while not merely a disease in the modern sense, is very much like a disease in at least two ways. First, it is significantly debilitating to one's well-being. Second, determining the causes is only valuable insofar as doing so is conducive to the end of restoring health. However responsible people may be for their addiction, addicts, too, need a cure.[34]

This section outlined a theological model for thinking about the sinfulness of addiction. This model, drawing from Aquinas, emphasizes the harmful destructiveness of sin in relation to happiness without discounting moral responsibility or blameworthiness in cases where that is appropriate. While rejecting a modern disease model of addiction, the sin model proposed here acknowledges that addiction is analogous to disease in at least the two important respects just mentioned. Having outlined a theological model for thinking of addiction as sin, I turn now to the cure for this sinfulness, which is the grace of God.

GRACE-ENABLED RECOVERY FROM ADDICTION

This section draws from Augustine's and Aquinas's interpretation of Romans 7:14–25 in order to explicate four stages in grace-enabled recovery from addiction. The first stage is healing from the addiction. The second is desiring the good to which the addiction is contrary. The third is enacting that good, and the fourth is persevering in it (ST I-II q. 111, a. 3).[35] We begin with Augustine.

In his early commentaries, Augustine reads Romans 7 as referring to a process. First, people discover that they are unable to fulfill the moral law. Second, they repent. Third, they seek the divine grace by which they are made able to fulfill that very law. However, Augustine later amended his view as he became increasingly convinced, largely but not exclusively by his own experience, that "grace plays the initiating role."[36] Paul's own conversion, for instance, does not follow

---

[34] For more on this topic, see Hanna Pickard, "Responsibility without Blame: Philosophical Reflections on Clinical Practice," *Oxford Handbook of Philosophy and Psychiatry* (Oxford: Oxford University Press, 2013), 1134–52.

[35] For more on this topic, see Bernhard Blankenhorn, OP, "Aquinas on Paul's Flesh/Spirit Anthropology in Romans" in *Reading Romans*, 1–38.

[36] Eugene TeSelle, "Exploring the Inner Conflict: Augustine's Sermons on Romans 7 and 8," in *Engaging Augustine on Romans: Self, Context, and Theology in Interpretation*, ed. Daniel Patte and Eugene TeSelle (Harrisburg, PA: Trinity Press International, 2002), 111. For more on this topic, see Karla Pollman and Willemien Otten,

such a pattern. Rather, it is an unrepentant Saul whom Christ first encounters on the road to Damascus. Whereas Augustine had previously held that the struggle with sin Paul speaks of in Romans 7 is before grace, he later holds that the primary struggle is after the infusion of grace. The first stage in recovering from sin in Augustine's later view is healing. I argue that the same holds with regard to the stages in recovering from addiction mentioned earlier.

Aquinas, too, holds to the primacy of grace. God's grace begins by healing. We do not, then, shift from wholly bad to wholly good as though in an instant. As Keenan observes, "Goodness…is really not *the* first movement. The first movement is from God who through Christ invites us to walk with him along his way by his grace."[37] Applied to addiction, I argue that it is in this stage that addicts are healed and go on to receive a strong desire to stop using as well as a newfound ability to enact this desire where they previously could not.

While in some instances the strong desire and the newfound ability to enact it may arise simultaneously, I do not think this is always or even normally the case when speaking of addiction. The healing stage I am concerned with here may involve a period where the addict strongly desires to stop but lacks the ability to do so. In this way, Keenan is right to point to a moment in the life of grace where the compulsive behaviors are concurrent with the graced motivations deep within the heart of the individual. The spiritually regenerated part of the person, or in Paul's language the "inward man," may regret still using. Disordered desires and compulsions persist. However, this is only because grace has not yet finished its work. Arising from the newness of life initiated by healing grace is also the strong desire to walk with God more ably. Thus, at some point, God's grace, having descended into the deep well of addiction to meet addicts, also lifts them out of it. Christ can go where others cannot. Christ can enter into the cemetery of addicts' souls in a way no one else can and encounter the inward affliction, crying out, self-bashing with stones, and, there, not only comfort them but also heal their minds and return them to their families to tell of all the Lord has done for them (cf. Mark 5:1–20).

That God can accomplish all of this is uncontroversial to those who hold to the traditional doctrines of Christianity.[38] What is, perhaps,

---

eds., *The Oxford Guide to the Historical Reception of Augustine* (Oxford: Oxford University Press, 2013). See also, J. Patout Burns Jr., ed., *Romans: Interpreted by Early Christian Commentators* (Grand Rapids, MI: Eerdmans, 2012).

[37] Keenan, "The Problem with Thomas Aquinas's Concept of Sin," 413.

[38] However, I pass over difficult theological questions here regarding addiction and the problem of evil. For more on this topic, see Gerald G. May, *Addiction & Grace: Love and Spirituality in the Healing of Addictions* (New York: HarperCollins Publishers, 1988).

more puzzling is the fourth stage, that of persevering in the good after having been led through the triumph of the first three stages. The giant of addiction has been knocked flat by God's grace. The new self, with God on its side, is now able to do good and resist evil in a manner that before seemed an impossible dream. Victory seems to have been attained. And yet the fight is not over. Indeed, if Augustine's reading of Paul is correct, the greater and more intense part of the struggle is coming down the road and not rather in the rear-view mirror as one would like to think.

In the stage of perseverance, the new self contends with sin in a way it could not before. In his sermons on Romans 6–8, Augustine, against Pelagius, insists on the continuing power of sin after conversion and therefore the need for even greater reliance upon the grace of God. The situation of the redeemed believer, in Augustine's view, is "not one of total victory."[39] When Paul tells us that he does the evil he does not want to do while failing to do the good he wills to do, he is describing the intensity and nature of the struggle in the stage of perseverance (7:15). Even in a state of grace, demonic powers or external events can assault the imagination to introduce *logismoi* into the mind—the destructive strands of thought about which the desert monks warned us. Augustine does not think we can entirely avoid the initial impressions made on the imagination by demonic powers, but he does think grace can fortify the mind against the impressions and the desires they incite.[40] Suggestion is ordered to arousing the passions for the sake of subduing the intellective will. However, the inner struggle depicted in Romans 7 complicates this schema.

In the first place, there are two opposite inclinations at work in the same person—one delights in God's goodness and another in sin. Augustine does not think the moral law of itself can bring delight in the good but only fear. Only the grace of the Holy Spirit can bring delight in the good. Now, the issue for Augustine comes with consent. When the will consents to and indeed enacts the good, the contrary desire is not dampened down but rather intensified. Thus, Augustine does not think that when Paul says he "does" the evil he does not want to do he is speaking of outward actions. He is not entirely relapsing and re-enacting the old addictions. Rather, he is fighting the desires that once fueled those addictions deep within himself. The inward man is fighting the rebellious old self that appears to grow stronger and louder each time we enact the opposite of that which it desires.

Augustine does not hesitate to use adversarial imagery when depicting the inner struggle: "He speaks of combat between opposing delights within oneself, of taking sides among delights, vanquishing

---

[39] TeSelle, "Exploring the Inner Conflict: Augustine's Sermons on Romans 7 and 8," 115.
[40] See Augustine's *De Trinitate* 12.12.17–18.

or being vanquished, dominating or being dominated, even killing."[41] And so, of course, does Paul: "For if you live according to the flesh, you will die, but if by the spirit you put to death the deeds of the body, you will live" (8:13). Indeed, Augustine even likens the inner struggle to the brutal death matches of Roman gladiatorial combat in which "all blows were permitted."[42] However, this match is in the "stadium of the heart," and Christ, who is its judge, will also come "to the aid of the Christian lying on the ground" (Augustine, *Sermon* 154 A, 3).

Aquinas, too, thinks Paul is referring to an inner struggle more than outward actions. The graced person is in a state of "war" between grace-enabled reason and "the disordered concupiscence of the flesh" (*Commentary on Romans*, 588).[43] The key for Aquinas is that Paul's "disordered desires do not come to fruition in an actual act of sin."[44] In Aquinas's view, Paul sins ("For I do not do the good I want") primarily in failing to take the proper precautions to avoid the rise of sinful desires. Thus, Paul "commits the venial sin of omission."[45] Persevering in grace, then, for both Augustine and Aquinas involves an intense inner struggle against sinful desires that are not entirely uprooted once and for all until the glorious freedom of the next life.

We have, then, four stages in grace-enabled recovery from addiction: the healing of the soul, the desire for the good to which the addiction is contrary, the ability to enact that good, and persevering through the ensuing struggle. However, these stages are only a matter of thinking about the reality of recovery. It is often very hard to tell what God is doing underneath the bandage and thinking too literally about the stages is likely to encourage presumption in some and despair in others. Recovering addicts, therefore, are not to be discouraged when they find old addiction or perhaps some new strands of it stemming from the same inner and outer sources, assailing the new person they are becoming. This is to be expected. There is even a lesson to be learned from it inasmuch as it reminds us that however far we think we may have come we are every bit as reliant upon God's grace as when we first began and perhaps even more so. In addition, this grace transforms how we respond to the reality of ongoing addictions in our lives and in the lives of others.

Addiction at in any stage is a spiritual struggle. It is a struggle that takes place in the depth of the heart. The battle is to be fought here,

---

[41] TeSelle, "Exploring the Inner Conflict: Augustine's Sermons on Romans 7 and 8," 122. For more on this topic, see James Wetzel, *Augustine and the Limits of Virtue* (Cambridge: Cambridge University Press, 1992), especially 112–60.

[42] TeSelle, "Exploring the Inner Conflict: Augustine's Sermons on Romans 7 and 8," 123.

[43] Aquinas, *Commentary on Romans*, 588. I use the translation in Raith, "Portraits of Paul: Aquinas and Calvin on Romans 7:14–25," (2012).

[44] Raith, "Portraits of Paul: Aquinas and Calvin on Romans 7:14–25," 244.

[45] Raith, "Portraits of Paul: Aquinas and Calvin on Romans 7:14–25," 249.

and God's grace makes it more intense but also makes victory attainable. Evil desires remain in us and war against the newness of life that Christ generously pours forth into our souls. Paul as redeemed sinner is indeed a model for the recovering addict. He struggles and hopes for the day when the struggle will be no more. He does not regard faith as the illusion that some people think it is. His faith is no human fabrication or mere concept but an experience of the heart that does indeed lead to moral improvement, however gradually.

The experience is of a God who does not require people to overcome their sinfulness in order to be loved but rather loves them in order they may overcome that very sinfulness. Paul comforts fighters in the stadium of the heart by assuring them that they remain God's children no matter how furiously sin rages on or even on occasion seems to have regained the upper hand. We may on occasion lose to the opponent, but we must not lose to the fear that invites us to end the struggle by acquiescing entirely. Above all, we must trust that, when we've truly given it all that we have and there is nothing left and feel overwhelmed and defeated, Christ will come to our side. He is faithful and does not give up on us even in our suffering. Therefore, after each failure, we can seek forgiveness, dust ourselves off, and try again. As C.S. Lewis once observed, this process of failing and trying again "cures our illusions about ourselves and teaches us to depend on God. We learn, on the one hand, that we cannot trust ourselves even in our best moments, and, on the other, that we need not despair even in our worst, for our failures are forgiven. The only fatal thing is to sit down content with anything less than perfection."[46]

Thinking about grace and addiction this way can also help guide us in how we interact with the addicts we may encounter in our own lives. Consider again a lesson from St. Paul: "Therefore, you are without excuse, every one of you who passes judgment. For by the standard by which you judge another you condemn yourself, since you, the judge, do the very same things" (Romans 2:1–2). In this little passage, Paul rejects the tidy but lazy and self-serving binaries we create to differentiate an imagined group of perfect people from ordinary human sinners. We do the same thing with the concept of addiction today. The world is supposedly divided into addicts and non-addicts. However, applying Paul's view of the universality of sinfulness to addiction results in the thesis that everyone is an addict. Is such a thesis defensible?

The answer depends yet again on how one defines addiction. If addiction is limited to behavior involving the ingestion of an external chemical into the body as with drug addiction or alcoholism, then the answer is clearly no. The net would widen if one introduced more

---

[46] C.S. Lewis, *Mere Christianity* (San Francisco: HarperCollins, 1952), 101–102.

chemicals into the mix such as nicotine or even caffeine. The net widens further still when one includes behaviors that do not involve the ingestion of external chemicals into the body but prompt the release of chemicals, primarily dopamine, from one's own brain. This could involve behavior as seemingly prosaic as seeking likes for your Facebook post or Tweet, jogging, golfing, going to church, or writing essays about addiction with the hope of getting them published. However, the thesis that anyone who routinely engages in a behavior they find pleasurable is an addict seems too general to have meaning.

There is, nonetheless, another way of thinking about addiction that may make Paul's statement more applicable. In order to do so we must, for the moment, move away from specific behaviors into issues concerning the enactment of rightly ordered goals. If one's chief goal is to love well, then any action genuinely done from that motivation and consistent with that end is good and right. Contrarily, any action that falls short of that end is wrong. In this sense, any continually occurring pattern of compulsive or semi-compulsive habitual behavior that routinely or occasionally prevents one from loving well may be thought of as an addiction.

Considered thusly, it may even be possible to heed the warning of the desert monks and consider addictions to certain harmful patterns of thinking.[47] We may become addicted to thinking in certain ways about ourselves or some other group of people to feed addictions that are deeper still. Lewis, for instance, noted the tendency of people to look for things in the media that fuel their own hatred remarking that some "actually find hatred such a pleasure that to give it up is like giving up beer or tobacco."[48] We may think here of cable news addicts and much of what one encounters in social media. We go looking for things we know will titillate our moral outrage feigning some apparently noble reason for doing so. But the phenomena can appear merely in one's head when the TV and phone are off—little, seemingly innocent chains of thought feeding resentments and self-pity, vindictive fantasies about the suffering of one's perceived enemies, delusional imaginings of one's own greatness. All this can then seep out through the most dangerous member of the body, the tongue, and finally announce itself in action and a way of being in the world (cf. James 3). This is why we can speak of having met a very resentful person without seeing directly into the nursery of their imagination in which those resentments are nurtured. Patterns of thought do not stay quarantined in some hidden place of the soul but eventually manifest in one's speech and conduct.

---

[47] For more on this topic and further examples, see Jason Byassee's *An Introduction to the Desert Fathers* (Eugene, OR: Cascade Books, 2007).
[48] Lewis, *Mere Christianity,* 120.

Thus understood, those of us who consistently succumb to patterns of thought, speech, or behavior (or more likely all three) that impede our ability to love well are addicts of one kind or another. May we still speak of degrees and make nuanced distinctions between people more or less addicted and addictions themselves as more and less dangerous? Certainly we can, and even should, but in so doing, we must remember that "whoever keeps the whole law, but falls short in one particular, has become guilty in respect to all of it" (James 2:10). The point, however, is not condemnation but rather a sensible basis for showing others that mercy that "triumphs over judgment" (James 2:13). For we judge others by a standard to which we ourselves fail to conform. The peculiarity of a friend or family member's specific form of addiction may indeed seem rather alien and unintelligible to us, but when we pretend as though we have no point of reference with the deeper struggle, we deceive the addict as well as ourselves (cf. ST II-II q. 161, a. 6).

Some might object to the expanded category for thinking about addiction I am proposing here. They may argue that such an expansion dangerously shifts attention away from the really treacherous addictions society should be focused on combatting, such as opioids. And given that addictions come with mortality rates, they may well be right. I have two responses. First, as I said before, there is nothing in my account that occludes the possibility of prioritizing some addictions as more dangerous and potentially harmful than others. Second, and this is the more important point, I think that addicts seeking help are far more likely to find it in those willing to be honest about their own struggle with the sinfulness that expresses itself in addiction.[49] The expanded category proposed in Scripture gives everyone, excluding the morally perfect, a genuine basis for adopting the former stance. It is also the approach I have found in the holier people I have known and in the lives of the saints. It is why we prefer going to them when we are struggling with our faith or some other matter as opposed to our bewildered religious friend who simulates holiness by pretending to be so far removed from sin as to be utterly perplexed at our weakness. Indeed, Christ's patience with our weakness is our model for patience both with our own weakness and that of others. Addicts are not to be cast aside and given up on but accompanied as they become better, just as Christ goes on ceaselessly helping us despite all of our wicked morals and deep imperfections.

---

[49] Of course, there is also a danger in the opposite extreme of presuming to understand the struggle of another person to a degree of which you are not really capable or viewing it too much through the lens of one's own struggle in a manner that is also not helpful. Listening is important.

Andrew Kim is Director of the Center for the Advancement of the Humanities (beginning July 2021) and Associate Professor of Theology at Marquette University. Having completed his Ph.D. at The Catholic University of America in 2013, Dr. Kim was an Assistant Professor at Walsh University prior to joining the Marquette faculty in 2017. His research and teaching focus on interdisciplinary, collaborative approaches to the theology of addiction and recovery. He has also written on virtue ethics and just war theory. His previous publications include the monograph *An Introduction to Catholic Ethics since Vatican II* (Cambridge University Press, 2015). His journal articles have appeared in *The Journal for Peace and Justice Studies, New Blackfriars, Studies in Christian Ethics,* and *The Journal of Moral Theology*, among other venues.

THANKS TO

Tyler Bussard, C'22 Mount St. Mary's University, intern, is from Clear Spring, Maryland. He is majoring in Forensic Accounting, Accounting, and Spanish with minors in Theology and Economics.

Christina Batt, a doctoral student in theology at The Catholic University of America.

Articles available to view
or download at:

https://jmt.scholasticahq.com/

The

Journal of Moral Theology

is proudly sponsored by

The College of Liberal Arts
at
Mount St. Mary's University

www.ingramcontent.com/pod-product-compliance
Lightning Source LLC
Chambersburg PA
CBHW070916160426
43193CB00011B/1479